Jim Crow Laws

Jim Crow Laws

Leslie V. Tischauser

Landmarks of the American Mosaic

 GREENWOOD

AN IMPRINT OF ABC-CLIO, LLC
Santa Barbara, California • Denver, Colorado • Oxford, England

Library of Congress Cataloging-in-Publication Data

Tischauser, Leslie Vincent, 1942–
    Jim Crow laws / Leslie V. Tischauser.
       p. cm. — (Landmarks of the American mosaic)
    Includes bibliographical references and index.
    ISBN 978–0–313–38608–4 (hardcopy : alk. paper) — ISBN 978–0–313–38609–1 (ebook) 1. African Americans—Legal status, laws, etc.—History. 2. Race discrimination—Law and legislation—United States—History. 3. African Americans—Social conditions—To 1964. I. Title.
    KF4757.T57   2012
    342.7308′73—dc23   2012007814

ISBN: 978–0–313–38608–4
EISBN: 978–0–313–38609–1

16 15 14 13 12   1 2 3 4 5

This book is also available on the World Wide Web as an eBook.
Visit www.abc-clio.com for details.

Greenwood
An Imprint of ABC-CLIO, LLC

ABC-CLIO, LLC
130 Cremona Drive, P.O. Box 1911
Santa Barbara, California 93116-1911

This book is printed on acid-free paper ∞

Manufactured in the United States of America

Contents

Series Foreword

THE LANDMARKS OF THE AMERICAN MOSAIC series comprises individual volumes devoted to exploring an event or development central to this country's multicultural heritage. The topics illuminate the struggles and triumphs of American Indians, African Americans, Latinos, and Asian Americans, from European contact through the turbulent last half of the twentieth century. The series covers landmark court cases, laws, government programs, civil rights infringements, riots, battles, movements, and more. Written by historians especially for high school students on up and general readers, these content-rich references satisfy more thorough research needs and provide a deeper understanding of material that students might only otherwise be exposed to in a short section in a textbook or superficial explanation online.

Each book on a particular topic is a one-stop reference source. The series format includes:

- Introduction
- Chronology
- Narrative chapters that trace the evolution of the event or topic chronologically
- Biographical profiles of key figures
- Selection of crucial primary documents
- Glossary
- Bibliography
- Index

This landmark series promotes respect for cultural diversity and supports the social studies curriculum by helping students understand multicultural American history.

Preface

THIS BOOK IS PRESENTED AS A REFERENCE WORK for students and general readers. Its purpose is to provide a chronological history of racial segregation in the United States from the end of the Civil War to the passage of the 1964 Civil Rights Act. The book includes biographies of key figures in the campaign against legal segregation, key documents presenting arguments for and against equal rights for all Americans, a glossary explaining the meaning of unfamiliar terms, and a bibliography assessing the important books on the topic and listing electronic resources suitable for student researchers. The major portion of this book describes the methods, purposes, and attitudes that created a legal system that separated people by race in schools, courthouses, busses, trains, and other public places where people might meet in more than one-half of American states. It also describes the legal strategies, demonstrations, marches, protests, and political activities that were used by supporters of equal rights for all Americans. Those combined actions eventually overturned the Jim Crow system. The fight against the legal segregation (which the Supreme Court declared constitutional in 1896) was long, bitter, many times violent, but eventually successful. The defeat of Jim Crow represented a victory for equal rights for all Americans. This is the story of that long struggle and its final victory.

I would like to acknowledge the help and assistance provided by my wife and best friend, Connie, and my sons Jeffrey and Michael. Without their encouragement and support this book would have been much more difficult to write and complete. And to the nurses and doctors in the intensive care unit at West Suburban Hospital, I offer my utmost thanks because without their dedication, kindness, and professionalism this book would never have been completed.

Introduction

FROM 1881 TO 1964, JIM CROW LAWS SEPARATED Americans by race in 26 states. The laws created *de jure* segregation or the legal separation by race of Americans. In most American cities, towns, and states, North and South, people lived in segregated neighborhoods and attended schools that were all white or all black. However, attitudes and history, not laws, created that separation or *de facto* segregation. The "majesty of the law" stood behind legal segregation in Jim Crow states. "The rule of law" imposed penalties and punishments on people who broke those statutes and ordinances mandating segregation. The most common Jim Crow laws made it illegal for anyone to marry someone of another race and demanded that business owners separate their customers by skin color and protected their right to legally refuse service to people because of their race.

Jim Crow America included the eleven states that seceded from the Union in 1861 and established the Confederate States of America. The Confederate states had one goal in mind when they broke away from the Union, the preservation of slavery and white supremacy. Abraham Lincoln went to war to preserve the Union and to end slavery. The Thirteenth Amendment added to the Constitution after the Civil War ended slavery in the United States. It had little impact on the attitudes and ideas used to defend and support the idea that holding other people as property and denying them freedom and any thoughts of equality was justified. Jim Crow laws were aimed at denying freedom and equality to the same group that had been enslaved, African Americans.

One idea topped all others, the supremacy of the white race, and in the racist mind it justified the abuse and inhuman treatment suffered for generations by Africans in the United States. If Africans were not human, or if they were an inferior or lesser part of the human race, they did not have to be treated like human beings. They did not have "human rights" because they were not part of humanity. They were cannibals, savages, and alien creatures coming straight out of the jungle. Biologically they stood closer to gorillas and apes than to human beings. The savagery and barbarism they had inherited from their ancestors for hundreds of years justified their enslavement. Their violent and murderous natures were not easily controlled. The chains of slavery were all that kept Africans from murdering white men and raping their wives and daughters.

The Civil War ended slavery and freed the slaves in the United States, but for most white Southerners, the war had ended nothing. Africans were not ready or able to live freely without the restraints offered by enslavement. They needed discipline and self-control before they could live freely next to whites, but preferably as far away from whites as possible. Without self-discipline and the ability to control their passions (mainly their sexual instincts), the freed blacks would unleash a campaign of violence, murder, and death such as the South had never before seen. The goal of Jim Crow laws was to create a legal system that offered the same protections against black "beastliness," that had been established by slave codes. Instead of chains, whips, and deadly fear, however, laws, jails, powerlessness, and the constant fear of death would provide those protections. Harsh laws separating blacks from whites, always backed up by fear of a lynch mob, a beating, or a severe, pain-filled punishment, would keep blacks from ever coming close to achieving equality. Demanding that black children go to separate schools than whites or that blacks not use the same washroom that whites used, or enter a building or room by a separate door—always in the back—was part of God's law, it was part of the natural order of the universe. Breaking those laws would destroy that entire universe and way of life, the "southern way of life," which outsiders never understood. For much of its history Jim Crow segregation had the protection of the U.S. Constitution and U.S. Supreme Court.

Jim Crow laws covered almost every possible area of human contact. A Georgia law made it unlawful for a white baseball team to play on any vacant lot or playground within two blocks of a playground devoted to the "Negro race." Another Georgia law made it a crime for the official in charge of a cemetery to allow "any colored person" to be buried on ground used for the burial of white people. A Louisiana law required separate buildings for black and white "blind persons" in state institutions for the disabled. That same state required all "circuses, shows, and tent exhibitions" to provide two ticket offices, two individual ticket sellers, and "not less than two entrances" to their performances. If the ticket offices were outside they had to be "not less than twenty-five feet apart." In Mississippi, "the Magnolia State," every hospital needed a separate entrance for white and "colored patients and visitors." According to a Louisiana housing law "any person who shall rent any part of a building to a negro person or a negro family when such building is already in whole or in part" occupied by a white person or family "shall be punished by a fine of not less than $25.00 nor more than $100.00 or be imprisoned not less than ten, or more than sixty days."

Florida (as did 37 other states) prohibited "all marriages between a white person and a person of negro descent to the fourth generation inclusive." (As a sign of their inferiority, Southern laws, newspapers, magazines, and schoolbooks always spelled "Negro" with a small "n.") North Carolina directed librarians to "fit up and maintain a separate place for the use of colored people." Alabama said "no person or corporation shall require any white female nurse to nurse in wards or rooms in hospitals, either public or private, in which negro men are placed." Blacks and whites in Alabama could be arrested for playing "together or in company with each other" at any game of pool or billiards. Any person in Mississippi "who shall be guilty of printing, publishing, or circulating printed, typewritten or written matter urging" or favoring "social equality or intermarriage between whites or negroes" faced a fine of up to $500 or imprisonment for up to six months "or both." As a final example of Jim Crow laws, the Alabama statute regarding restaurants said that white and colored persons could be served in the same room but only if they were "effectually separated by a solid partition extending from the floor upward to a distance of seven feet or higher and unless a separate entrance from the street is provided for each compartment."

Jim Crow laws might produce some laughter in the twenty-first century but they had a serious purpose, to prevent any possible contact between black and white U.S. citizens out of fear that contact would be the first step on the road to equal rights for all people. The laws had the full backing of the U.S. Supreme Court until 1964, when Congress outlawed all discriminatory legislation passed by any state legislature, county board, or city council (in the Civil Rights Act of that year). More than two dozen states had discriminatory laws at that time, but in the American South Jim Crow laws established an entire way of life, the "southern way of life," with whites having the status of the "master race" and people of color having nothing but low wages, hard work, and very few chances for improvement.

Members of the master race felt that segregation gave Southerners of all colors exactly what they wanted, peace and security. "The Negro had not been segregated merely for political or race advantage, but . . . for his good and the country's good, and speaking broadly, for our own salvation," a white North Carolina U.S. senator explained in 1906. After more than 95 percent of African Americans lost their right to vote because of the poll tax and literacy test imposed by his state, a white Mississippi member of Congress declared that his state's electorate was now restricted "to those, and to those alone, who are qualified by intelligence and character for the proper and patriotic exercise of this great franchise" (Newby, 1965, p. 151). Taking away the right to vote from African Americans was not the result of white prejudice and bigotry, as "outsiders" claimed, but of black ignorance, criminality, laziness, and sexual immorality, a Mississippi state senator boasted.

Booker T. Washington and his followers thought that "good white" people in the South would support equal rights for African Americans once blacks had demonstrated their ability to work hard, run a business or a farm, and improve their economic status. It might take a long time, a couple of generations, for the better class of whites to come to that understanding, the Wizard of Tuskegee believed, but some day they would. Until that time, African Americans would be better off pursuing economic opportunities and improving their job skills rather than fighting for political and social equality. Washington's view matched exactly the ideas expressed by the most extreme white racists. "Political equality," beginning with the right to vote, according to white extremists, led directly to the thing they feared the most—"social equality"—because the racists believed that social equality had one horrible consequence: interracial marriage and the mongrelization of the white race.

Thomas Dixon, the white Southern novelist and defender of the Ku Klux Klan, suggested the following experiment to measure a person's commitment to equality, "If a man really believed in equality," and in Dixon's view no white Southerner ever believed in the equality of all races, "let him prove it by giving his daughter to a negro in marriage. That is the test. When she sinks with her mulatto children into the black abyss of negro life, then ask him" if he believes in social equality. Dixon had no doubt as to what the answer would be. The real problem with the idea of equality, another Southerner explained, "is not black warriors, but colored brothers-in-law" (Newby, 1965, p. 365).

The fight against Jim Crow segregation and for full constitutional rights for all Americans began in the courts and moved to the streets, and then into Congress. It ended successfully, but the struggle took more than 80 years and was filled with bloody lynchings, massacres, murders, humiliations, discriminations, unequal treatment, protests, demonstrations, boycotts, congressional debates and filibusters, racist court opinions, racist police brutality, and the total loss of all constitutional rights and privileges. Jim Crow created a totalitarian, racist society in 11 U.S. states. The African Americans living in those states suffered great stress and trauma during those times. Thousands lost their lives, and thousands more lost any sense of fairness and justice. As one elderly black Mississippi woman described her life in Jim Crow America, "The white man had everything. We had nothing" (Litwack, 1998, p. 271).

The story of the fight against Jim Crow and for equal rights and justice for all Americans begins with the ending of the Civil War.

References

Litwack, Leon. *Trouble in Mind: Black Southerners in the Age of Jim Crow*. New York: Alfred A Knopf, 1999.

Newby, I. A. *Jim Crow's Defense: Anti-Negro Thought in America, 1900–1930*. Baton Rouge: Louisiana State University Press, 1965.

Chronology

1865 April 9: General Robert E. Lee surrendered to General Ulysses S. Grant, ending the Civil War.

April 15: John Wilkes Booth assassinated Abraham Lincoln, making Southerner Andrew Johnson president.

May 1–3: White mobs and police in Memphis, Tennessee, killed 46 African Americans.

June 3: Police killed 40 African Americans and wounded more than 100 attending a Republican Party convention in New Orleans.

November 22–29: Mississippi enacted the first "Black Code."

December 15: The Thirteenth Amendment, outlawing slavery "except as a punishment for crime," was ratified.

December 24: The Ku Klux Klan was formally organized as a "social club" for Confederate soldiers in Pulaski, Tennessee.

1868 July 28: The Fourteenth Amendment, granting citizenship to all persons born in the United States, was ratified.

September 28: An estimated two hundred to three hundred African Americans were massacred in Opelousas, Louisiana.

1870 March 30: The Fifteenth Amendment, declaring that race could not be used to prevent a U.S. citizen from voting, was ratified.

1873 April 14: In the *Slaughterhouse Cases* the Supreme Court severely reduced the protections offered citizens by the Fourteenth Amendment. In a 5–4 decision, the justices said that actions by states could not be struck down by federal courts because the "privileges or immunities" of citizens protected by the amendment did not apply to states but only to federal government actions.

1875 March 1: Congress passed the Civil Rights Act of 1875. It guaranteed equal rights to all Americans regardless of race.

September 4: Whites in Clinton, Mississippi, killed more than two hundred African Americans.

1876 November 7: The presidential election ended with neither candidate, Republican Rutherford B. Hayes nor Democrat Samuel Tilden, getting the constitutionally required majority of electoral votes. Congress established an electoral commission to determine who should receive the disputed votes.

1881 March: Tennessee passed the first Jim Crow law in the nation. It segregated railroad cars.

1883 October 15: In the *Civil Rights Cases*, the Supreme Court declared the Civil Rights Act of 1875 unconstitutional. The Fourteenth Amendment made it illegal only for states, not private citizens, to discriminate.

1886 March 17: A white mob killed more than 20 African Americans in Carrollton, Mississippi.

1890 November 1: The "Mississippi Plan" was approved by the state constitutional convention. It created literacy tests to keep African Americans from voting.

1891 January 15: The Lodge Bill was defeated in the U.S Senate. Senator Henry Cabot Lodge had proposed a bill that would have sent federal supervisors into congressional districts to investigate charges of racial discrimination in voter registration.

1895 September 18: Booker T. Washington delivered his "Atlanta Compromise" speech advocating "accommodationism" and "gradualism" in solving "the Negro problem."

1896 May 18: The Supreme Court issued its *Plessy v. Ferguson* decision declaring that students could be separated by race in public schools. This ruling made Jim Crow laws constitutional.

1898 November 10: Whites killed eight African Americans during a race riot in Wilmington, North Carolina.

1899 October 30: The Supreme Court decided unanimously in *Cumming v. Richmond County Board of Education* that the "separate but equal" doctrine did not require school boards to fund schools for both black and white students if they had only enough money to fund one school system. If blacks were denied a school, they had to prove that the only reason the board made that decision was "hostility to the colored population because of their race." The unanimous court found no evidence of racial discrimination in this case.

1901 March 4: Congressman George H. White, the only African American in Congress, left the House of Representatives after losing his bid for reelection. The next black in Congress was not elected until 1928.

October 16: Booker T. Washington had dinner at the White House with President Theodore Roosevelt.

1906 August 13: A racial disturbance in Brownsville, Texas, witnessed the death of one white man. Three companies of African American soldiers stationed outside of Brownsville were dishonorably discharged by the Army for alleged involvement in the killing.

September 22–24: During a race riot in Atlanta, Georgia, ten African Americans and two whites were killed.

1908 July 2: Thurgood Marshall was born in Baltimore, Maryland.

August 14–16: Eight African Americans were killed in a race riot in Springfield, Illinois. Two thousand more were driven out of the city, most would not return to their homes for a year.

In *Berea College v. Kentucky*, the Supreme Court ruled that a Kentucky law making it a crime to educate white and African American students in the same building was constitutional.

1909 February 12: The National Association for the Advancement of Colored People (NAACP) was organized in New York City.

December 19: The Baltimore City Council approved a law that established boundaries for white and black neighborhoods. Other cities soon followed. (The Supreme Court declared such laws unconstitutional in 1917.)

1911 In *Bailey v. Alabama*, the Supreme Court struck down criminal penalties for "breach of labor contracts."

1913 April 11: President Woodrow Wilson ordered the segregation of all federal government offices, lunchrooms, and restrooms in the United States.

1915 June 21: The Supreme Court found that an Oklahoma law establishing a "grandfather clause" that allowed anyone to register to vote if he had been eligible to vote in 1867 without having to pay a poll tax or take a literacy test, before ratification of the Fifteenth Amendment, was unconstitutional.

November 14: Booker T. Washington died.

In *The United States v. Reynolds*, the Supreme Court declared laws making it a crime to break a labor contract unconstitutional.

1917   July 1–3: White rioters killed 40 to 300 African Americans in East St. Louis, Illinois, and drove 6,000 blacks from their homes.

August 23: Two African Americans and eleven whites died in a race riot in Houston, Texas. Twenty-nine African American soldiers were executed for participating in the riot.

November 5: In *Buchanan v. Warley*, the Supreme Court declared a Louisville city ordinance mandating segregated neighborhoods unconstitutional.

1919   In the "Red Summer," 26 race riots occurred between April and October, including riots in Chicago; Charleston, South Carolina; Longview, Texas; Washington, D.C.; and Elaine, Arkansas.

1921   May 31–June 2: A race riot in Tulsa led to the deaths of 60 to 300 African Americans and 21 whites.

1922   December 4: The Senate failed to pass a federal antilynching bill because of a Southern filibuster.

1923   January 4: The all-black town of Rosewood, Florida, was burned and destroyed by a white mob.

1928   November 6: Voters in Chicago elected African American Republican Oscar De Priest to the House of Representatives. He was the first black in Congress since 1901.

1931   April 6: The Scottsboro Boys were arrested in Alabama and charged with raping two white girls.

1932   May 2: In *Nixon v. Condon*, the Supreme Court found that a Texas law preventing African Americans from voting in primary elections was unconstitutional.

October 10: The Supreme Court, in *Powell v. Alabama*, threw out the conviction of Ozzie Powell, one of the Scottsboro Boys, because he had not been provided with adequate legal counsel during his trial.

1935   April 1: The Supreme Court, in *Norris v. Alabama*, ruled that the Scottsboro Boys had been denied fair trials because African Americans had been excluded from the juries.

1936 February 17: The Supreme Court announced its decision in *Brown v. Mississippi*. Evidence obtained through the use of torture could not be used in court.

1938 December 12: The Supreme Court, in *Missouri ex rel. Gaines v. Canada*, declared that if states had a law school for white students they must also provide a law school for African American students.

1941 June 25: President Franklin Roosevelt established the Fair Employment Practices Committee (FEPC).

1943 June 24: Twenty-five African Americans and nine whites were killed in the Detroit, Michigan, race riot.

1944 April 3: The Supreme Court, in *Smith v. Allwright*, decided that whites-only primary elections were unconstitutional.

1946 June 3: In *Morgan v. Virginia*, the Supreme Court declared segregation on interstate buses unconstitutional.

1948 July 26: President Harry Truman issued Executive Order 9981, desegregating the armed forces.

In *Shelley v. Kraemer*, the Supreme Court ruled that state and local governments could not enforce racially restrictive covenants.

1950 June 5: In *Sweatt v. Painter*, the Supreme Court decided that the Fourteenth Amendment required Texas to admit an African American student to the all-white University of Texas Law School because the school it constructed for blacks was inferior and inadequate.

1951 May 24: The Supreme Court ruled that racial segregation in Washington, D.C., restaurants was unconstitutional.

December 25: Ku Klux Klansmen killed Harry T. Moore, a leader of the Florida NAACP, and his wife.

1952 Tuskegee Institute reported no lynchings during the year. For the first time in 71 years, no American had been lynched.

1954 May 27: The Supreme Court issued its opinion in *Brown v. Board of Education* outlawing segregation in public schools.

1955 May 31: In *Brown II*, the Supreme Court said that schools must begin to desegregate "with all deliberate speed."

August 28: Two white men beat 14-year-old Emmett Till to death in Money, Mississippi.

December 1: Rosa Parks refused to give up her seat to a white man in Montgomery, Alabama, and was arrested, leading to the Montgomery Bus Boycott.

1956   February 29: Autherine Lucy, the first African American student to attend the University of Alabama, was expelled after white students rioted on campus.

November 13: The Supreme Court banned segregation on intrastate buses, trains, and other forms of public transportation in *Browder v. Gayle.*

1957   August 29: Congress passed the Civil Rights Act of 1957.

September: President Dwight Eisenhower ordered federal troops into Little Rock, Arkansas, to protect nine African American students and to ensure the enforcement of a federal court order to desegregate Central High School.

1958   January 12: Martin Luther King Jr. established the Southern Christian Leadership Conference (SCLC) in Atlanta, Georgia.

1959   April 26: Two white men lynched African American Mack Charles Parker in Poplarville, Mississippi.

1960   February 1: Four African American students in Greensboro, North Carolina, began a nonviolent sit-in at the lunch counter in a Woolworth's store, demanding service.

April 15: Students organized the Student Nonviolent Coordinating Committee (SNCC) in Raleigh, North Carolina.

May 6: President Eisenhower signed the Civil Rights Act of 1960.

1961   May 4: Eleven members of the Congress of Racial Equality (CORE) left Washington, D.C., on the first Freedom Ride.

September: White students rioted on the campus of the University of Georgia after the first two African American students enrolled in the school began attending classes.

1962   October 1: James Meredith became the first African American student to attend the University of Mississippi. White students rioted that evening and two people were killed.

1963   April 16: Martin Luther King Jr. wrote his "Letter from Birmingham Jail."

May 3: Birmingham police used dogs and fire hoses to attack civil rights demonstrators.

June 11: Governor George Wallace blocked the door to the registrar's office in an attempt to prevent the enrollment of two black students at the University of Alabama.

June 12: White supremacist Byron De La Beckwith assassinated Mississippi NAACP field secretary Medgar Evers.

August 28: Three hundred thousand demonstrators gathered in the nation's capital for the March on Washington for Jobs and Freedom.

September 15: Ku Klux Klan terrorists killed four African American girls, ages 11 to 14, in the bombing of the Sixteenth Street Baptist Church.

1964 June: SNCC sponsored the Mississippi Freedom Summer Project.

June 21: Ku Klux Klan terrorists murdered three civil rights workers in Philadelphia, Mississippi.

July 2: President Lyndon Johnson signed the 1964 Civil Rights Act, making Jim Crow laws illegal.

1965 March 7: Alabama state troopers assaulted civil rights marchers in Selma, Alabama, on the Edmund Pettus Bridge.

March 21–25: Martin Luther King Jr. marched with thousands of demonstrators from Selma to Montgomery, Alabama, to demand voting rights.

August 6: Lyndon Johnson signed the Voting Rights Act of 1965, which banned literacy tests, into law.

1967 June 12: The Supreme Court in *Loving v. Virginia* declared all state laws barring interracial marriage unconstitutional.

July 13: Thurgood Marshall became the first African American justice on the Supreme Court.

ONE

Jim Crow Laws—Meaning, Origins, and Purpose

THE TERM "JIM CROW" refers to a series laws and ordinances passed by Southern states and municipalities between 1877 and 1965 legalizing segregation (the physical separation of individuals based on race, gender, religion, or class) within their boundaries. It also refers to an entire way of life in which whites and blacks lived in two vastly unequal communities in the South. One of them—the white—had all the power, wealth, and privileges while the other—the black—faced daily, seemingly unending incidents of terror and humiliation, with hardly any freedom, very little wealth, and absolutely no justice.

The name Jim Crow came from a song and dance routine performed by an actor in one of the very popular minstrel shows touring the country from the 1820s to the 1870s. In one of the travelling shows, Thomas Dartmouth "Daddy" Rice, a white actor, portrayed an elderly black slave, Jim Crow. Rice appeared on stage in "blackface." He darkened his face and hands with burnt cork, wore shabby overalls, shuffled across the stage in bare feet, and carried a banjo. His routine included jokes and a song and dance number performed in a white version of black dialect titled "Jim Crow." The complete song had at least 44 verses. The first verse began

Come listen all you gals and boys,
I's jist from Tuckyhoe,
I'm goin to sing a little song,
My name's Jim Crow.

And during the chorus the all-white actors in front of the all-white audience would dance around the stage, shuffling and singing in the black dialect of slaves they had heard:

Chorus
Weel about and turn about and do jis so,
Eb'ry time I weel about and jump Jim Crow.

Rice said he first heard the song while walking down an alley in Louisville, Kentucky. The singer, an elderly black slave, worked in a blacksmith's shop and was called Jim. Rice picked "Crow" because crows are black (Emerson, 2010, 21–30).

Big Daddy's performances in all regions of the United States made him very popular and wealthy in pre-Civil War America. After the war, he turned to alcohol as his fortunes declined. The song captured the popular and misinformed white image of slaves, who were always happy, smiling, dancing, lazy, and dim-witted—Africans who found a home on the "ole Marster's" plantation, far away from the cannibalism and savagery of their home in Africa, the "Dark Continent." By the mid-1830s, "Jim Crow" had become a term used by whites to refer to all blacks, along with "coon." It came from "Zip Coon," another offensive and degrading minstrel show character played by a white actor with his face coated with charcoal who amused white audiences.

How the Jim Crow name became associated with segregation laws remains unknown, but by the 1890s, it referred to an entire way of life. It stood for an entire culture based on violence, racism, and fear that affected the life of every African American living in the South. Until the 1920s, 90 percent of the black population of the United States lived in the 11 states of the old Confederacy. In the early Jim Crow decades (1880–1900) of the nineteenth century, white mobs lynched hundreds of African Americans, and the black community saw all of the political, legal, and citizenship rights it had gained since the Civil War (1861–65) disappear. For whites Jim Crow meant fun, laughter, and amusement. In African American homes the name meant humiliation, degradation, and cowardice.

Relegating blacks to second-class citizenship had a long history in the United States, dating back to 1619 when the first Africans were sold as slaves in Virginia. By 1750, every British colony in North America, including all 13 colonies that would break away from the British Empire in 1776, had legalized slavery and created law codes that treated slaves differently than whites, with harsher punishments imposed no matter what the crime.

The Virginia Slave Codes of 1662 and 1705 served as models for other colonies. Owners possessed absolute authority over their slaves, who the law considered "real estate," just like a barn, a house, or a field, rather than a human being. The code said that all "Negro, mulatto, and Indian" persons in the colony "shall be accounted as slaves." Race made one a slave, nothing else. White persons could not be enslaved. If your mother were a slave, you would be a slave. If a slave "resisted his master," the master could "correct" him or her in whatever way he deemed appropriate. Slave owners had the full protection of the law no matter how cruelly or brutally they treated their "property." If a slave died because of the punishment he received from his master, the law treated the owner "as if such accident never happened." Slaves and whites were hung for murder or rape; however, for lesser crimes, such as robbery or "insolence," slaves received 60 lashes while whites seldom got more than 30. For running away, a slave could have one of his or her feet slashed off, or lose his or her ears.

For "minor offenses," such as "associating" with whites or refusing to "work hard enough," the code allowed slaves to be whipped, branded with a hot iron, or "maimed," which generally meant losing a foot, a hand, or an ear. All slaves on a plantation witnessed the administration of these punishments and the screams and cries they heard supposedly acted as a deterrent to any unlawful actions they might consider. Such demonstrations of brutality and cruelty would remind the witnesses of how helpless, alone, and insignificant they were.

Not all Africans in North America lived in slavery. A small number (about 5% of the total slave population) were "free blacks" or "free people of color," as whites called them. They became free by various means. Africans volunteering to fight against the British during the Revolutionary War received their freedom, and during that War for Independence (1775–83), most Northern states abolished slavery. No matter where they lived, however, freed slaves faced strict laws segregating them by race—called Black Codes—severely limiting their conduct and behavior. Most states prevented free blacks from voting, serving on juries, or testifying against whites in court. Free black children in Northern states received their education in segregated schools, free black convicts served their sentences in segregated prisons, and free blacks who died were buried in segregated cemeteries. Laws segregating free Americans by race existed long before the era of Jim Crow.

Even in states where slavery remained legal, Africans managed to become free either by purchasing their freedom from a willing owner or through manumission, the legal process of becoming free. Slave owners could manumit their slaves with few restrictions, but slave rebellions usually led to a crack down on freeing slaves and after the 1830s, manumission became almost impossible. Most Southern states required manumitted slaves to move out of the state after becoming free, while Louisiana required that free blacks leave the United States. In the U.S. slave states of Alabama, Arkansas, Delaware, Florida, Georgia, Kentucky, Louisiana, Maryland, Mississippi, Missouri, North Carolina, South Carolina, Tennessee, Texas, and Virginia, free blacks lived in small, isolated, impoverished communities barely better off than slaves living on nearby plantations. Any "free Negro" who married a white person faced severe punishment, including being sold to the highest bidder as a "servant" for seven years. A black convicted of raping a white woman faced castration or death.

Northern states such as Indiana and Illinois enacted "exclusion laws" prohibiting free blacks from buying land or opening a business within their boundaries. Ohio required blacks to post a $500 bond with the secretary of state guaranteeing their good behavior as long as they lived in the state. Ohio also required separate schools for black children. According to Indiana law, only white students could attend its public schools. Why? When black parents sued and asked for permission to enroll their child in an all-white school, a state court denied their request. The judge explained that the Indiana legislature had decided that "black children were deemed unfit associates of whites as school companions," and that was sufficient reason for excluding them (Litwack, 1965, 73–74).

The "exclusion" laws, separate school laws, and white-only voting laws received support from overwhelming majorities of citizens in the slavery-free North. Though not always enforced, the segregation laws stood as reminders to blacks that the white community did not want them in their neighborhoods, cities, and towns. Supporters of antiblack laws included many people with liberal views such as the utopian founder of New Harmony, Indiana, Robert Dale Owen. Though he dedicated his colony to eternal peace and justice, the Scotch philanthropist favored Indiana's discriminatory school and exclusion laws. In an 1850 speech, he asked if any decent American wished "the continuance among us of a race to whom we are not willing to accord the most common protection against outrage and death?" (Litwack, 1965, 75). The greatest fear possessed by whites concerning African Americans was their alleged uncontrollable instinct to attack and sexually violate whites, especially white women. This fear lasted well into the Jim Crow era and had a long-term impact on race relations in the United States. Gunnar Myrdal, the great Swedish sociologist who studied Southern race relations in the 1930s, concluded in his *An American Dilemma: The Negro Problem and American Democracy*, published in 1944, that the fear of interracial sex and marriage, or miscegenation as whites called it, was the most important worry in their racial thinking.

Voting rights, equality before the law, and competition for jobs were extremely worrisome ideas, but none came close to fear of interracial sex in truly frightening white men and women. The history of Jim Crow laws provides great support for Myrdal's conclusion.

Northern states slowly but eventually repealed their Black Codes, but then they reemerged in a much more violent and extreme form in the American South after the Civil War. When the fighting stopped in April 1865, 19 of the 24 states that fought to keep the Union together had laws forbidding blacks from voting, serving on juries, or testifying against whites in court. The war ended slavery in the United States, but prejudice and discrimination remained. Although the Northern laws were repealed long before Jim Crow laws disappeared, they demonstrated that Northerners opposed slavery but at the same time feared the presence of African Americans.

Ending unfree labor had been extremely costly in terms of lives and money for the North; huge losses of life affected every region of the nation. Union army deaths exceeded 350,000 while Confederate losses reached just below 260,000. The Confederate states, where most of the fighting had taken place, lost more than 40 percent of their combined wealth. This did not include the vast fortunes lost because of the death of slavery. And the gains? Four million slaves were now free in the United States, but legally they were not citizens. Freed slaves lacked any constitutional rights because of the Supreme Court's decision in the 1857 *Dred Scott* case. In that ruling, Chief Justice Roger Taney, a Southerner and strong defender of slavery, speaking for the court majority, declared that blacks had never been citizens and could never become citizens; they were property in his view of the Constitution, not human beings. However, did any of that legal standing change now that slavery no longer existed? That question proved very difficult to answer.

Some Americans believed that freedom for the former slaves meant having exactly the same rights and privileges as all other Americans had. The newly freed human beings deserved all the privileges of citizenship. The freed people certainly wanted the rights denied them as slaves: education, for example, and the ability to move about freely without interference, and, of course, economic and political self-determination. Those privileges were what American freedom meant, and if they continued to be denied to the newly freed people, then all the deaths and all the destruction that took place during the bloody war meant nothing.

The period of U.S. history known as Reconstruction was about to begin. It involved a long political and constitutional debate that frequently became violent. It concerned the question of what rights former slaves deserved.

Many Northern Republicans, the party of Abraham Lincoln, believed that the freed men and women deserved full citizenship and the same constitutional rights guaranteed to other citizens. Most Democrats disagreed. Before the war they had defended slavery, and during the war they became the "peace party." As recently as the 1864 presidential election, the Democratic platform called for a quick end to the fighting on whatever terms the slave states wanted. As for blacks, few Democrats, North or South, wanted equal rights or felt that the slaves deserved them.

Political divisions also existed on the question of what should happen to the Confederate soldiers. Had they not committed treason, many Republicans argued, so did they not deserve severe punishment? On the other hand, moderates argued that losing the war was punishment enough. Abraham Lincoln hoped to restore as quickly as possible the constitutional rights of Confederates, including their right to vote, especially if they took an oath of future loyalty to the Constitution. The "Radical Republicans" in Congress, led by Senator Charles Sumner of Massachusetts and Representative Thaddeus Stephens of Pennsylvania, believed that all Confederate army veterans should never again be allowed to vote and supported a bill favoring that idea.

Radicals argued that simple freedom was not enough and that the freedmen and women needed quick economic assistance to prevent starvation and exploitation by their former owners. Radical Republicans proposed giving the freed people land taken from wealthy plantation owners, so they could farm it and provide for their own needs. They also wanted immediate action granting former slaves all the privileges and rights enjoyed by other Americans, including the right to vote, the right to move about freely, the right to a job, and the right to an education. Democrats, on the other hand, seemed more concerned with restoring the rights of former Confederate soldiers. They wanted them to have their rights as Americans restored immediately, without more punishment or delay. The freed slaves had received all the help they needed; they had their freedom and now they had to learn how to take care of themselves.

President Lincoln's assassination five days after the ending of the Civil War resolved none of these issues. The new president, Andrew Johnson, had owned slaves in his native state of Tennessee and held a life-long prejudice against blacks. He had been the only Southerner to remain in the Senate when the war began. He did not support voting rights for freed slaves, believing that the Constitution gave states alone the power to determine who could vote. In his view, the slaves had their freedom and they needed no other government help. Freedom was enough.

Johnson believed the Union had been restored with the surrender of the Confederate army; nothing more was needed to confirm that point. Confederates needed to have their constitutional rights quickly restored, and he as president had the power to restore them. In one of his first acts as president, Johnson authorized elections in the former Confederate states. All citizens eligible to vote before the war began in 1860 could cast ballots in 1865—in other words, only white males over 21. Under those guidelines, in the first postwar elections many former Confederate soldiers and government officials ran for office, and Confederate veterans flocked to the polls and elected their war-time leaders as their new governors, legislators, and local officials. These new governments hurried into action passing new laws effecting race relations, including a series of very restrictive "Black Codes," modeled after those discriminatory laws found in Northern states before the war.

The Thirteenth Amendment, ratified in December 1865, outlawed slavery, but by that time many former Confederate states had laws of their own creating a system of labor and race relations as close to slavery as constitutionally possible. White Southerners believed that blacks would work only if forced to by strict laws and brutal punishments. Mississippi and South Carolina enacted some of the harshest laws in the ex-Confederacy, mandating that former slaves either get jobs or go to jail. They required all blacks to sign a labor contract with a plantation owner every year and to work for him for the entire year. Quitting was not allowed; it became a crime. Sheriffs had the authority to arrest a black person found without a labor contract or proof of a job and charge him or her with vagrancy (defined simply as "not working"). Punishment included a $50 fine or up to a year in prison. In addition, sheriffs could lease out prisoners to local cotton growers. On the plantation, prisoners worked long and hard without pay and the sheriff kept the lease fee. County jails used to fill up around planting and harvesting time with people convicted of "vagrancy."

Alabama's code allowed blacks to testify in courts but "only in cases involving 'people of color.' " It prohibited blacks from owning guns and did not allow black children to attend school with whites. Florida and Texas enacted laws requiring railroad companies to have separate cars for white and black passengers. No former Confederate state gave blacks the right to vote or to serve on juries. They all, however, outlawed marriages between blacks and whites. Conviction for the crime of interracial marriage in Mississippi called for a sentence of life in the state penitentiary for the offenders.

The Black Codes followed the tradition established by the slave codes and the Northern Black Codes; they created a legal "color line," which placed harsh penalties on anyone who tried to cross it. The codes lasted for less than a year, however, because Congress acted quickly to repeal them.

When Congress reassembled in January 1866, Republicans controlled large majorities in the House and Senate, and passed the Civil Rights Bill of 1866, which restricted the influence of the Black Codes. President Johnson vetoed the bill, arguing that it violated states' rights. Congress overrode his veto with the necessary two-thirds majority, making the Civil Rights Bill the law. The new law gave citizenship to all freed slaves and provided all U.S. citizens with the same rights as others, including the right to make and enforce contracts; to sue; to give evidence in court; to inherit real estate and property; and to purchase, lease, and convey real and personal property. It also gave the federal government the right "to intervene" in states that denied these constitutional rights to U.S. citizens.

Shortly after passing the Civil Rights Act, Congress passed the Fourteenth Amendment and sent it to the states for ratification. The amendment repeated many of the clauses found in the 1866 Civil Rights Act, to counter any claims of representatives who argued that the act was unconstitutional. It also overturned the *Dred Scott* decision that blacks could not become citizens. It established two methods by which an individual became a citizen—he or she was either born in the United States or went through the naturalization process (as established by Congress), if the person came from another country. It also guaranteed all citizens the same rights as others and said, "No State shall make or enforce any law, which shall abridge the privileges and immunities of citizens of the United States." The amendment did not list what "privileges" or "immunities" citizens enjoyed, and arguments over the meaning of those words divided the Supreme Court for the next hundred years.

The amendment gave Congress authority to reduce a state's representation in the House if it denied voting rights to any of its citizens, though this provision was never enforced, even as Southern states denied voting rights to several million people for almost an entire century. The ex-Confederate states bitterly resisted the Fourteenth Amendment, so they, except for Tennessee, refused to ratify it. This refusal made it impossible to reach the constitutionally required two-thirds majority of states needed to ratify an amendment.

Congress responded to the Southern action by abolishing the nonratifying states (they had committed "state suicide" when they seceded from the Union, the amendment's supporters argued, and had not yet been rightfully returned to its life). They were placed under military control. If they wanted back into the Union, Congress required the former slave states to ratify the amendment. As a result of that demand and to hasten an end to "military occupation," all states in the South ratified the Fourteenth Amendment in time for the 1868 presidential election. For the first time in the history of U.S. elections, all male citizens over 21 years of age, regardless of race or color, could vote for a candidate of their choice. African American voters turned out in large numbers, in spite of the violence and harassment they faced throughout the South, to cast their votes for Ulysses S. Grant, the Republican candidate for the White House. Grant ran on a platform calling for equal rights for all Americans. He defeated Horatio Seymour, Democratic governor of New York, who ran a racist campaign that attacked the idea of giving voting rights to "ignorant" blacks.

In state and local elections, black candidates in the former Confederate states received electoral support from two groups of whites: carpetbaggers, Northerners who moved into the South when the war ended, and scalawags, that small group of Southern white voters who supported equal rights and the Republican Party. Election results saw Republicans win governorships in all but two Southern states, Louisiana and Georgia. In another first, African Americans won seats in state legislatures and gained control of many local offices, from sheriff to county commissioner (by the turn of the century more than six hundred blacks had served in those roles). Voters chose no black governors, but they did elect one black lieutenant governor, in South Carolina, making him the highest-ranking African American state official. The Mississippi legislature sent two black U.S. senators to Washington (the only two African Americans to serve in the Senate until the 1960s), and two members of the House of Representatives, one from Georgia and the other from South Carolina, were black. Altogether, 16 African Americans served in the House from 1868 to 1902.

From 1868 to 1870, in the only two years the party controlled a majority of the ex-Confederate states, the new Republican governments brought new programs and ideas to South, such as public schools, public hospitals, and expanded use of public funds for road building and railroad construction. Called "Radical Republicans" by their Democratic opponents, who started referring to themselves as "redeemers," the new governments sought economic growth and diversity by encouraging Northern industrialists to move their companies and jobs south. The all-white Democrats planned to "redeem" the South from "corrupt, black-controlled" governments and the economic and political goals they pursued. The "radical" governments hardly seemed radical to the carpetbaggers and industrialists. They supported programs that included state-funded public school systems and public hospitals, and laws outlawing racial discrimination in public transportation and accommodations. To finance their projects, they sold bonds and borrowed millions of dollars to promote economic development and the building of a "New South." The 1868 election brought a brief period of economic development and integrated government to the South. It could not last.

White opposition to equality grew rapidly and became increasingly violent. The Ku Klux Klan (KKK) and other terrorist groups had organized a massive terror campaign to stop the reforms. By the time the next elections came around, killing, beating, burning, and whipping blacks who dared to vote reached epidemic levels. The KKK produced the most violence. Established in Pulaski, Tennessee, shortly after Lee's surrender, the KKK began its campaign of violence against what it came to call "negro misrule" in 1868.

Klan violence, terror, and membership spread across the entire South by 1869. Some Confederate states returned to white rule (or were "redeemed") by the end of that year. To restore order in the bloodiest counties, Congress passed a series of Enforcement Acts in 1870–71, which gave President Grant authority to use the army to arrest Klan leaders and restore peace. The president sent the army into South Carolina several times over the next two years to end to the beatings, whippings, and murders that took place almost daily in many areas of the South. Republican governors in North Carolina and Arkansas (both "carpetbaggers") used state militia units to protect citizens from the violent disorder.

In other states, including South Carolina, Georgia, Mississippi, and Alabama, the army and federal marshals arrested hundreds of Klansmen. Federal judges sent dozens of Klan leaders to prison. These arrests significantly reduced Klan activity by 1872. By then, however, white-only governments had taken control of all but five ex-Confederate states. The others took more time, but by 1875, all former Confederate states, except for three—Georgia, Mississippi, and South Carolina—had been "redeemed." No other Republican governments survived the terrorist violence.

The white Democratic return to power in the Southern states benefited greatly from decisions of the U.S. Supreme Court. The justices helped restore white rule to the white South by severely weakening the meaning and coverage of minority rights provided by the Fourteenth Amendment. The court began its campaign against equal rights with the so-called *Slaughterhouse Cases* in 1873. In this 5–4 decision, the majority ruled that the Fourteenth Amendment, which supposedly guaranteed that every U.S. citizen possessed "certain privileges and immunities" that no state could take away, did not mean what most supporters thought that meant. Instead, the court severely limited the meaning of that phrase. It covered only a few minor privileges such as the right to use the navigable waters of the United States and the right to travel freely to and from the nation's capital, but nothing beyond that. "Privileges" of more significance such as the right to vote or to serve on juries, according to the court's definition, came under the jurisdiction and protection of state governments. The national government had no right or power to interfere in decisions made by state governments concerning those "privileges" protected by the Fourteenth Amendment.

The *Slaughterhouse Cases* involved a relatively minor Louisiana law that gave one slaughterhouse the sole right to butcher cattle and hogs in the city of New Orleans. Butchers working for other companies in the city sued in federal court, arguing that an exclusive grant to slaughter animals in the city took away their right to work—one of the rights, they argued, guaranteed to Americans by the Fourteenth Amendment. In its 5–4 verdict, the court ruled against the butchers and in favor of the monopoly. The majority said that the right to labor (or a job) was not one of the rights protected by the amendment's "privileges and immunities" clause. "The one pervading purpose" of the Fourteenth Amendment, the court majority announced, was to guarantee "the rights and freedoms" of black Americans, and neither butchering animals or the right to a job were included among those rights.

The decision in the *Slaughterhouse Cases* had a major impact on the question of what rights and privileges Americans possessed, and who or which level of government had the responsibility of protecting them. The next important case involving the question of rights, *Cruikshank v. United States*, 92 U.S. 542 (1876), arose out of the bloodiest incident of mass murder in the entire Reconstruction era, the Colfax Massacre of 1873. In that year on Easter Sunday in Colfax, a tiny Louisiana town on the Red River close to the Texas border, a white mob burned, shot, and killed more than one hundred African Americans. The massacre took place following a disputed mayoral election in which both blacks and whites participated. After officials counted the ballots they proclaimed a victory for the all-white Democratic ticket. The Republicans (all-black) in Colfax charged that the Democrats had stolen the election in an effort to take over the city government, and they decided to fight that outcome by whatever means necessary.

The blacks took dramatic action. More than one hundred armed black men took over the courthouse, holding it for three weeks. Then more than three hundred armed whites attacked, setting the courthouse on fire. As the African Americans raced out of the burning building, the whites shot and killed more than 20 of them, "arrested" the others, and turned them over to the sheriff.

While awaiting trial in the city jail, another white mob attacked the imprisoned black Republicans. The mob killed over one hundred of the prisoners in their cells, dragged their bodies out to the lawn, and buried them in a mass grave. The governor sent in investigators to find out what happened. They reported back two days later describing how they found "fifteen to twenty" bodies, all black, floating in the Red River. They had not found the grave containing the many other victims. No white person they interviewed had any knowledge of any mass grave or even of the reported "massacre." The exact number of victims remains unknown, but Louisiana erected a plaque on the one hundredth anniversary of the massacre dedicated to the memory of the "105 blacks and three whites" who died on that bloody Easter Sunday.

When federal marshals, sent by President Grant, arrived on the scene a few days later, they reported some success in getting black citizens to talk, and eventually arrested seven of the whites involved in the killings, including a man named Cruikshank. They were charged with violating the Enforcement Act of 1870. A federal jury in Louisiana convicted Cruikshank and two other defendants of depriving the murdered victims of their constitutional rights and they were sentenced to federal prison for five years, the maximum penalty allowed by the law.

The defendants took an appeal of their conviction to federal court and eventually to the U.S. Supreme Court, which heard their case in 1876. In a unanimous (9–0) decision, the court ruled that the crimes committed came under state, not national government jurisdiction. Therefore, neither federal agents nor federal courts had any legitimate interest in the case. Louisiana alone had the authority to bring charges in such cases and only its courts could try the accused and determine their guilt or innocence. The likelihood that the state would take legal action against the white mob members was very small, and shortly after the Supreme Court ruled, all convicted parties in the Cruikshank case walked free from prison. The Supreme Court's decision in *Cruikshank* encouraged more racial violence in the South. Federal authorities had no right to become involved in criminal acts, including murder, unless committed on federal property, and state authorities refused to act. The Supreme Court had effectively deprived blacks in the South of their rights and liberties. African Americans found that they were on their own in an increasingly violent post–Civil War South. The *Cruikshank* decision had deadly consequences for many of them.

Republicans in Congress did not give up in their quest to protect African Americans in the South. In 1875, they passed a Civil Rights Act, sponsored by the greatest friend of African Americans in Washington, the sick and dying Senator Charles Sumner of Massachusetts. After quick passage by the House and Senate, President Grant signed the act into law. It banned "racial discrimination" in hotels, public conveyances (such as streetcars and trains), stores, restaurants, and all "places of public amusement." The Senate bill had originally included a section requiring integration of public schools, but the House voted to eliminate that clause. A section forbidding the exclusion of blacks from juries remained in the legislation despite intense opposition from Southern representatives (Gerber and Friedlander, 2008, 93). The new law offered needed protection to black Americans, but only if federal authorities enforced the law's provisions, and that enforcement appeared questionable as the nation grew further away in time from the Civil War. The Supreme Court decisions and growing disinterest among Northerners towards race problems in the South made the likelihood of action on the Civil Rights Act ever more remote by the mid-1870s.

The protections erected by the 1875 Civil Rights Act to outlaw discrimination against the freed slaves faced increasingly intense, always more violent opposition in the South. Mississippi was one of three Southern states with a majority black population—57.7 percent of the state was African American, according to the 1890 census. South Carolina counted 59.8 percent of its population black, while in Louisiana that percentage was 50.1. These were the only Southern states with African American majorities. Mississippi exploded in violence in the fall of 1875. White mobs killed unknown hundreds of African Americans as the state Democratic Party launched a new strategy (called the "Mississippi Plan") to "redeem" their state from "Yankee control" and "black power." Democrats, though a minority of the population in the state, wanted to return the white race to its "proper" position of strength and control. The first major violence took place in the Mississippi River town of Vicksburg in December 1874 when hundreds of heavily armed whites went on a two-day rampage, shooting and killing more than three hundred blacks and wounding hundreds more. White losses amounted to two dead and four wounded.

Republican governor Adelbert Ames called for the Grant administration to send military assistance as quickly as possible, but the president took no action. Then, at a Republican political rally in Clinton, a mob of drunken whites began what a local newspaper called "an indiscriminate assault on blacks," killing at least 30 African American men, women, and children, before returning to their homes. One of the whites explained what motivated the attack; it was part of a "glorious struggle against the mongrelism, ignorance, and depravity" of Republican rule and represented a victory for

"Anglo-Saxon supremacy." After the deaths of dozens more blacks across the state in the first months of 1875, the *Yazoo City Banner* boasted, "Mississippi is a white man's country and by Eternal God we'll rule it" (McMillen, 1989, 160).

Racial killing increased in the Magnolia State as the election for governor grew nearer. On Election Day, black voters stayed home by the thousands, fearful of the deadly violence that afflicted the state and seeing political activity as a threat to their lives. Results of the election gave the Democratic Party control of both houses of the Mississippi legislature— by four to one majorities (despite the state's majority black population)— and a year later it won five out of six seats in the House of Representatives in Washington. The "Mississippi Plan," as some called it, of open violence directed against African Americans had worked. The state had been "redeemed." Voters had restored white supremacy. The Democratic Party controlled Mississippi government for the next hundred years. To celebrate its first victory, the Democratic-controlled legislature impeached the Republican African American lieutenant governor, Alexander K. Davis, and forced Republican governor Adelbert Ames to resign.

Along with Mississippi, white Democrats now controlled the governments in Tennessee (1870), Georgia (1871), Virginia (1873), Texas (1873), Alabama (1874), and Arkansas (1874). In only four states, Florida, Louisiana, and North and South Carolina, did the Republican Party retain a reasonable chance of winning an election. The movement towards one-party domination in Southern states meant that the fight for equal rights was rapidly ending, unless the national government provided immediate help to the struggling black community. However, after the 1876 presidential election even that possibility disappeared.

At the national level, Congress, the president, and the Supreme Court seemed unwilling to take any meaningful action to protect African Americans in the South. With the death of Charles Sumner, Congress lost its most important voice supporting equal rights. Then, after the election of 1876, not just Congress but even Republican presidents lost interest in protecting voting rights for blacks, and the only decisions the Supreme Court announced reduced rather than expanded the meaning of civil and constitutional rights.

The disputed presidential election of 1876 affirmed the retreat from the protection of political and constitutional rights of African Americans that the Republican Party had offered since the end of the Civil War. The popular vote in 1876 went to Democrat Samuel Tilden over Rutherford B. Hayes, the Republican. However, the Electoral College failed to produce a winner since neither candidate had won the required majority of votes in that body.

Who had won the electoral votes in four states—Florida, Louisiana, Oregon, and South Carolina—remained in dispute. Congress, with the Senate controlled by the Republicans and the House by the Democrats, created a 15-member electoral commission to resolve the issue and determine who would get the electoral votes. Tilden needed one additional electoral vote to win, while Hayes needed all of the twenty-one disputed votes.

The commission had five House members, five Senators, and five justices of the Supreme Court. Seven of the members were Democrats, seven were Republicans, and one of the justices, David Davis of Illinois, was an independent. Before the commission met, however, the Illinois legislature elected Davis to the Senate. His replacement on the commission was a solid Republican. After reviewing the evidence, the commission voted 8 to 7, along straight party lines, to give all of the disputed votes to Hayes, making the Ohio governor the new president. One obstacle remained in the way.

The commission decision required congressional approval. How would Republican Hayes win approval in the Democratic-controlled House? Here is where the future of race relations in the South was firmly settled for the next 90 years. Hayes went to Southern Democrats in the House, telling them that if they supported the decision of the electoral commission he would withdraw all remaining federal troops from the South. This would mean that Southern states—all now controlled by white Democrats—would have total control of race relations within their boundaries. After listening to Hayes's offer, the Southern congressional representatives quickly agreed to support him for the presidency, and Hayes entered the White House. After taking his presidential oath, Hayes ordered federal troops withdrawn from South Carolina, Louisiana, Florida, and all other Southern states. Now, black Americans were totally without protection.

Whites had regained control of just about every elected office in the ex-Confederacy; one problem, however, remained. White supremacists had won great victories but largely through campaigns supported by guns, violence, and death. "The old men of the present generation can't afford to die and leave the elections to their children and grandchildren, with shot guns in their hands, a lie in their mouths and perjury on their lips in order to defeat the negroes," a white Mississippian sighed. Could the victory for white domination be maintained without the un-Christian, uncultured, and uncivilized use of guns and lies? "There must be devised some legal defensible substitute for the abhorrent methods on which white supremacy lies," a newspaper editor suggested (Lears, 2009, 131–32). White supremacy maintained by law rather than terror appeared less barbaric and savage, more civilized than brutal killing and violence. The Klan and the 1875

Mississippi Plan used illegal, "abhorrent" methods to gain their victories. Good, educated, decent Christian men needed something better to pass on to their children than a history filled with the bodies of dead African Americans littering the ground.

Now that whites had regained political supremacy, they needed something else. "And what is it we want to do?" asked a delegate to the Alabama constitutional convention of 1901. "Why, it is within the limits imposed by the Federal Constitution, to establish white supremacy in this State," he answered (Perman, 2001, 193). Mississippi and the KKK had shown that killing and bloodshed could establish a white supremacist state. However, white supremacy could also be established legally. The white race could establish a society based on white supremacy and do it constitutionally, depending on the interpretation of the term "states' rights" by the Supreme Court in Washington. Unless, that is, anyone at a higher level of authority paid attention to how Americans, all Americans, were being treated and actually cared about it. From 1877 until around 1955, however, few people at that higher level seemed to care or seemed even aware of what Southern whites were creating in Jim Crow America.

References

Emerson, Ken. *Stephen Foster & Company: Lyrics of America's First Great Popular Songs*. New York: The Library of America, 2010.

Gerber, Richard A., and Alan Friedlander. *The Civil Rights Act of 1875: A Reexamination*. New Haven: Connecticut Academy of Arts, 2008.

Lears, Jackson. *Birth of a Nation: The Making of Modern America, 1877–1920*. New York: HarperCollins, 2009.

Litwack, Leon. *North of Slavery: The Negro in the Free States*. Chicago: University of Chicago Press, 1965.

McMillen, Neil R. *Dark Journey: Black Mississippians in the Age of Jim Crow*. Urbana: University of Illinois Press, 1989.

Perman, Michael. *Struggle for Mastery: Disfranchisement in the South, 1888–1908)*. Chapel Hill: University of North Carolina Press, 2001.

TWO

From the *Civil Rights Cases* to Legal Segregation, 1883–1896

JIM CROW LAWS ENJOYED the legal protection of the U.S. Supreme Court, which laid the constitutional foundation for the era of Jim Crow. In three decisions it made in interpreting the legal status of separating people by race—the *Slaughterhouse Cases* (1873), the *Civil Rights Cases* (1883), and *Plessy v. Ferguson* (1896)—the court provided the ex-Confederate states the constitutional backing they needed to construct a completely segregated society. The "Jim Crow laws" remained constitutionally protected until President Lyndon Johnson signed the Civil Rights Act of 1964. In its post–Civil War rulings, the highest court in the nation provided a legal substitute for the "abhorrent methods" (such as lynchings and murder) Southerners had used since the end of Reconstruction to keep African Americans "in their place," away from whites. No longer would the ex-Confederates have to resort to fraud, intimidation, and mob violence to keep African Americans in a separate and unequal society, without equality, opportunities, justice, or full constitutional rights.

Southern whites feared that the government in Washington might intervene in "local matters," such as whether their children would have to attend school with blacks. Jim Crow laws empowered whites in the South to keep blacks, considered an "innately inferior and savage race," from registering to vote, serving on a jury or a school board, or running for political office. The Supreme Court enabled whites to deprive African Americans, a people "much closer to the anthropoid apes" than to human beings according to a popular Southern "expert" on the black race, of such basic freedoms as deciding where to eat, whom to marry, or where to sit on a train or streetcar. Because of decisions made by the Supreme Court, racial segregation became lawful (*de jure*)—not just a matter local customs, or traditions, but a reality, a fact (*de facto*). Racial separation in Southern states was taken to be as true as the fact that the sky was blue. Courts and the law of the land, not just mobs, kept blacks "in their place," as servants, field hands, common laborers, or in other low-paying jobs. White supremacy now had legal and constitutional standing, protected by the principle of "states' rights." At the same time, if the law ever failed to maintain the correct racial order and etiquette, the mob always stood ready to enforce the rules.

The *Slaughterhouse Cases* had limited the civil and political rights (or their "privileges and immunities" as the Constitution put it) of citizens guaranteed by the Fourteenth Amendment, and weakened the role of the national government in protecting the rights of Americans. Those rights, according to the highest court in the land, were limited to the right to vote and to use the navigable waters of the United States, and a few other relatively minor freedoms The 1883 *Civil Rights Cases* reduced the role of the national government even more. The "cases" referred to involve the meaning of the Thirteenth and Fourteenth Amendments and the constitutionality of the Civil Rights Act of 1875. That law, written by the outspoken abolitionist senator from Massachusetts, Charles Sumner, made racial discrimination in places of commerce in the United States, such as stores, restaurants, theaters, and trains, in violation of federal law. The violations considered in the 1883 decision took place in California, Kansas, Missouri, New York, and Tennessee. That only two of the states (Missouri and Tennessee) were "Southern" demonstrates that states outside the South had discriminatory laws too—and the court said that was perfectly legal. Americans could not have the right to discriminate and treat other people unfairly taken away from them by any legislature, judge, or constitutional amendment.

The California incident involved an alleged violation of the 1875 Civil Rights Act. A San Francisco theater refused to seat a black patron, Charles Green, who had purchased a ticket to a concert by the all-black Tennessee Jubilee Singers from the state's all-black Fisk University. Green sued in federal court after being removed from the theater by a police officer, claiming that his rights as an American had been violated. At the trial, the theater's attorney argued that a private business had the right to deny service to anyone it pleased for any purpose. The judge agreed and acquitted the theater owner of all charges, but Green appealed to the U.S. Supreme Court, which accepted the case in 1876. Seven years later it offered its opinion, not only in that case but six other similar cases.

The second act of alleged discrimination covered by the *Civil Rights* decision involved an incident in a theater in New York City. In 1879, a black man, William R. Davis, claimed that an usher refused to let him enter the main floor of New York City's Grand Opera House because of his race.

When Davis refused to leave, the usher called a police officer and explained to Davis that the opera house did not admit blacks. "But the laws of this country do," Davis shouted, as he was escorted out of the theater. The next day he filed suit with the U.S. Attorney's Office in New York, claiming that the theater's policy violated his rights as a U.S. citizen guaranteed by the 1875 law. In court, Davis's lawyer argued that the opera house had denied his client the "full enjoyment" of his rights as a U.S. citizen by denying him his seat. The two-judge panel hearing the case could not agree on a verdict, however, and the case went to the U.S. Supreme Court.

The third case, the Tennessee incident, involved the refusal of a conductor for the Memphis & Charleston Railroad to admit a black woman who had purchased a first-class ticket entrance to the "ladies" car. The conductor said it was open to white women only. The black woman sued, but the federal district court judge rejected her claim of discrimination, so she decided to appeal the decision. Before the federal appellate judges, the railroad attorneys argued that the conductor had followed a state law that allowed only white women to sit in the "ladies" car. The Tennessee law dated to 1881—it was the first Jim Crow law adopted by any state—and required railroads to provide "separate but equal" facilities for passengers on all trains. After the appellate court found in favor of the state, the Supreme Court accepted the case on appeal and added what eventually became the *Civil Rights Cases*. The two other cases, both involving the refusal of hotels in Kansas and Missouri to provide rooms to African Americans, were eventually added to the final decision. All five incidents, according to the lawyers handling the appeals, had denied African Americans access to public places—theaters, train cars, and hotels—in violation of the 1875 Civil Rights Act. Those denials represented another form of slavery, or a "badge of slavery," they argued, which violated the Thirteenth Amendment.

In its 8–1 decision, the court rejected the argument made by the defendants' lawyers and instead declared that the Civil Rights Act of 1875 was unconstitutional. Justice Joseph P. Bradley, writing for the majority, wrote that any idea or suggestion that discrimination based on race was "a badge of slavery" and therefore was somehow connected to the Thirteenth Amendment did not deserve consideration. "Such an act of refusal had nothing to do with slavery or involuntary servitude," he asserted. Free blacks, he pointed out, had obeyed many discriminatory laws before the Civil War when slavery legally existed, so how could such laws now become a "reminder of slavery?" The Thirteenth Amendment outlawed slavery, nothing else. The Civil Rights Act made only discriminatory actions taken by the federal government a violation of the law; it did not apply to acts committed by private individuals or corporations. Americans had the right to discriminate.

In his dissent, Justice John Marshall Harlan maintained that the Fourteenth Amendment had created something new for all Americans—a "national citizenship," with certain rights protected by the Constitution that no states could deny to any U.S. citizens. All citizens of the United States, by birth or naturalization, had all the rights guaranteed by the federal Constitution. No state could deny U.S. citizens any of those constitutional rights. Such rights, in Harlan's view, included equal access to theaters, railroads, hotels, restaurants, stores, courthouses, or other buildings open to the public. U.S. citizens were free from any denial of their rights because of skin color, race, or religion. The court majority rejected Justice Harlan's view and adopted a much narrower definition of citizenship rights. In their view, states' rights trumped constitutional rights, and they numbered very few, though they did not list what even their narrow list of rights included. In the majority's opinion individuals were citizens of the state they lived in first, and subject to its laws, not federal laws. The state that citizens lived in governed their lives, even if their laws treated people differently. States' rights protected Jim Crow, according to the U.S. Supreme Court.

The court in its 1883 decision followed a tradition in nineteenth-century law that rigidly distinguished areas under state or local authority from those areas subject to the control of the national government. States controlled education, prisons, elections, road building, and hospital construction (if any), while the national government conducted foreign affairs and protected the country from invasions. The Fourteenth Amendment provided citizens of the United States with "privileges and immunities" that could not be "abridged" or denied. Since it did not provide a list specific "privileges and immunities," the 1883 Supreme Court constructed its own narrow list. Future courts never completed that list either.

Had the Supreme Court considered actual living conditions for African Americans in the former Confederate states in 1883, which the justices did not consider, they would have found immense poverty, hopelessness, fear, anger, bitterness, and despair within the entire community. With the withdrawal of federal troops after the election of Rutherford B. Hayes, white supremacists ruled in every ex-Confederate state, including the three states with African American majorities, Louisiana, Mississippi, and South Carolina. Black voting participation declined dramatically after 1876, though a few African Americans managed to cast ballots in a few states. In Virginia African Americans served in the state assembly until 1891, and in North Carolina voters sent more than 50 blacks to the state legislature between 1876 and 1892. The Georgia and South Carolina state legislatures had black members until 1902. In Washington, D.C., the U.S. Congress had black members (usually no more than two or three at a time) in every session from 1869 to 1901. By 1900, only one black congressman, from North Carolina, survived, and after the next election, he was gone. Several states had already begun campaigns, dominated by acts of terror and violence, to exclude African Americans from the voting booth. As early as 1880, the number of registered African American voters in Mississippi had declined by 66 percent from the previous presidential contest. That was still too many "ignorant savages" turning out to cast ballots according to many white Mississippians, so they continued their antiblack campaign.

Laws and poll taxes keeping blacks away from the voting booth did not yet exist. However, other methods proved very successful at keeping them away from the polls in the ex-Confederate states. The most effective methods included terror, force, and fear; the KKK and similar groups scared many blacks away with ropes, bullets, and fiery crosses; fear of losing a job, or a house, or a life, worked well in reducing black voter participation. In some states in the South, the all-white legislatures designed increasingly complicated rules for voters to follow and incorporated them into laws and the state constitution.

In 1883 South Carolina imposed an "Eight-Box Ballot Act" upon its citizens. This measure required separate ballots for every office voted on, from county coroner to governor to president, and demanded that voter's place the individual ballots provided for each office in the correctly labeled ballot box. If a vote for "governor" ended up in the box for "lieutenant governor," or if a voter placed his ballot in the box for "state representative" instead of the box for "state senator," precinct judges would not count those votes. Aimed at making voting especially difficult for the 70 to 80 percent of African Americans in the state considered illiterate, the Eight-Box system worked very well. Black voting declined rapidly. It had been against the law in slave states to teach slaves how to read or write, so most African American adults had never learned to read. The postwar public schools for blacks in South Carolina rarely met for more than three months a year—compared to six months for white schools—and black adults rarely attended those schools. Thousands of illiterate white farmers and sharecroppers also lost their votes because of this system. State legislators knew that would happen but willingly accepted the loss of poor whites' votes in exchange for an almost totally lily-white electorate.

Georgia, Virginia, Florida, and South Carolina all began collecting poll taxes by 1884. This tax required voters to pay for part of the cost of running elections, as defenders of the tax explained. Though small, usually $1.00 or $2.00 a year, the tax reduced the number of black voters by as much as 60 percent in states that required such a payment. (Yearly incomes for African Americans rarely rose above $75 to $80 in any Southern state at this time.) Of course, thousands of impoverished whites failed to pay the poll tax or any other state taxes and lost their right to vote, too. Sacrificing some white voters, mainly the poor whites and the white trash, in return for keeping almost all African Americans from the polls seemed worth the costs, in the eyes of white politicians.

The new voting requirements achieved their goal of making it difficult if not impossible for African Americans to cast ballots. The states of the former Confederacy went beyond passing election laws to "keep blacks in their place," however. More and more laws, the Jim Crow laws, restricting human behavior because of race made their way into Southern law codes. Legislation that established rigid rules defining who could or could not get married were added in all states of the Old South. So were laws restricting where a person could sit on a train or streetcar based on skin color. By 1884, all 11 ex-Confederate states had laws banning "miscegenation," a word that meant interracial marriage. Laws establishing segregated public school systems, parks, cemeteries, theaters, prisons, and libraries quickly found their way into their codes.

These laws prevented African Americans from entering "sacred" places that whites intended to protect from blacks and their inherited traits of "mongrelism, ignorance, and depravity." Trains and streetcars became important places to legally segregate because they were among the few places that whites and blacks came close to each other in their daily lives. People could move away from others on streets and sidewalks but not in confined places such as train cars or streetcars. Segregation laws soon protected white women from having to sit next to the "smelly brutes" with their "pushy" ways who now travelled by train.

The motivation for separating people by race emerged from several sources. Blacks, most Southern whites insisted, were born with criminal and violent natures that were incurable. Not even schooling could lessen these criminal tendencies. Education only increased black criminal instincts and desires. A governor of Alabama insisted that schools for African Americans were "turning out thieves and vagrants in companies, battalions, and armies" (Newby, 1965, 132). The notorious convict-leasing system, which proved deadly for many of its victims but profitable for the states that adopted it, was based on the view that harsh penalties were necessary to keep black criminals from destroying white civilization, and as a side benefit the state also made money. The system was also constitutional. The Thirteenth Amendment abolished slavery and involuntary servitude "except as a punishment for crime." States could legally enslave prisoners according to the Constitution.

Mississippi acted first in leasing prisoners. For $1.75 a day payable to the state, plantation owners seeking desperately needed field hands could rent slaves, and there were a lot of prisoners available. Men and boys as young as eight years old convicted of relatively small crimes, such as drinking too much or gambling in the state served a minimum five-year sentence. So many cotton growers were willing to pay the small price required that the state ran out of prisoners every year. The state legislature responded to that problem by passing a law that made it easier to increase the supply of convicts. The "Pig Law," as it became known, labeled stealing a pig—or anything worth more than $10.00—"grand larceny," subject to a five- to ten-year prison sentence. During debate on the proposed law, supporters made it clear that the crimes described in it, such as stealing a pig or public drunkenness, were illegal acts that African Americans were much more likely to engage in than whites. The law, passed in 1876, increased the prison population from three hundred to more than a thousand within two years. Blacks made up 90 percent of the new prison population, and by 1884 money collected from the system contributed almost half of the state's budget.

Since the new prisoners came from an already despised population, few people protested the treatment they received. As a railroad executive explained concerning the high death rate among convicts in the lease system, "Why so high? Because he is a convict and if he dies it is a small loss." A historian concluded that because of convict leasing, "A generation of black prisoners would suffer and die under conditions far worse than anything they had ever experienced as slaves" (Oshinsky, 1996, 53). However, the system made money for the state and no one protested, except sometimes the convicts. The prisoners in Mississippi slept outside on the ground without blankets or shoes, and sometimes even without clothing. They worked 16- to 20-hour days in extreme heat, a pace so hard that one out of four convicts died every year. The state made no distinction between prisoners based on age, so 25 percent of Mississippi's prisoners were under sixteen years of age, some as young as eight or nine years old.

In Alabama, convicts worked in coal mines where an astounding 35 percent of them died every year. Most had never been inside a mine before their prison sentence and the conditions they worked in were horrible, even for the coal mine industry. In the view of the mine owners, convicts made an ideal workforce; they were cheap, docile (even sleeping in their chains and drinking muddy water without complaint), and they would never go on strike. (However, that last point did not always prove true. In Tennessee in 1892 in what became known as the Convict War, prisoners and free miners joined in a strike that required the governor to send in the state militia before it ended, after many miners were shot and killed.)

The death rate and inhuman conditions were found in almost every place and industry that used convict labor. The pain and agony the system inflicted on prisoners fell most heavily upon the black population. Ninety percent of the leased prisoners in Alabama were African American. They began working in chains at 3:00 a.m. and kept shoveling and dynamiting coal until 8:00 p.m. They ate meals out of their shovels. Almost every day a prisoner died and had his body dumped into a pit, without any record kept of who he was and why he died. Someone else always came along to take his place. In Texas, prisoners received food "that even buzzards would not eat," according to one visitor. Alabama, Mississippi, and other states eventually abolished the convict-leasing system after a newspaper investigation into the death of a young white prisoner in Florida, but the end did not come until the 1920s. Even then the system still survived in Louisiana until after World War II. Most states replaced convict leasing with chain gangs.

Laws and attitudes established a color line in the South long before the Jim Crow era began. Frederick Douglass, the great African American antislavery leader, made a speech in 1883 celebrating the twentieth anniversary of Abraham Lincoln's Emancipation Proclamation. Commenting on the current state of race relations in the United States, he lamented, "In all relations of life and death, we are met by the color line. It hunts us at midnight . . . denies us accommodation . . . excludes our children from schools . . . compels us to pursue only such labor as will bring us the least reward."

National politics played a key role in the creation of the Jim Crow system in the Southern states. Because of the events of the Civil War and Reconstruction, the Republican Party became the party favored by black Southerners. The Democratic Party had opposed the war and the Reconstruction goals of making full citizens of the former slaves. The Democrats fought against giving freedmen the right to vote and became the white man's party in the South, a position it held until the 1960s. When Republicans controlled both the presidency and both houses of Congress, the possibility of protecting African Americans and their rights became improved even after the 1876 election. Rutherford B. Hayes kept his promise and did little to protect black Americans. Neither Presidents James

Garfield nor Chester Arthur, both Republicans, took much interest in promoting civil rights, and Congress generally remained split with Democrats controlling the House and Republicans the Senate for most of the period following Reconstruction.

In 1884, Democrat Grover Cleveland won the presidency and two years later his party gained control of both houses of Congress. In 1887, the Democrats tried but failed to repeal all laws concerning or protecting the right to vote. In the 1888 election, the Republicans returned to power with Benjamin Harrison entering the White House and Republicans for the first time since 1868 gaining control of both the House and Senate. During his first year in office, President Harrison called for new laws strengthening federal protection for black voters in the South. Congress began considering that issue in 1890.

Republican representative Henry Cabot Lodge of Massachusetts became the strongest voice favoring equal rights. He presented a Federal Elections Bill to the House in June 1890. The proposal allowed one hundred citizens in any congressional district to petition for federal supervisors, appointed by a federal judge, to oversee election procedures of any kind, from registration to counting the votes in their district. It also authorized the president to send in federal troops to prevent violence during election campaigns. White Southern Democrats labeled Lodge's bill "the Force Bill," the same thing they had called the Ku Klux Klan Acts of 1871. During debate Representative John Langston, one of only three African Americans in the House, asked the central question raised by Lodge's bill, "Under our amended Constitution . . . shall every American citizen . . . be permitted to wield a free ballot?" A Texas Democrat warned that as far as his constituents were concerned the bill was "destined to retard our progress, destroy confidence, impair development, engender bitterness, relegate us to the dark and deplorable conditions of reconstruction, and produce only evil" (Perman, 2001, 275). The House passed an elections bill but it ran into trouble in the Senate, where Democrats engaged in a weeklong filibuster that prevented its passage. This would be the first of many filibusters Southerners would use to protect their system of Jim Crow inequality. Their successful demand to retain "local control" meant that white supremacy would continue to rule the South.

In 1890, Mississippi held a constitutional convention to revise its old document. One delegate explained why the elected delegates had come together: "Let us tell the truth if it bursts the bottom of the universe. We came here to exclude the negro." African Americans had already been excluded from the political process in Mississippi, of course, but not quite totally or legally. Since the early 1870s, white Mississippians had resorted many times to terror and violence to "keep negroes in their place." Whites had controlled the political behavior of African Americans through mob action, lynching, and fraud for years. But some whites had trouble with those methods of control. Newer, less violent methods of restricting black freedom had to be found, and some states had already tried out those methods and they had succeeded.

Some states had adopted laws aimed at keeping African Americans "in their place," at the bottom of the economic and political ladder. Tennessee and Arkansas had imposed a poll tax and the secret ballot the year before the Mississippians met. Poverty and illiteracy took an immediate toll on voter registration in those states. The $1.00 poll tax proved difficult if not impossible for many impoverished farmers and sharecroppers (white and black) to come up with. Secret ballots posed another major problem for citizens of voting age because more than 60 percent of African American adults, and a large number of whites, had never been to school. Secret ballots assumed voters could read, but many could not. Adoption of the secret or "Australian" ballot (because Australia was the first nation to use them) proved an enormously effective method of keeping illiterate voters away from the polls.

Adding a literacy test to the requirements for registration made signing up to vote even more difficult for many people The tests demanded more than just knowing how to read and write. They also required knowledge of U.S. history and government and asked potential voters to prove that they "understood" specific parts of the U.S. and state constitutions. Alabama's literacy requirements included passing an 80-question multiple-choice examination on the state and federal constitution. In states that adopted literacy testing, turnout in elections dropped immediately and by huge numbers. The secret ballot turned out to be a very effective method of preventing already registered voters from voting. As one Nashville newspaper reported, "Many negroes went to the polls, and because they could not prepare their own ballot and would not acknowledge their ignorance by asking the assistance of the judges, returned home without voting." White sharecroppers faced problems similar to African Americans under the new voting requirements and their numbers fell dramatically too, but no state had yet come up with a method of protecting their right to vote (Perman, 2001, 183).

Mississippi's new constitution listed four new registration requirements specifically aimed at excluding African Americans from the polls. First came a high poll tax of $2.00, which voters had to pay by the February before the election. They needed to have some reading ability because the new rules included a secret ballot. Also, any conviction for a crime the convention delegates thought blacks committed more frequently than whites (so-called "negro crimes") including arson, bigamy, bribery, burglary, embezzlement, forgery, and murder, disqualified potential voters for the rest of their lives. The new regulations included an "understanding clause," which gave county clerks authority to ask questions concerning U.S. history and government, and then the same white registrar graded the answers. This supposedly provided an opportunity for poor whites to meet voting qualifications, because local registrars presumably graded whites more generously. These provisions, supporters pointed out, did not violate the Fourteenth or Fifteenth Amendments because anyone registering to vote, white or black, had to meet them. Twenty years later the U.S. Supreme Court agreed with the advocates of a more "educated" electorate: taxes and literacy tests did not involve discrimination since all potential voters had to pay the same tax and take the same test.

The new constitution laid the basic framework for the "Second Mississippi Plan." The First Mississippi Plan in 1875–76 advocated force and violence to keep African Americans in their place and away from the polls. This new plan depended on law, not violence, to accomplish the same goal. Mobs, according to a Mississippi newspaper, were "no longer necessary because the [new] laws are so framed that the Democrats can keep themselves in possession of the governments" of any state by following the Mississippi example. In the view of a white Mississippi lawyer, the new constitution "had solved for the state the problem of negro suffrage" for all time, peacefully and legally, although the mob always stood ready to move at any time if called upon (Perman, 2001, 87–88).

Any fear that federal marshals might come to protect the right to vote for African Americans disappeared when Democrats took control of Congress in 1894. In the congressional election that year, the "white man's party" gained large majorities in the House and Senate, and a Democrat, Grover Cleveland, first elected in 1892, sat in the White House. In 1895 Congress repealed all federal election laws remaining in federal law books. The threat from what South Carolina senator Benjamin "Pitchfork Ben" Tillman called "the black snake" of "negro domination" now disappeared. "This is a white man's country," Senator William Bate of Tennessee informed his colleagues, "and I believe that God, in His wisdom, has destined it to remain a white man's country" (Perman, 2001, 23, 25).

One group of black leaders in the South tried to get the black community to accept Jim Crow and live as quietly as possible within a culture devoted to the doctrine of white supremacy. Booker T. Washington (1856–1915), born a slave in Virginia to a black mother and a white father, led this group. He called upon African Americans to accept white rule and the supremacy of the white race, at least temporarily. Once blacks had demonstrated their ability to work hard and prosper, white Americans would support them in achieving their goals of political and social equality. In 1881 Washington, educated at Hampton Institute, a teacher-training college in Virginia, was appointed the first leader of Tuskegee Institute in northern Alabama. Here, and for the next 34 years, students received training in agriculture, business, and education while learning Washington's philosophy of subordination to a superior race. "The opportunity to earn a dollar in a factory just now," he explained, "is worth infinitely more than the opportunity to spend a dollar in an opera house" (Harlan, 1972, 65).

Invited to speak at the Atlanta Cotton States and International Exposition in 1895, Washington outlined his position on race relations for the largely white audience. The few blacks in attendance sat in segregated seats. For African Americans trying to better their lives in the South, he offered helpful advice. "To those of my race who depend on bettering their condition . . . or who underestimate the importance of cultivating friendly relations with the Southern white man who is their next door neighbor, I would say, cast down your bucket where you are, cast it down making friends, in every manly way, of the people of all races by whom you are surrounded. . . ." The audience broke into enthusiastic applause when the "wizard of Tuskegee" assured them "the wisest among my race understand that agitation of questions of social equality is the extremist folly." Accommodationism, a term used to describe Washington's philosophy, included an assurance to white plantation owners and business executives, "You and your families will be surrounded by the most patient, faithful, law-abiding, and unresentful people that the world has seen." He gave white supremacists great comfort when he concluded, "In all things purely social we can be as separate as the fingers, yet one as the hand in all things essential to mutual progress." In his "Atlanta Compromise" address, Washington never challenged the two central principles of white racism—first, whites belonged to a superior race, and second, African Americans therefore accepted their inferiority and still lived their lives very happily. Accommodationists seldom challenged their second-class status in society. Washington did question the campaign for disfranchisement, however, though he supported keeping illiterates out of the voting booth.

Washington's philosophy of "uplift" for his race meant acceptance of political and social subordination. However, as the editor of the militant

African American Washington, D.C., *Bee* commented, "It is a notorious fact, that the utterances of Mr. Washington are [aimed at] nothing more than to make himself rich by assuring the white people of this country that the Negro's place is in the machine shop, at the plow, in the washtub and not in the schools of legal and medical professions, that he has no business to aspire to those places, as they are reserved for the Caucasian" (Anderson, 1988, 65). Yet, Washington's philosophy remained extremely popular not only among white Americans but also African Americans, North and South. It was safe—accepting black inferiority kept the lynch mobs away. But not totally—white mobs lynched 369 African Americans in Southern states in 1894 and 1895 alone, according to the NAACP.

The age of Jim Crow had begun. However, were segregation laws constitutional? As long as there were any doubts, Southern political leaders would have to worry about possible federal government "interference" in their local affairs. A court case in Louisiana offered the U.S. Supreme Court an opportunity to rule on their legitimacy. In 1890, the legislature passed a law forbidding any passenger from entering a railroad "coach or compartment to which by race he does not belong." Other states had a similar statute; Tennessee acted first in 1881 by passing a similar statute and several other states had followed suit in the late 1880s. No one had challenged these laws in court, however. Then in June 1892, Homer Adolph Plessy, an African American shoemaker from New Orleans and a member of the Citizens' Committee to Test the Constitutionality of the Separate Car Law, bought a ticket and entered the "whites only" car. He approached the conductor and said, "I have to tell you that according to Louisiana law, I am a colored man." His race may not have been obvious to others as he was very light-skinned because he was seven-eighths white, but under the state code that made him "colored." When he refused the conductor's demand to move to the "colored car," he was arrested.

These events followed a plan. The Citizens' Committee had sent Plessy to buy a ticket, sit in the whites only car, and have himself arrested so a court could rule on the constitutionality of the 1890 separate car law. The law, an early example of a Jim Crow law, ordered trains to provide "equal but separate" accommodations for white and black passengers. At the trial, state criminal court Judge John H. Ferguson (hence, *Plessy v. Ferguson*) found Plessy guilty and ordered him to pay a fine. He ruled that Louisiana, under its "police powers," could assign seats in railroad cars as a method of keeping order. Plessy decided to appeal the judge's verdict to the state supreme court. The Citizens' Committee found a team of nationally known lawyers to handle the appeal, including Albion Tourgee, a white novelist and army officer who had served in Louisiana during Reconstruction, and the former solicitor general of the United States, Samuel Phillips.

The five members of Louisiana's highest court ruled unanimously against Plessy. Backing up their decisions with two precedents from Northern court decisions, which Southern courts always enjoyed doing, the Louisiana justices ruled that segregation on railroads was not discrimination. In the first case, *Roberts v. City of Boston* (1849), the decision noted, the Massachusetts Supreme Court had upheld a city ordinance requiring black and white children to attend separate schools. The "Yankee" judges upheld the ordinance because it by itself did not cause prejudice; it simply reflected the attitudes of a majority of the city's population. "This prejudice, if it exists," Chief Justice Lemuel Shaw wrote, "is not created by law and cannot be changed by law." The segregation rule represented the will of the people and should stand. The Louisiana judges failed to acknowledge, however, that the Massachusetts legislature outlawed segregation five years after the *Roberts* decision.

The second verdict cited by the Louisiana court came from an 1867 ruling of the Pennsylvania Supreme Court. It also found that separating people by the color of their skin did not constitute discrimination. In the Pennsylvania decision, the Northern judges upheld the right of a railroad to seat white and black passengers in different sections of its passenger cars or in separate cars because that practice alone did not qualify as discriminatory. "To assert separateness is not to declare inferiority . . . It is simply to say, that, following the orders of Divine Providence, human authority ought not to compel these widely-separated races to intermix," the Pennsylvania court ruled. In other words, God demanded segregation; it was part of his creation. Moreover, the Northern judges pointed out, all sections of the country separated people by race in certain areas of life, more proof of that practice's legitimacy. The Louisiana legislature had acted properly in passing the separate car law, the state's Supreme Court concluded. "The separation of races in public conveyances . . . is in the interest of public order, peace, and comfort," according to the court, as long as both races had equal access to transportation.

Plessy and his attorneys then appealed to the U.S. Supreme Court, which accepted the case in 1893. Because of a huge backlog of appeals, however, the court did not hear arguments in the case until three years later. In 1896, in a 7–1 decision (one of the justices fell ill and did not participate in deliberations), the majority rejected all arguments made by Albion Tourgee in his appeal. Justice Henry Billings Brown, author of the majority opinion, explained that the Louisiana law did not violate the Thirteenth Amendment, as Tourgee argued, because his concept of discrimination being a "badge of slavery" had no foundation in law. Brown maintained that the amendment prohibited "slavery and involuntary servitude" and nothing more. It said nothing about anything like a "badge of slavery." Discrimination was not slavery. "It would be running the Thirteenth Amendment into the ground to make it apply to every act of discrimination," Brown ruled, echoing the view of Justice Bradley (no longer on the court) in his 1883 decision on the *Civil Rights Cases.*

Brown then rejected Tourgee's assertion that the Separate Car Act violated the Fourteenth Amendment's "privileges and immunities" clause. That phrase applied only to the right to vote and the right to serve on a jury, nothing else. The amendment protected only those political rights and did not include or imply protection of any others, including any "social rights," such as the right to an education, or the right to use public facilities, or the right to interracial marriage. Discrimination in these areas was "in the nature of things," Brown argued. In support his of argument, Brown cited the work of William Graham Sumner, professor of sociology at Yale University, especially his theory of how societies made their laws.

Societies based their laws on the fundamental beliefs and principles held in common by their members. Laws had their source in *folkways,* Sumner explained, which he defined as the shared behaviors and beliefs common among people. These shared beliefs emerged over long periods of history and changed very slowly. Folkways included religious beliefs, racial attitudes, and ideas concerning what to eat and how to dress. Folkways eventually evolved into *mores.* Mores come from folkways, but include ideas of such high value to a people, such as a ban on incest, murder, or interracial marriage, that breaking them produces such horror and revulsion among the society's members that it justifies punishment of the violator. Effective laws must comply with these mores; otherwise, people will not obey them. In Brown's interpretation of Sumner's theory of social change, racial segregation based on the idea of the inferiority of the "African race" had become a custom of Southern society, which laws could not abolish or change. "If one race be inferior to the other socially, the Constitution of the United States cannot put them upon the same plane," he believed.

Justice Brown concluded that Louisiana's separate car law did not violate the U.S. Constitution. Discrimination was "in the nature of things," he said, and the court majority agreed. The law did not "stamp" any race or individual "with a badge of inferiority," as Plessy's lawyers asserted. If people felt "inferior" because a law separated them from others because of their skin color, the law could not be blamed. Any sense of inferiority came about only "because the colored race chooses to put that construction upon it."

In the lone dissent, Justice John Marshall Harlan, the lone dissenter in the *Civil Rights Cases* 13 years earlier, called for a "colorblind constitution." As he argued, if a state separated people by race, why could it not separate them by religion, Protestants on this side, Catholics over there? Harlan did not believe in the equality of all, however; even the dissenter agreed with the majority's white supremacist view on one point, "the white race is undoubtedly" dominant "in prestige, in achievements, in education, in wealth and power" and it would be for all time. That status did not give whites any extra rights or privileges and it took none away from African Americans. "In respect of civil rights," he held, "all citizens are equal before the law" no matter what their intelligence, wealth, or standing in society. He concluded with a warning that the majority's decision "would stimulate aggressions . . . upon the admitted rights of colored citizens" as well as encouraging states to pass laws to "defeat the beneficent purposes" of the Constitution. The flood of segregation laws passed by Southern legislatures in the decade after the announcement of the *Plessy* decision proved Harlan very right. In *Plessy*, the court made segregation legal everywhere in the United States, and it remained that way for 57 more years.

The court proclaimed that segregated facilities were legal. The decision said nothing about "equal" or "separate but equal." Any train ride through the South would have proven any such guiding standard to be false. William F. Fonville, an African American journalism student from North Carolina, described conditions on a Jim Crow car he rode on during a trip through the South in 1893. He wrote about the conditions he experienced on Southern trains in *Reminiscences of College Days*, published in 1903. The Jim Crow car, he wrote, "is divided into two compartments. The end next to the baggage car is the 'Crow' car . . . the other end is a smoker." In the "smoker" white and black passengers could smoke cigars or pipes whenever they wished. Smoking on regular cars was not allowed. Black passengers paid the same fare as whites yet "sat amid smoke and coal dust, packed in with luggage." Conductors sent noisy, cursing, drunken white passengers to the Jim Crow cars to sober up. The Jim Crow car usually was attached as the first car behind the coal car, which sat right behind the engine, so black smoke constantly blew through open windows and the engine noise made it difficult to hear passengers sitting right across the aisle.

References

Anderson, James D. *The Education of Blacks in the South, 1860–1935.* Chapel Hill: University of North Carolina Press, 1988.

Harlan, Louis. *Booker T. Washington: The Making of a Black Leader, 1856–1901*. Urbana: University of Illinois Press, 1972.

Newby, A. I. *Jim Crow's Defense: Anti-Negro Thought in America, 1900–1930*. Baton Rouge: Louisiana State University Press, 1965.

Oshinsky, David M. *"Worse Than Slavery": Parchman Farm and the Ordeal of Jim Crow Justice*. New York: Free Press, 1996.

Perman, Michael. *Struggle for Mastery: Disfranchisement in the South, 1888–1908*. Chapel Hill: University of North Carolina Press, 2001.

THREE

Jim Crow Triumphant, 1896–1918

SEGREGATION HAD DIVIDED THE SOUTH from almost the very beginning of British settlement. Slavery, introduced in 1619, was based on race. Only Africans and Native Americans could be enslaved under colonial law. Similarly, Jim Crow laws separated the races by laws that legalized the racist habits and customs of white Southerners. But segregation was not limited to the South. Many Northern and Western states had Jim Crow laws, too. Forty-two states in 1950 had legislation separating people by the color of their skin in places from schools to telephone booths. However, Southern states had the most of such laws, and legal authorities enforced them more consistently and vigorously in Dixieland. From the first years after the Civil War, African Americans faced laws that separated them from whites in almost every area they could possibly meet. Through Jim Crow laws, Southern legislatures attempted to reestablish the racial rules that applied during slavery times. "Jim Crow" meant more than the laws that created the system, however; the term really referred to an entire way of life, an entire culture.

Jim Crow culture tried to prevent all contact between black and white people through laws rather than by mob action or lynching. Jim Crow laws segregated public transportation (trains and street cars), public education (elementary schools, high schools, and colleges), courtrooms (some states required separate Bibles so black and white witnesses would not have to place their hand on the same book), housing, restaurants, hotels, parks, golf courses, playgrounds, swimming pools, circuses, barbershops, hospital emergency rooms, prison cells, factories, offices, movie theaters, libraries, cemeteries, water fountains, public washrooms, and any other places whites and African Americans might possibly come in contact with one another. It all was legal. The U.S. Supreme Court backed it up and protected it. Legal segregation did not violate or deny any American of any color his or her civil rights, at least according to *Plessy v. Ferguson.*

Jim Crow laws alone did not create segregation in the South (or North or West), they just legalized it, and made it more legitimate. Blacks and whites would have gone to separate schools, lived in separate housing, eaten in separate restaurants, watched plays and movies in separate areas of theaters, and moved about in separate sections of streetcars with or without laws. The Jim Crow system of prejudice and discrimination reflected the attitudes of the vast majority of Southern whites who wanted nothing from African Americans except that they remain in the home and provide a cheap supply of labor. It was just "in the nature of things" and God had made it so. "When you ask me why I do not associate with a negro," a white Texan explained in a magazine article aimed at explaining white racial attitudes to Northern readers, "I do not say it is because the negro is poor and dirty and ragged and uneducated. I and all the white men I know object to a negro because he has a black face." The huge number of African Americans living in the Old Confederacy, he continued, had created enormous trouble for the police and courts and threatened the peace, happiness, and prosperity of all white Southerners. Those "troubles" came directly from the criminal and violent nature of the entire "African race" and neither education nor religious instruction had an impact on those traits because blacks were born with them. Crime and bad behavior were in their blood (scientists might have said "in their genes") and only harsh discipline restrained those passions. Along with being born criminals, Africans were naturally lazy and stupid and worked only when threatened by a whip or beaten by a club. Old-time "darkies," meaning those who had survived slavery, still understood their inferior human status, but the new generation of "Afro-Americans" seemed to believe that they were born equal to whites in every area of their lives. This new breed needed daily reminders that they could never achieve that goal; they could never achieve equality with the Anglo-Saxon race. They needed to be constantly aware of their inferiority and their worthlessness. Jim Crow laws fulfilled that need (Newby, 1965, 116).

Jim Crow's defenders argued that segregation laws actually reduced racial violence by keeping the races away from each other. Segregation helped blacks accept the reality of their inferior status in society. It prevented them from mistakenly and foolishly trying to rise above their natural, God-created unequal and limited mental capacities. Racial peace in the South depended on black acceptance of their inferiority. One of the first historians of American slavery, William A. Dunning, attributed the "peace" found in the South before the Civil War to one crucial fact:

the Negro, when enslaved, went "more or less cheerfully about his affairs, evincing little interest in his 'rights' or 'wrongs.'" Instead, slaves accepted the common rules and etiquette of conduct in race relations and did not resist them. When meeting a white man, for example, never shake his hand; when talking with a white man, always remove your hat, bow courteously, address him as "Mister" or "Boss," and always say "sir" when responding to a question. Expect a white man or woman to call you "boy," no matter what your age. Most importantly, never say anything to a white woman unless she asks you a question or speaks to you first, and always be humble.

In a book called *Race Orthodoxy in the South, and Other Aspects of the Negro Question*, published in 1914, Thomas Pearce Bailey (1867–1949), a white Southern educator and writer who many Southerners considered an "expert" on race relations, provided a list of 12 rules governing the racial thinking of whites in the South during the era of Jim Crow:

1. The white race must dominate.
2. The Negro is inferior and will remain so.
3. There will be no social equality.
4. There will be no political equality.
5. In the matter of civil rights and legal adjustment, give the white man, rather than the colored man, the benefit of the doubt; and under no circumstances interfere with the prestige of the white race.
6. In educational policy let the Negro have the crumbs that fall from the white man's table.
7. Let there be such industrial education of the Negro as will fit him to serve the white man.
8. Remember: only Southerners understand the Negro question.
9. The status of peasantry is all the Negro may hope for, if the races (are to) live together in peace.
10. Only the South can settle the Negro question.
11. Let the lowest white man count for more than the highest Negro.
12. The above statements indicate the leanings of God.

As long as blacks abided by these rules, racial peace prevailed. When broken, violence usually followed (Newby, 1965, 4, 116, 155).

White Southerners believed that they and no one else, especially Northerners, understood African Americans; that they alone knew what blacks wanted and needed, and even what made them happy. Segregation did not begin because of prejudice or discrimination. John Rankin, a white member of Congress from Mississippi, asserted at the end of one of his speeches defending Jim Crow and lynching, "I have no antipathy for the

Negro as a race. I have no prejudice against him because he is a Negro. . . .
But I understand him; I know his weaknesses, his shortcomings, and his
limitations. I want to see him protected in the enjoyment of his life, liberty,
and the pursuit of happiness." Such "happiness" came from working for the
white man and his family. Black men found happiness by doing the jobs
considered too nasty and dirty for whites. African American women
entered white homes (through the back door), cooked their meals, cleaned
their houses, and nursed their children because those activities suited their
nature and never implied equality. Women in the superior, more intelligent
race did not engage in such dreary tasks, while black women's minds were
exactly fit for doing those very things. An elderly black woman summed up
the African American attitude toward whites when she told a reporter, "The
only thing that you be thinking of" when coming across white people was
"that they were the ones who had everything" (Litwack, 1998, 7).

Jim Crow attitudes affected every aspect of daily life in the post–Civil
War South. In educational policy, white taxpayers followed Bailey's rules
by establishing and paying for two separate systems of education, one for
whites and another—underfunded, vastly inferior, and incessantly vocational—for African Americans. In public elementary schools from Virginia
and North Carolina to Texas, the curriculum for black students emphasized
subjects that would teach them how to remain "in their place"; how to live
quietly and submissively, as subordinate, inferior people; and how to lead
law-abiding lives in a system where the law treated them brutally. Black children needed to know just one thing especially well, how to work hard and
long hours. A Georgia law stipulated that African American students receive
only industrial education. Along with this "job training," strictly limited to
jobs that did not compete directly with the jobs whites filled, black children,
according to a 1907 report from the Southern Education Association, a
liberal reform group founded to improve black schools, benefited most from
courses that stressed good character, good behavior, and citizenship—moral
training. They needed to be taught things they never learned at home, "honesty, truth, chastity, industry, and respect for the Sabbath," according to
one white school principal assigned to a black school.

Other white educators argued that any attempt at such moral reform
in African American classrooms wasted money and time. Education of
African American children, because of their naturally low intelligence,
should aim at accomplishing only a few limited goals—such as how to fix
a pair of shoes or sew a pair of trousers. Schooling could never make "the
negro . . . a white man by cultivating his brain, since they are what God
made them and will remain so" (Newby, 1965, 167). Any belief or notion

that a black boy or girl could reach the ability level of the average white student was unreasonable and unrealistic. Therefore, as Mississippi governor and long-time senator James "White Chief" Vardaman asserted, education of blacks should only proceed so far, not only because of their limited brain power, but because more highly educated African Americans (meaning those with more than three years of schooling) usually became more dangerous and criminal than the illiterates. During his successful campaign for governor in 1904, he called for the elimination of all funding for "negro education."

Most Southern white educators shared Vardaman's opinion. Howard Odum, for example, a sociologist, was considered an "expert" on the African American population. By time he founded the University of North Carolina School of Public Welfare in the early 1930s, he had changed his mind; however, his early view of the African American character reflected that of traditional racist thinking. In his 1910 book *Social and Mental Traits of the Negro*, he wrote "the young educated negroes are not a force for good in the community but for evil. . . . They sneer at the idea of work, and thus spread dissatisfaction among the members of their race." A white Alabama lawyer summarized his state's educational philosophy regarding black students when he wrote, "It's a question of who will do the dirty work. If you educate a negro, he won't stay where he belongs." Where "they belong" meant to provide them with barely any education at all—and Alabama fervently worked to meet that standard.

Racist assumptions and attitudes, held by the always-white assistant education superintendent in charge of "colored schools," justified public funding for white schools that reached levels from five to sixteen times as high as it was for black schools. In 1915, South Carolina provided $16.22 for each white student in its public schools compared with $1.93 for every black student. Over the first half of the twentieth century, the state legislature gave white South Carolina schools an average of ten times as much money as it did black schools.

During the Jim Crow era, African American students in North Carolina made up almost one-third of the state's elementary school population yet they received only 13 percent of the state school funds. Georgia's white students received about seven times as much in state aid every year from 1900 to 1950 as the legislature provided for black elementary students. Black parents frequently resorted to what they called "double taxation" to support their local schools. This meant that after paying their state and county taxes at the same rate as whites, they contributed more money to a special fund raised by church groups and local women's clubs to buy the desks, chalk, books, and other supplies for their one-room school. Parents also provided room and board for black teachers—the Peachtree State paid teachers at African American schools $30.00 a month while white teachers made almost three times as much. Parents cooked supper for their children's teachers and helped clean and maintain the one-room schoolhouse.

An investigator for the white "Women's Association for the Betterment of Public School Houses in North Carolina" described a "Colored School" he visited in a rural county in these words, "The school house is a shabbily built board structure, one story high. . . . There are no blinds and no curtains in the windows. The desks are homemade, with perpendicular backs and seats, all the same size. There is a dilapidated wood stove, but no wood box. The stove is red with rust and dirt, never having been polished and cleaned since it was placed in position for use. . . . There is no teacher's desk or table. There is one chair. The walls and windows are covered with dust and seem never to have been washed. The children's hats and coats are hung on nails around the room. All their books are soiled and look much like their surroundings. There are no steps to this school. An inclined plane of dirt serves that purpose. The yard is very muddy during the winter, and the general appearance of the place anything but attractive." The teacher taught all six grades. Few states provided more than six grades for black students; school boards felt they did not need any more than that for the types of work available to them (Harlan, 1958, 20–21).

School boards consistently paid white teachers two or three times as much as they paid black teachers. (In one Georgia county white teachers received $89 a month while black teachers in the same county got $30.) Teachers in African American schools seldom had more than a seventh or eighth grade education themselves. States built few "normal schools" to train African American teachers, and the teacher-training institutions that did exist seldom provided more than high school–level courses. State and public universities refused to admit African American students. Booker T. Washington's Tuskegee Institute and the Hampton Institute in Virginia, both financed by Northern churches and philanthropists, trained teachers but only in limited numbers and with a limited philosophy of education. Tuskegee and Hampton concentrated on the economic development of the African American community and stressed job-training skills in their curriculum. The "Tuskegee Way" emphasized vocational training and moral discipline.

Black children taught by Tuskegee graduates learned to how "love" their jobs and to understand the importance of hard work. With these skills, they could become more productive citizens, and that would significantly improve the image of their race in white eyes. Only a few black schools, mainly church-affiliated private academies, provided a traditional, classical set of courses that emphasized liberal arts, the humanities, and sciences.

The Tuskegee method meant that students learned to accept disfranchisement, political powerlessness, and inequality. Then, after showing a long history of progress and success, the "good whites," in Booker T. Washington's view, would recognize the worthiness and abilities of African Americans and support their campaign for political power and equal rights. But first, blacks had to demonstrate that they could do the work required for success. The accommodationists taught that African Americans needed education, but a certain kind of education and extreme patience to reach that goal. They needed to learn a trade, develop technical skills, and discover how to make and save money. Then they would earn the respect of at least the better-educated, more prosperous class of whites.

History did not provide much evidence to support the accommodationist view. Local white school boards rarely focused much attention on black education at the elementary level. In many districts schools remained open for less than three months a year. And after fifth or sixth grade, education generally stopped. Most African Americans in Dixie never attended high school. Southern states refused to spend money on them. In 1890, less than 1 percent of black children attended school beyond the elementary level, and 20 years later, that total had increased to only 2.8 percent. White students did better than blacks, but only by a small margin.

Education just did not seem to matter to any taxpayers in the "New South" supposedly emerging in the early part of the twentieth century. Only 10 percent of whites between the ages of 15 and 19 attended high schools in the American South in 1915. Mississippi had 112,527 African Americans aged 15 to 19 that year, but just 390 attended a public high school in the state. In Louisiana, of 76,868 eligible black teenagers, exactly 98 attended the only public high school the state provided for blacks. Not a single state in the entire South had a mandatory school attendance law before 1920. Little public support existed in favor of such laws, and most business leaders and agricultural interests argued against such laws. Public schools simply cost too much money. Jobs in coal mines, cotton fields, and cotton mills seemed more productive and valuable.

These attitudes accounted for the limited quality and quantity of education available in every Jim Crow state, and that fact had been true seemingly forever. Public education simply did not exist in slavery days. Sons and daughters of the wealthy received instruction from private tutors, while poor whites and slaves received nothing. Before the Civil War, laws barred teaching slaves to read and write. If slaves learned to read, they might come across something about freedom or justice or something equally dangerous. Why would slaves need to know how to read, anyway? Somebody could read the Bible to him or her. Working in the cotton fields did not require much knowledge. Children of slaves needed to know how to work. To teach them to read would be a true waste of money, according to slave owners.

After the war the experiment in public education during Reconstruction lasted only briefly before traditional attitudes came back. Education funding suffered severely after the return of white power. A Mississippi plantation owner explained why he and his neighbors showed little support for black education: "What I need here is Negroes who can make cotton, and they don't need education to help them make cotton" (Anderson, 1988, 189–92).

Refusing to educate African Americans, whites believed, kept them forever quiet, ignorant, and unequal. A white newspaper editor explained the real significance of Jim Crow, "Our civilization and safety require the social bar to be forever preserved between the races. Education of negroes tends to throw down the bar. It is preparing the way for social equality," and that could never be allowed. Education gave blacks the dangerous idea that they were equal to whites. It motivated them to question their subordinate status in U.S. society, and education moved them "to rebellious protest and sometimes to violent revenge." Quality education, or really any education at all, for African Americans was extremely dangerous for the future of the white race, warned the editor of the *Atlanta Constitution*. It could lead blacks to consider the ultimate rejection of their natural inferiority, interracial marriage—miscegenation, as some called it—and such race-mixing could only lead to the mongrelization and eventual degrading and disappearance of the Anglo-Saxon race (Litwack, 1998, 98–99).

Black parents in Georgia raised the threat of equality in the state in 1897. That year African Americans in Augusta filed a lawsuit against their county school board after it voted to close Ware High School to save money. As the only high school in the state for blacks and one of only four "Negro" high schools in the entire South, Ware represented something important for African Americans in the city, a chance to demonstrate their ability to achieve just as much as white students. The board acted because it needed the school's yearly $845 budget to hire new teachers for its four black elementary schools, which were becoming overcrowded. The black schools had to turn away more than four hundred students the year before because they were unable to provide seats or teachers for them. The building housing Ware High School offered enough space for about two hundred of those black children and in the board's view providing them with classroom space where they could be furnished "with the rudiments of education" was a better use of resources than teaching the "sixty high school pupils" currently attending Ware. The board refused to close the white high school, however, which really angered the black community.

Lawyers for the black parents asked the Superior Court of Richmond County to close the white high school until the board of education found enough money to reopen the black high school. The county superior court issued an opinion favorable to the African American parents, but the Georgia Supreme Court overturned that judgment, without offering any explanation. The parents then took their case to the U.S. Supreme Court.

Before the Supreme Court, white former Reconstruction senator George F. Edmunds, now in charge of the black parents' case, argued that under the Equal Protection Clause of the Fourteenth Amendment, if a school district provided a high school for whites it also needed to have a high school for blacks. Justice John Marshall Harlan, author of the dissent in *Plessy v. Ferguson* three years earlier, authored the unanimous decision of the court in *Cumming v. Richmond County Board of Education* (1899), and rejected the appeal. In Harlan's view, the black parents had not shown that the school board members had reached their decision because of any "hostility to the colored population," but simply out of economic necessity. Racial discrimination had nothing to do with that decision. Yes, the board could have voted to shut down both the black and white schools, he acknowledged, but had the members reached that decision it would have "needlessly hurt" the white students who had done nothing to deserve that fate.

For the parents to prove racial discrimination and a denial of equal protection under the Fourteenth Amendment they needed to show that the board had acted solely because of race, and they had not done that. In essence, this ruling meant that school boards did not have to provide high schools for African Americans if white students suffered harm because of such a decision. Harm to black students did not seem to matter. Augusta did not reestablish its high school for blacks until 1945, and most Southern counties did not provide secondary education for African Americans until the late 1940s. White students suffered no harm.

If Jim Crow states refused to provide some of their citizens with an education, perhaps private philanthropists could fill in the gap. A few wealthy Northern business leaders and industrialists contributed money to Southern black communities seeking to upgrade their Jim Crow schools. In 1895 Julius Rosenwald, one of the founders of the Sears, Roebuck

Company, established a fund to build schools in the rural South, especially for black children. To qualify for the money, black parents had to contribute at least half of the cost of the construction projects. Between 1914 and 1927, the Rosenwald Fund gave $3,032,000 to the program, while black families raised $3,550,000. With this cash, the fund built more than 3,700 elementary and high schools in 14 states. According to the fund's regulations, local Jim Crow school boards controlled the curriculum, but at least the classrooms were new (Johnson, 2010, 129–30).

As noted before, Jim Crow elementary and high schools provided manual training and industrial education for their students. Louisiana always was among the last of the Jim Crow states to provide public money for black residents. The Orleans Parish School Board established an "industrial" high school for African Americans in 1930—the first high school for blacks in Louisiana history. The school had a clear and racist mission, "to educate negroes in trades and in positions to which negroes are best qualified, and under no circumstances to educate them to compete with white labor in this city." When the board of education in Columbus, Georgia, decided to build a high school for African Americans, the white consultant it hired to oversee the project advised the board not to offer a traditional curriculum or college preparatory classes. Eliminating traditional classes, such as mathematics, biology, history, and others made sense, he explained, "especially for the negroes whose opportunity to make use of such traditional subjects" was very "limited" (Anderson, 1988, 212–24).

Black teachers and parents complained about the limited scope of education the Jim Crow high school made available to their sons and daughters, but their objections had little influence on the final decision. The all-white board agreed to classes in bricklaying, cooking, shoe-repair, and other occupational courses that "meet the needs of the child," but offered nothing in typing, bookkeeping, or stenography—or history, literature, or the sciences. The primary reason for denying "commercial" courses to black students was the nature of the job market; white businesses would never hire black secretaries or typists, the board informed the parents. Teaching commercial subjects would not lead to a job; it would only result in "keen disappointment" for the black students, who would be refused employment because of the color of their skin. This statement was true because of the Jim Crow nature of the job market in Columbus and every other Southern city, but still very disappointing for the African American community. It simply reflected the very old and tiresome image of inferiority that so deeply troubled and insulted the black community. The "needs" of black students, they were being told, included little more than training for the lowest-paid employment opportunities, the "n——jobs," as whites called them, which were limited to cooking, cleaning house, picking cotton, or polishing shoes on busy street corners.

Public institutions of higher education such as colleges and professional schools for blacks in the Jim Crow South hardly existed. Moreover, no public white colleges or universities would accept African American applicants. In 1900, only 3,880 black students in the entire South attended college, and exactly 105 black men and 22 black women received degrees. Qualified blacks students from Southern states enrolled in private and state universities in the North and the few African American schools that trained teachers, such as Hampton Institute, Tuskegee College, and Fisk University in Nashville. Baptist, Methodist, and Presbyterian missionary societies had established a few small colleges that stressed courses in carpentry, printing, and other trades, but some of them also provided liberal arts classes, professional training, and other educational courses aimed at developing a leadership class to fight for equality and justice.

The traditional black colleges saw industrial training and the development of a business class as their chief mission and tended to ignore political and social questions. Instead, they taught how to work and survive as second-class citizens in a society dominated by white supremacists. However, most of the black institutions, no matter what their mission, always suffered great financial and academic hardships.

Northern philanthropic agencies interested in supporting black higher education, such as the Slater Fund and the Laura Spelman Rockefeller Memorial Fund, gave monetary assistance to black colleges in the South but in return they usually demanded an emphasis on job training. A white member of the Tuskegee Board of Trustees expressed this vocational, job-oriented view of education for African Americans when he said, "except in the rarest of instances I am bitterly opposed to the so-called higher education of Negroes," especially that kind emphasizing liberal arts and humanities. Education in those areas of learning never helped anyone get a job, he explained. In terms of the extremely small amounts of money provided for black higher education and the almost universal insistence upon a vocational curriculum, a large number of white citizens in the Old Confederacy agreed with his point of view (Anderson, 1988, 146–47).

In a key ruling with wide influence in legitimizing the Jim Crow system, *Berea College v. Kentucky* (1906), the U.S. Supreme Court once again upheld a state law that barred all educational institutions, public and private, from offering a fully integrated education. Berea, a small college in the hills of the eastern part of the state, announced it would accept black students and that they would sit in the same classrooms as whites. The state legislature responded to that announcement almost immediately by passing a law requiring segregation in all classrooms in the state. When the case came before the Supreme Court, the judges ruled in a 7–2 decision that Kentucky had the right to segregate all schools and institutions by race. Separation by race, the majority argued, in no way deprived any students or citizens of their constitutional rights. Instructors could teach their students in separate rooms at different times or in different places under the law. As long as professors provided students with similar information and training, racial segregation did not matter. Education meant learning something or being taught something; it had nothing to do with race or discrimination. The *Berea* decision meant that states could legally segregate public institutions or places, private or public, that they wanted to segregate. They no longer had to worry about interference from federal courts or Congress in creating a Jim Crow society. Over the next few years, the Jim Crow states proceeded to pass segregation laws with the utmost zeal and without any opposition from the government in Washington, D.C.

In some ways, Jim Crow schools met the basic ideals established by advocates of progressive education. "Education for Life," as progressive reformers called their philosophy, meant preparing students to live in a modern industrial society through career training and teaching them civic responsibility. For African Americans in Jim Crow states that meant learning how to live in the oppressive, prejudiced, and violent culture they saw existing around them. In their Jim Crow schools, in the view of progressive Southern educators, black students learned how to accept their inequality and powerlessness, and to stay "in their place." They learned how to accept second-class citizenship. Blacks, whether middle class or desperately poor, had no way of having their voices heard or objecting to their mistreatment, because they could not vote or run for office. The white, elected school boards made decisions affecting both black and white schools in their district, but blacks could not vote. Therefore, the always-white board members had no reason to pay attention to any protests or suggestions from African American critics.

Black parents paid local taxes to support education but had no control over how to spend that money. Their schools had no blackboards, books, or desks, but their complaints could just be ignored. If the local board decided to spend ten or twenty or a hundred times as much money on white students, black parents could not protest, even in counties where they made up the majority of the population. Poll taxes and literacy tests had taken away their right to vote, and without the power of the ballot, African

Americans had no influence on white politicians or the policies they made at the local, state, national, or any other level. Black neighborhoods had dusty, trash-filled streets, no streetlights, no fire hydrants, broken sidewalks (if there were any sidewalks at all), broken playgrounds (if there were any), and no police protection. The registered voters elected local sheriffs in the Jim Crow states and counties, while in cities that did not elect police officials, the always-white mayors appointed always-white police chiefs. The all-white deputies the chief appointed and the all-white police force the mayor employed arrested thousands of blacks but otherwise seldom went into their neighborhoods. Crime flourished.

The national government backed away from enforcing the Fifteenth Amendment's protection of the right to vote after Congress failed to pass the Lodge Bill in 1891. That left it up to local always-white registrars to decide who could and who could not cast a ballot. Few Southerners (or Northerners) seemed troubled by the disfranchisement of their African American neighbors or complained about their unequal political or social status The Jackson *Clarion-Ledger* expressed a common view: "If every negro in Mississippi was a graduate of Harvard . . . he still would not be so well fitted to exercise the rights of suffrage as the Anglo-Saxon farm laborer" (McMillen, 1990, 34).

The highest court in the land and the document it interpreted decided that the entire Jim Crow system of inequality and discrimination met constitutional standards. In 1898, the U.S. Supreme Court considered a case, *Williams v. Mississippi*, that challenged the constitutionality of two key parts of the Jim Crow system, the literacy test and the poll tax. An all-white jury in Mississippi had sentenced an impoverished, illiterate African American sharecropper, Henry Williams, to death for killing his white landlord. Williams's attorney appealed and argued that the state had violated his client's right to a fair trial because no blacks had served on the jury. Jurors in the state came only from lists of registered voters, and because blacks could not meet the requirements for registering to vote, no names of African Americans appeared on those lists. The state constitution required potential voters to pay a poll tax and pass a literacy test before registering, leaving it up to local county clerks to determine who met the qualifications. This practice almost totally eliminated blacks from the registration process and therefore kept them off from the jury rolls. Mississippi's registration procedures had reduced the number of eligible black voters from 147,205 to 8,615 only 10 years after they were adopted.

Race, according to the unanimous decision handed down by the court in the *Williams* case, played no role in preventing blacks from serving on juries. Members of both races, the court reasoned, had to pay the same tax and take the same test. Williams had not shown that election officials had intentionally resorted to racial discrimination in any of their decisions determining who could vote. The registration requirements did not prevent African Americans from voting because of race but because of other factors, such as their failure to pay the poll tax and their inability to pass a literacy test. The same rules applied to white men.

Along with the required tax and test, Mississippi law also made it illegal for persons convicted of certain crimes to register to vote. That restriction did not discriminate against anyone, the Supreme Court ruled, because it applied to "weak and vicious white men as well as weak and vicious black men." The court did not consider the legislative intent of the framers of this clause at Mississippi's 1890 constitutional convention. Had the justices considered that discussion they would have found good reasons to reconsider their unanimous/decision. Supporters of the exclusion had specifically selected crimes they "knew" blacks committed more frequently than whites, though they offered no evidence in defense of their assertion. Excluded crimes included bigamy, gambling, rape, robbery, and murder. The court ruled that all of the regulations concerning voter eligibility in Mississippi were constitutional because none were based on race. They applied equally to whites and people of color, so the court refused to overturn Williams's death sentence even though the jury that convicted him of murder had been all white and a black person had never served on any jury in the state's entire history.

Within 10 years, most Southern states wrote new constitutions or passed new laws that copied the voter registration provisions in Mississippi. The new rules had an immediate and devastating impact on the participation of black voters. In Louisiana, the number of eligible black voters dropped from 130,344 to 5,320 the year after the new requirements went into effect. Alabama removed 95.4 percent of African Americans previously registered to vote from its lists within a year of ratifying its new constitution. Southern political leaders proudly announced that the disfranchisement of black Americans had been accomplished without violence or fraud. "Honest" methods of keeping blacks home on Election Day, the Alabama governor proclaimed, now existed. "The law" had replaced fraud and terror as the most effective way to eliminate black voting power, and laws proved just as effective as had the older, violent methods in accomplishing that goal. Even more impressive, the highest court in the United States had found the new means of voter exclusion constitutional and legitimate. Total white power had been achieved.

Jim Crow laws deprived African Americans of their right to equal educational opportunity and of their right to vote, and had done so without any protest or interference from the president, Congress (the last African American member of Congress lost his reelection bid in 1902 and the next black member did not enter the House of Representatives until 1921), or the courts. At the state and local level, white Southern governors, legislators, judges, mayors, school board members, county commissioners, sheriffs, and tax collectors stood solidly behind the discriminatory laws. Political, judicial, and police officials supported the Jim Crow laws and their goal, removing "the negro as a factor" in the life of the South, as one election official explained.

The last effort of any major American political party to protect black citizens from discrimination and abuse came in 1904. That year the Republican Party platform called for states to lose seats in the House of Representatives if they denied African Americans their right to vote. However, the party's presidential nominee, Theodore Roosevelt, never raised the issue during the campaign, and no one expected anyone running for office as a Democrat to even mention the issue. No white group or individual voiced any objections to the disfranchisement of black citizens in the South or the terrible conditions in the region's "colored" schools. The only objections came from W. E. B. DuBois in the pages of African American newspapers, such as the Chicago *Defender* and the Washington *Bee*. Thirty years after the end of Reconstruction, inequality had become constitutional and legal everywhere in the United States.

Of course, blacks in the South experienced far more prejudice, discrimination, and violence in the Old Confederate States than they did in the North. Ignorance, illiteracy, and poverty helped enormously to keep them "in their place," way at the bottom of society. The same factors kept a huge supply of cheap labor available for white plantation and business owners to exploit. Fear and violence played a key role in preserving the vast social and economic inequality found in the "New South." Race riots in Wilmington, North Carolina (1898), New Orleans, Louisiana (1900), Brownsville, Texas (1906), and Atlanta, Georgia (1906) showed the power of white violence. Whenever whites felt that African Americans threatened their political power or economic status, vicious mobs easily came together to protect white supremacy.

A white mob killed 10 blacks in the Wilmington, North Carolina, riot of 1898. Wilmington was an unusual Southern city because it had a population of 17,000 African Americans and 8,000 whites. The city had a Republican African American government until November 1898, as had been true for more than a decade, but then white Democrats shot their way into power. The day after the city election, which the Republicans had won once again, six hundred armed whites rushed through the black section of town setting fire to houses and stores, including the building housing the African American newspaper, which had "insulted white women" in one of its stories. As the rioters raced through the neighborhood, they randomly shot dozens of people, including children, who just happened to be in the streets. Blacks had their own guns in Wilmington, however, and shot back, beginning a two-day war with the white invaders. The bloodshed ended only after the governor sent in the state militia "to disarm the blacks." When the fighting ended, anywhere from seven to thirty African Americans had been killed (no one knows the true number) and three whites lay wounded, though none had died. A few weeks after the militia restored "law and order," the North Carolina legislature imposed a literacy test on its citizens and most blacks lost their right to vote.

Two years later another violent conflict brought blood and death to the New South. In New Orleans, Robert Charles, son of a sharecropper in Copiah County, Mississippi, shot 27 whites, including 7 police officers, during a self-proclaimed war against the white race. A supporter of the back-to-Africa movement led by Bishop Henry M. Turner of the African Methodist Episcopal Church in Atlanta, Charles sold copies of the group's newspaper, *Voice of Missions*, in the poorer neighborhoods of New Orleans. In its pages, Bishop Turner proclaimed that African Americans had the right to defend themselves with guns if they felt threatened by white mobs or the white police. Charles's reasons for his personal war against white police and civilians can be traced to his experiences and hatred for living in a Jim Crow society.

Charles had witnessed and been the victim of white hate from early in his life. Copiah County had been the scene of more lynchings than any other county in his home state. He had fled to New Orleans to escape the racist hatred he felt in his impoverished rural birthplace. He thought he had gotten away from Copiah in what many people considered the relative peace and security he found in New Orleans. But then in its 1898 constitution, Louisiana imposed literacy tests and poll taxes on its citizens, the same thing Charles had witnessed in his home state eight years earlier. The outcome had been a 90 percent decline in the number of African Americans registered to vote. Now he saw it happening again, and as one of his friends explained to a New Orleans reporter, "he deeply resented the disfranchisement of his race."

More than simply the loss of political power moved Charles to begin his war. Outrageous acts of brutal violence against members of his race inspired Charles's deadly revolt. In April 1899, a lynching in Georgia stirred him so deeply that he began reading about and considered joining the back-to-Africa movement. The absolute brutality of the lynching moved him deeply and he felt "beside himself with fury." He became so angry, Charles told one of his coworkers that he decided "it was the duty of every Negro to buy a rifle and keep it ready." The Georgia victim, Sam Hose, had allegedly killed a white man. Hose, a 21-year-old black field hand, had been tortured mercilessly and then burned alive before a crowd of thousands of cheering, laughing whites, including many women and children. The whites then cut his body open and hacked out his heart and sliced it into pieces. The pieces were then sold for souvenirs. Hose was only one of the 114 people lynched in the American South in 1899; 106 of the victims were black. As was true in all other 113 cases, no one was arrested for killing Hose even though the crime took place in the daylight in front of thousands of witnesses.

Charles's shooting spree began on a very hot day in July after a policeman tried to arrest him. Charles knocked him down and ran to his apartment, where over the next five days he fought his war against white racism. Dozens of police surrounded the rooming house where he lived in a second-story apartment. A white mob, led by the mayor, who yelled, "I have killed a Negro before and . . . I am willing to kill them again," came to "help the police." The mob of three thousand angry, screaming whites swept through the black neighborhood, killing at least five African Americans, one of them a young boy on crutches. Fifty blacks were severely beaten as the rioters moved along. The beatings and shootings continued into the next day when the rioters killed two more black victims, both elderly black men. The police eventually set fire to the house occupied by Charles and shot him to death as he tried to escape, ending the New Orleans riot. Charles had killed seven people (four of them police officers), seriously wounded eight (three of them policemen), and slightly wounded twelve civilians. All the victims were white (Hair, 1976, 171–72).

A riot in Brownsville, Texas, in the summer of 1906, known as the Brownsville Raid, served as another reminder of the racial hatred that infected the United States. On the evening of August 12, a white woman claimed a group of black soldiers from nearby Fort Brown had attacked her. That same night, a shooting in a bar claimed the life of a white bartender and injured a white police lieutenant. Neighborhood residents claimed they had seen black soldiers running through the streets randomly shooting out windows and streetlights shortly after the bar shooting.

The next morning a white citizen's committee met with the white commander of Fort Brown demanding an investigation of the previous night's violence. The commanding officer told his all-black troops that if they did not identify the men responsible for the shooting and killing, he would have them all arrested, court-martialed, and dishonorably discharged. The soldiers maintained their innocence, but the army accused them of a "conspiracy of silence." A military court convicted all 167 black enlisted men stationed at Fort Brown with participation in a murder. All but one received long prison terms and dishonorable discharges. The soldiers petitioned President Theodore Roosevelt to review their case, but he refused to overturn the verdict.

A Senate investigation followed and its report indicated that the evidence against the soldiers seemed "contradictory, insufficient, and biased." However, the army refused to overturn the verdict of the court-martial, and the soldiers went to jail. In 1972, Congress reopened the case and awarded honorable discharges for all of the soldiers, though without back pay. The one soldier still living received compensation of $25,000 and an apology from the army for the lifetime of trouble and distress he suffered because of the wrongful verdict (Lane, 1972, 146–48).

Just five weeks after the Brownsville Raid a major riot erupted in Atlanta, Georgia. On the evening of September 22, white mobs murdered at least 25 African Americans (the exact number remains unknown), and injured hundreds more. A police investigation listed white deaths as two, with perhaps twenty wounded. The riot followed months of rising racial tension aroused by a campaign for governor that pitted the publishers of two Atlanta newspapers against each other. Race played a major role in each candidate's campaign. The city council had recently passed the city's first Jim Crow laws. They segregated streetcars, parks, the courthouse, and other places where blacks and whites might brush against one another. Streetcars were required to post signs reading: White People Will Seat from the Front of the Car Toward the Back and Coloured People From Rear Toward Front. Elevators in all buildings were to be labeled: This Car for Coloured Passengers, Freight, Express and Packages.

White attitudes toward blacks had been inflamed by comments from the two gubernatorial candidates, Hoke Smith, the publisher of the *Atlanta Journal*, and Clark Howell, the editor of the *Atlanta Constitution*. Smith called for a state literacy test to disfranchise African Americans and "keep them in their place." Howell accused Smith of being "too friendly towards blacks" in his newspaper editorials and asserted that he could do a better job in promoting and protecting white supremacy in the state. The inflammatory comments made by the candidates included warnings about "black beasts" roaming the streets. During the summer both papers carried daily headlines about supposed attacks by "black brutes" on white women, none of which happened to be true.

Newspaper hysteria appeared to be one of the main causes of the deadly riot. The blood started to flow on a hot Saturday evening. Extra editions put out by both newspapers appeared with stories, never confirmed, concerning four attacks by black "brutes" upon white women in the afternoon. A crowd of thousands of white men and boys gathered downtown and moved through a largely middle-class black neighborhood armed with guns, clubs, bats, and rocks. The first violence occurred when a gang of whites attacked a black barbershop and beat five customers, all black, to death. Thirteen-year-old Walter White, future executive secretary of the National Association for the Advancement of Colored People, witnessed a group of whites attacking and clubbing to death a young black youth "with a withered foot."

When the all-white police arrived in the neighborhood, followed the next day by the all-white state militia, instead of stopping the still raging mob, they assisted it in burning and looting black-owned homes, churches, and stores. The fires burned and the violence continued for five more days before it ended. The police had arrested more than 250 black men and confiscated their weapons. Ten African Americans and two whites died during the rioting. Hundreds more were wounded. In the aftermath of the blood and fire, the Georgia legislature passed a law requiring a literacy test for voters. It also imposed statewide prohibition. African Americans always consumed more liquor than whites did, according to supporters of the law ending the sale of alcohol in the state. Many whites blamed "drunken negroes" for the death and destruction during the riot. Without alcohol, life would be safer for everybody, the white leaders felt.

The bloody, antiblack violence that stained the United States during the first decade of the twentieth century included 962 lynchings. These public murders were accompanied by an almost complete loss of voting power for African Americans, and a rapidly growing list of Jim Crow laws. The legal system consisted of mostly prejudiced judges, almost always all-white law enforcement officers, and all-white juries. There were also the problems of terrible, vastly underfunded schools, almost universal poverty, racist state governments, and a national government seemingly unconcerned with the rights and lives of African Americans in the South. Most of them lived their lives quietly searching for jobs, and law and order, and wondering whether any of that could be changed.

On February 12, 1909, a group of Northern white liberals joined with a small number of African American lawyers, doctors, and educators in New York City to create a new organization to fight for that cause, the

National Association for the Advancement of Colored People (NAACP). The meeting was called after a race riot in Abraham Lincoln's hometown of Springfield, Illinois, left six people dead (two blacks and four whites) and hundreds of black families homeless after white mobs burned down the city's entire black neighborhood.

At its first meeting, the NAACP delegates adopted a series of resolutions announcing the group's goals, including a call to fight racial segregation, Jim Crow laws, and disfranchisement in the South. The 47 founders committed the organization to work through the courts to challenge racial discrimination and segregation. The civil rights group originally feared moving directly against the Jim Crow system. The NAACP thought that openly challenging the race issue in the South would lead to nothing except more lynchings, more violence, and cost the lives of many African American supporters. However, early in its history, a letter arrived at the group's New York office outlining the case of Pink Franklin, an illiterate black sharecropper in South Carolina who had killed a white deputy sheriff and been sentenced to death.

Franklin had moved away from the property of a landowner he agreed to work for and who had given him a few dollars of his promised wages—so he could feed his family—before he did any work. That moving away violated a state law, which made it a crime for a worker to leave a job before repaying any advanced wages. Franklin's employer got a warrant from a local judge, and two white sheriff's deputies showed up at Franklin's shack at 3:00 a.m. to serve it. They entered the cabin without any warning and with their guns drawn. Franklin jumped out of bed, found his rifle, and fired several shots at the unknown intruders, killing one of the officers and seriously wounding the other. A quick trial before an all-white jury found him guilty of murder, and he was sentenced to death. He decided to take the verdict on appeal to a higher court.

Franklin's two black attorneys took his appeal first to the South Carolina Supreme Court and then to the U.S. Supreme Court. Both courts rejected the appeal. Booker T. Washington became involved in the case and began a campaign to persuade the governor to commute Franklin's sentence to life imprisonment. The NAACP joined in the drive, and the governor commuted the sentence shortly before Franklin was supposed to die. Five years later Franklin received a pardon. Though small, the association could claim a part in this victory for justice.

Almost all Southern states had statutes similar to South Carolina's law on advanced wages. Alabama's 1885 "false pretenses law," for example, made it a crime for any worker to obtain money before doing a job and then leaving it "without repaying" the advance. The law said he should be punished "as if he had stolen it." However, the Alabama Supreme Court ruled the law unconstitutional because it did not require proof of "intent to defraud." In 1903, the state legislature made it a crime *prima facie* (on the face of it; meaning just doing it is a crime, intentionally or not) for any person to take money and fail to pay it back. No evidence of intent to defraud was required. That same year, Florida and Georgia passed similar laws. Within a short time, hundreds of black men in each state found themselves serving time in prison for violating the new "false pretenses law." Were such laws creating a new type of slavery?

In the view of an attorney with the U.S. Department of Justice in Alabama, some of them, especially certain contract labor laws, violated the Thirteenth Amendment's ban on "involuntary servitude." Between 1900 and 1905, Justice Department lawyers brought more than one hundred cases involving "peonage" before federal judges in Southern states. In the first successful prosecution, a federal court in Florida convicted Samuel Clyatt of using forced labor in violation of the 1867 Peonage Abolition Act, a law aimed at preventing plantation owners from forcing former slaves to work for them to pay off a debt. Two African Americans owed Clyatt some money and he had them arrested when they failed to repay it. A local judge convicted them of violating a Florida law that made it a criminal act not to repay a debt. The judge sentenced the two men to work on Clyatt's plantation until they paid off their debt. They appealed to the U.S. Supreme Court, which overturned their conviction and declared all peonage laws, which it defined as "forced servitude for debt," unconstitutional. They violated the Thirteenth Amendment, which banned "involuntary servitude."

The decision in *Clyatt v. the United States* led to a concerted campaign to end imprisonment for debt across the United States. In the spring of 1908, an illiterate and impoverished African American named Alonzo Bailey filed suit in federal court in Birmingham, Alabama, claiming that the state's law on contracts violated the Thirteenth Amendment. A week before, Bailey had been imprisoned for violating that law. He had contracted to work for a plantation owner and received a $12.50 advance on his wages. He agreed to repay that money at the rate of $1.25 a month deducted from his salary of $15.00 a month. He left his job, however, before paying back the advance. His employer had him arrested and a state judge sentenced him to 136 days of hard labor on a chain gang. (Chain gangs provided an alternative to the state's convict lease system.)

Bailey's white attorneys took the appeal of his conviction before the Alabama Supreme Court, which ruled that the law was an appropriate method of punishing "fraudulent practices." From there an appeal went to the U.S. Supreme Court, which heard arguments in October 1910. In the following January, Chief Justice Edward White read the 7–2 majority opinion in *Bailey v. Alabama* (1911) that declared Alabama's labor law unconstitutional. It violated the Thirteenth Amendment's ban on involuntary servitude, according to the majority, and the Peonage Abolition Act of 1867. The court declared peonage, defined as forced "labor for another in repayment of a debt," in violation of the Constitution, and ordered Alabama to release Bailey (Daniel, 1972, 76–77).

In 1914, in *United States v. Reynolds*, the Supreme Court declared a second Alabama labor law unconstitutional. A jury had convicted Ed Rivers, an African American, of petty larceny and fined him $15.00 and court costs of $43.70. Since he could not pay either the fine or the costs, the judge sentenced him to prison. However, as had been true since Reconstruction, Alabama's "criminal surety law" allowed anyone in the state to pay a fine along with the court costs of someone convicted of a crime who was unable to pay the judgment against him. After the court received its money the guilty person had to repay the debt by working for whoever paid his fine. J. A. Reynolds, a local white farmer, paid Rivers's court costs and fine. Rivers then signed a contract to work for Reynolds for nine months, but quit after just three months. Reynolds had Rivers arrested for violating his contract, a jury brought back a guilty verdict, and the judge fined him one cent but required Rivers to pay court costs of $87.50.

After state courts rejected their appeals, Rivers's attorneys took the case to the U.S. Supreme Court, which ruled that the Alabama criminal surety law was unconstitutional. This form of Jim Crow justice—almost all of the men convicted under these laws were African Americans—was now eliminated, a rare court victory for the black population of the United States. Despite the court's rulings, however, Georgia and Florida maintained their "peonage" laws until 1944; the Justice Department never seemed to have time to take any cases from those states—and there were many of them— to court. So hundreds of blacks convicted of violating the "surety laws" suffered in miserable conditions and performed backbreaking labor in turpentine camps, in snake- and mosquito-infested swamps (building roads and railroads), and plantations of all kinds, for breaking laws that violated the U.S. Constitution and should never have been enforced.

Jim Crow laws and Jim Crow justice flourished in the American South for almost a hundred years with little interference from "outsiders," the white Southern term for federal government officials, liberal federal judges, and Northern whites who just did not understand "the Negro" like white

Southerners did. African Americans felt they had no alternatives to their desperate situation in Jim Crow country. "There is nothing we can do about it. Because if we do anything about it, they will kill you," a black mother in Mississippi explained to her son (Litwack, 1998, 446–47).

References

Anderson, James D. *The Education of Blacks in the South, 1860–1935*. Chapel Hill: University of North Carolina Press, 1988.

Daniel, Pete. *The Shadow of Slavery: Peonage in the South, 1901–1969*. Urbana: University of Illinois Press, 1972.

Hair, William Ivy. *Carnival of Fury: Robert Charles and the New Orleans Race Riot of 1900*. Baton Rouge: Louisiana State University Press, 1976.

Harlan, Louis R. *Separate and Unequal: Public School Campaigns and Racism in the Southern Seaboard States, 1901–1915*. Chapel Hill: University of North Carolina Press, 1958.

Johnson, Kimberley. *Reforming Jim Crow: Southern Politics and State in the Age before* Brown. New York: Oxford University Press, 2010.

Lane, Ann J. *The Brownsville Affair: National Crisis and Black Reaction*. Port Washington, NY: Kennikat Press, 1972.

Litwack, Leon F. *Trouble in Mind: Black Southerners in the Age of Jim Crow*. New York: Alfred A. Knopf, 1998.

McMillen, Neil. *Dark Journey: Black Mississippians in the Age of Jim Crow*. Urbana: University of Illinois Press, 1990.

Newby, I. A. *Jim Crow's Defense: Anti-Negro Thought in America, 1900–1930*. Baton Rouge: Louisiana State University Press, 1965.

FOUR

From the Great Migration to the Great Depression, 1915–1933

BETWEEN 1910 UNTIL 1930, more than 1,750,000 African Americans decided to move north to escape the Jim Crow system. Most of the migrants went to Boston, Chicago, Cleveland, Detroit, Indianapolis, New York City, Philadelphia, and other Northern industrial cities. Black populations in Northern cities such as Chicago and Detroit increased by as much as 40 percent during that 20-year period, leading to intense competition for housing and jobs. The migrants encountered bitter white racism in the North that mirrored what they had left behind in the Jim Crow states; however, in the North black men had the right to vote (and after 1919 so did black women), lynch mobs were rare, and African Americans could move around freely, as long as they stayed in their neighborhoods. Jobs were also available and employers rarely refused to hire someone because of his or her skin color. The meatpacking, steel, and construction industries needed unskilled workers, and after 1915 jobs in war-related industries grew in great numbers. As the war in Europe expanded, immigration stopped. After the United States entered the war in 1917 and Congress authorized a draft, even more jobs became available, and they paid much better than any jobs in the South.

The collapse of the Southern cotton industry forced many families, black and white, from their homes. The rapid spread of a quarter-inch-long bug with wings—the boll weevil (*Anthonomus grandis* Boheman)—heading north from Central America disrupted the economy of the cotton-producing South. The boll weevil quickly reduced land values and wiped out thousands of jobs in the cotton fields usually held by African American men, women, and children. The destructive insect spread north from its home in Central America through Mexico, reaching Texas in the 1890s, and by 1915, it had devastated fields across the entire Cotton Belt, from the Rio Grande to South Carolina. It left behind hundreds of devastated counties and towns. No insecticide existed that could stop its advance. The weevil bankrupted hundreds of cotton growers throughout the entire region. But, as the future gospel singer Mahalia Jackson, then growing up in rural Mississippi, remembered, many blacks felt that the bug produced at least one good thing "Thanks to the boll weevil, a lot of those thieving plantation people died out, too" (Litwack, 1998, 176).

Weevils feed only on cotton plants, spending their whole lives on them or inside them, first destroying the leaves, then causing the whole plant to turn brown and wither away. Planters had no defense against the destruction, no poison or insecticide to kill it (not until the 1970s did scientists develop a successful method of control). Within five years of the bug's first arrival in the United States, production of cotton fell by more than 50 percent. After a field became infested, it took 10 years to recover from the damage and return to normal production. Wealthy plantation owners usually had enough savings to survive for a decade; African American cotton pickers did not.

Because of the damage to their crop, the white plantation owners no longer needed large numbers of African American field hands to tend and pick their cotton. By the time the fields recovered, machines existed that could do the work of 10 human beings. The Cotton South provided few other jobs for the unskilled, uneducated, illiterate workforce the Jim Crow system of law and education had produced. High unemployment resulted in every county in the Cotton Belt. Migration to the North or to the nearest large city provided one solution for many former field hands. Moving meant that African Americans could not only escape the boll weevil, they could also get away from Jim Crow.

Black families in the Carolinas and Georgia took the closest train heading north and ended up in New York City, Philadelphia, or New England. Victims of the agricultural depression not wanting to move that far from home streamed into Atlanta, Birmingham, or Charleston. Impoverished tenant farmers and sharecroppers from Alabama and Tennessee boarded trains taking them to Cleveland, Detroit, or Indianapolis. The Illinois Central Railroad brought thousands of destitute, unemployed field hands from Mississippi and Louisiana to St. Louis and Chicago. The Great Migration, as historians called it, doubled and sometimes tripled the African American population in every Northern industrial city between 1915 and 1920 (Wilkerson, 2010, 161–63).

The boll weevil pushed many African Americans out of the South. World War I provided another stimulus to the Great Migration. Jim Crow, however, followed closely behind. As blacks moved north and west, the whole country adopted the Jim Crow system of race relations, from the White House to the Pacific coast. President Woodrow Wilson, who entered the White House in 1913, ordered that all government offices segregate their workforce shortly after taking his oath of office. Born in Georgia, Wilson shared the Jim Crow attitudes of most white Southerners. African Americans, according to that view, belonged to a backward, savage, inferior breed of humanity. If properly educated they might one day become "civilized," but acquiring the attitudes and values required for civilized living would take a long, long time. As a Democrat, Wilson had been elected by and now led the "white man's party," for which he offered no apology or compromise. Jim Crow would rule in the White House as long as Wilson remained president.

The changes in racial attitudes resulting from the World War I experience led to renewed efforts to challenge and defeat Jim Crow segregation and the constitutional interpretation that protected it. The possibility of dying for one's country, even a country that treated you as a second-class, inferior citizen, inspired many black veterans to demand equal justice and the same rights enjoyed by white Americans. After the United States entered the war in Europe in April 1917, about 367,000 African Americans served in the armed services, most of them drafted. By time the war ended in November 1918, more than 200,000 black soldiers had gone to France and seen duty on the Western Front, most of them as cooks, construction workers, truck drivers, and gravediggers. Because of the Jim Crow attitudes of military commanders, only a few thousand blacks were allowed to directly fight the Germans. Strict segregation ruled in the military. Until almost the very end of the war, when the first black officers appeared in France, only white officers commanded African American units. Army policy-makers and planners in Washington and on General John "Black Jack" Pershing's staff in France were convinced that African American troops, because of their naturally low intelligence and inherent tendency to run away from battle (as many had supposedly done in the Spanish-American War of 1898 and the war in the Philippines, according to army evaluations of military preparedness), should never be used in combat. So, just as the French and British used Africans from their colonies to dig trenches and latrines, Americans used their blacks to dig their trenches and latrines.

White officers often assigned African American troops to a job considered beneath the dignity of whites, picking up the bodies that littered the "no-man's-land" separating the Allied and German trench lines after major battles. The military, however, found that it needed more officers as the

war grew longer, and the army began sending African Americans to officers' training school. The War Department built a separate, segregated
school for blacks chosen for officers' training, with all-white instructors.
Located outside of Des Moines, Iowa, it trained several hundred blacks
before the war ended. After graduation, the black officers received their
assignments, all of them in lower-level administrative and supply positions.
They could not be trusted in combat, the army insisted, so they rarely commanded troops (Schneider, 2002, 7–11).

Black soldiers faced the same prejudice and discrimination in the military that they found elsewhere in U.S. society. French civilians were not
quite as rude and disrespectful, however, and for many African Americans,
this was a first. Kindness and respect from whites was something they
rarely experienced in their hometowns. U.S. military officials attempted to
persuade the French government to keep whites and blacks from eating
together in restaurants, sleeping together in the same tents, or even shaking
hands, but generally failed in that effort. African American soldiers found
more freedom and kindness in Paris than they had ever experienced anywhere in their homeland. The same was true on the battlefield. No matter
how many times French officers ordered their men to respect the racial
customs of the United States, they frequently failed.

On the home front the war for freedom and democracy had little impact
on traditional racist attitudes and behaviors. Jim Crow ruled. In the summer
of 1917, two bloody riots reminded African Americans of the dangers they
faced living in a Jim Crow society. On July 1, East St. Louis, Illinois, not geo-
graphically in the South, but mentally—in terms of its racial attitudes—not
very far from Dixie, exploded into one of the deadliest race riots in U.S. history. Angry over reports that an African American had shot and killed a
white storekeeper, three thousand whites burned and looted black homes
and churches in a weeklong campaign of violence fueled by alcohol and
intense racial hatred. On July 2 an unmarked police car drove into the burning African American neighborhood but then was stopped by a gang of
armed black men who surrounded it, set it on fire, and beat to death two
white police officers trying to escape. During the night, white gangs invaded
the black neighborhood, shooting and killing more than one hundred
African Americans and burning hundreds of homes to the ground. In the
midst of this attack, the white rioters shot and wounded a black child, then
picked him up and threw him into a blazing house where he burned to
death.

When the death and destruction came to an end, most of the city lay in
ruins. After an investigation, the state's attorney charged seven white police

officers and ten black civilians with murder. Convicted by an all-white jury of murder, each of the policemen were ordered by the white presiding judge to pay a fine of $150—the only punishment handed out to any whites involved in the riot. All-white juries convicted the ten African Americans of murder and each was sentenced to 14 years in prison.

The next month on August 23, twenty people (sixteen whites and four blacks) died in Houston, Texas, during a night of gunfire and murder. Many of the African American rioters belonged to the all-black Twenty-Fourth U.S. Infantry, a unit that had recently arrived at Camp Logan in Houston from their home base in Columbus, New Mexico. The killings began when police arrested a black soldier for interfering with the arrest of a black woman. A rumor reached Camp Logan alleging that the police had killed the soldier and that a huge, armed white mob was approaching the camp, where they were going to kill all blacks they found. The soldiers grabbed their rifles, and more than a hundred of them headed toward downtown Houston, killing sixteen whites, including five police officers, on the way. Four members of the Twenty-Fourth died on the way, two of whom had been accidentally shot by other members of their unit.

Army authorities indicted 118 soldiers from the Twenty-Fourth, accusing them of murder. After the court-martial hearings, the military jury returned 110 guilty verdicts. The eight found not guilty had testified against the others. Nineteen of those convicted received death sentences, sixty-three were sentenced to life imprisonment, and the remaining defendants got lesser terms. Houston authorities brought no whites to trial nor charged them with any role in the violence. (By 1930, all of the imprisoned soldiers had been pardoned or paroled except for two. The two remained in prison until they were released in 1938, thanks to the continuing efforts of the NAACP.)

The war with "the Huns" produced an outpouring of patriotic excess. Many Southern cities and counties passed "work or fight" laws specifically aimed at their black citizens. Apparently, the local authorities, believing that African Americans would try to avoid the draft, were ready to send any who tried to run away from their patriotic duty to prison, or put them to work on chain gangs. Jim Crow draft boards in each Southern county made sure that most of the men they called into the military were black. Very few blacks refused to serve, preferring to follow W. E. B. DuBois's advice to "close ranks . . . shoulder to shoulder with our own white citizens and allied nations that are fighting for democracy" (Schneider, 2002, 8–11).

Some whites had reservations about the wisdom of teaching blacks how to use rifles; if they learned how, these white critics of the draft explained, they might return from the war demanding better treatment as U.S. citizens. Knowing how to use a rifle, they would be able to back up that demand with bullets. By the same token, if some African Americans fought and died in France, other white racists warned, the whole community might begin demanding equal rights. Perhaps this fear of the consequences of patriotism and sacrifice inspired the tremendous flood of racial violence and lynching that swept across the United States when the war ended. Whites needed to remind African American veterans to remember their place in society and to forget about challenging or raising that status. A few casualties or deaths in France were not enough reason to challenge white supremacy. Equality was still the worst thing imaginable. That any black person could even aspire to such a goal was an idea that had to be extinguished. Whites would have to fight together to keep that dream from becoming reality.

Shortly after returning home, African American veterans confronted an epidemic of racial violence. The summer of 1919—the "Red Summer," according to some observers, referring to the blood that flowed in U.S. streets along with the alleged involvement of Communist Reds in the chaos—witnessed racial hatred and violence in every area of the country. Communism caught the attention of Americans the year before because of the success of the Russian Revolution. The racial violence in the United States had little to do with communism. The violence in the United States included 25 race riots and 83 lynchings, up from an average of 46 during the war years. One of the lynching victims was a woman, eleven were soldiers, and fourteen were burned, eleven of them alive. All but seven of the victims were black. Not a single person was charged in any of these crimes. The Ku Klux Klan established branches in almost every state in the Union.

Major race riots hit Washington, D.C., not too far from the White House; Chicago; Omaha; Charleston, South Carolina; Longview, Texas; Knoxville, Tennessee; and Elaine, Arkansas. The first riot began on July 19, 1919. Seven people (four African Americans and three whites) were killed and more than seventy injured during three days of mob chaos in the nation's capital. White soldiers, sailors, and marines went on the attack after hearing rumors—all found to be false—that black soldiers had assaulted four white women that day. A week later, four days of rioting took the lives of 38 people, including 23 blacks and 15 whites, and destroyed large sections of Chicago's African American neighborhoods. The Great Migration had tripled the city's African American population between 1915 and 1919. However, the area in which blacks could buy or rent homes had hardly grown at all. The riot started when whites killed a black teenager on the city's lakefront after he had accidentally crossed an unmarked line separating the one "black beach" from the white beaches. Within hours, white mobs invaded the black community, setting fires to homes and businesses, dragging black people off streetcars, beating several of them to death, and seriously injuring hundreds more. After three days of such violence, Illinois National Guard troops regained control of the city and restored peace, though much of the black neighborhood was still on fire. The fires set by white gangs left more than one thousand black families homeless. Within six months of the racial violence, the Ku Klux Klan had established a large presence in the city. The Chicago Klan reportedly had more than 50,000 members by 1922.

The deadliest racial conflict in 1919, and perhaps the worst incident of racial killing in U.S. history, took place in the little town of Elaine, Arkansas. The exact number of deaths remains unknown, although the estimated number of African Americans killed by whites ranges anywhere from one hundred to three hundred. The white total reached five killed. The killings began on September 30, 1919. That night about one hundred black sharecroppers gathered in a church in Hoop Spur, three miles north of Elaine, to listen to an organizer from the Progressive Farmers and Household Union of America. The union wanted higher payments from white landlords for the cotton they grew. Whites believed that union represented a dangerous threat to the future of the United States, seeing it as part of the communist conspiracy to overthrow capitalism. An armed group of white sheriff's deputies drove to the church to break up the meeting and chase the organizer out of Phillips County. The black farmers had brought guns with them and exchanged shots with the deputies as they tried to enter the church. Three whites died in the gun battle, including a deputy sheriff.

The next day the Phillips County sheriff sent nine deputies back to the church to investigate the shooting and to find those responsible for the deaths. Rumors spread rapidly through the white population of the county and neighboring areas in Mississippi and Tennessee, reporting that a communist-inspired black revolt had begun and that hundreds of armed blacks were roaming the countryside killing whites. By mid-afternoon more than one thousand whites gathered in Elaine to hunt down the black "rebels" and restore order. A deputy sheriff wired the governor's office in Little Rock reporting that blacks had attacked the courthouse in Elaine with guns drawn, shooting wildly, resulting in numerous casualties among the white population. A later investigation found no deaths or injuries among the white residents of Elaine. Instead, as a newspaper reported from the scene on the day of the alleged attack, "at least fifteen negroes were lying in the streets and outskirts of the town," presumably dead, and there were probably many more bodies in the surrounding woods. Eyewitnesses recalled seeing whites cut the ears and toes off many of the dead to carry home as souvenirs. Other observers told reporters that the killers dragged the bodies of their victims through the streets of Elaine as though they were hunting trophies.

The Arkansas governor asked the army authorities in Washington, D.C., to send troops to Phillips County to prevent further deaths. The soldiers were sent, and they arrived on October 2. They assisted the sheriff in arresting hundreds of African Americans, but no whites, placing them in prison camps, where they were brutally tortured by the guards. Some African Americans in Elaine claimed they saw U.S. Army soldiers join in the shooting and killing of blacks in Phillips County, but army authorities denied that charge. After the violence ended, military investigators reported that not one of the hundreds of black prisoners they interviewed mentioned torture. A week after the killings stopped, a grand jury charged 123 African Americans with various crimes, including murder and "nightriding."

The trials began in late November in a courthouse surrounded by armed national guardsmen. The judge provided the impoverished black defendants with a team of local white lawyers, but during the several trials none of them ever asked a question or called a single witness. By the end of the month, juries had convicted 12 of the blacks of murder and sentenced them to death (the "Elaine Twelve"). In separate trials in November, other all-white juries convicted 65 black men of either second-degree murder, which carried a 21-year sentence, or "nightriding," which called for a year in prison. The prosecutors dropped the cases against the remaining prisoners. At the conclusion of the final trial, the NAACP announced it would represent the Elaine Twelve in their appeals. The association hired Scipio Jones, a black attorney from Little Rock, to handle the case. The Arkansas Supreme Court upheld six of the death sentences; however, because of a technical error, it ordered new trials for the remaining six. At their retrial, an all-white jury quickly convicted the six defendants once again, and the judge sentenced them to death. He set the executions for July 23, but the governor granted a stay of execution so they could file an appeal in federal court.

After three years of appeals in the lower federal courts, the Supreme Court finally heard oral arguments in January 1923. NAACP lawyers explained that mob justice had prevailed at the Arkansas trials and that evidence presented by black "eyewitnesses" to the killings had been obtained only after they were tortured by the police. A month later the court, in *Moore v. Dempsey*, ordered another trial for the six prisoners because the "mob-dominated trial" they first received had denied them "due process of law." The Arkansas Supreme Court granted their release from prison, though the other six men remained under sentence of death. Two years later, after negotiations with state authorities, Scipio Jones gained their freedom. On his last day in office, the governor authorized their release, ending their six-year ordeal. This decision represented the first major victory for the NAACP in its long campaign against Jim Crow justice and violence (Stockley, 2001, 24–26, 215–16).

Black soldiers had faced discrimination in their training camps before the war, in France during the war, and when they returned to the United States when the war ended. One new experience while overseas, however, opened their minds to something many veterans had never experienced or even thought possible before the war. While in Europe the relatively free and unprejudiced response they received from whites in France showed them what life could feel like in a relatively open society. (Not totally open—Africans from France's colonial empire had achieved equality and yet still felt the sting of prejudice in their African homelands, and they felt terribly aggrieved.) That new insight inspired some African American veterans to challenge the Jim Crow inequality they came out of in the American South. At a minimum, men who put their lives on the front for their country deserved the right to vote. First, however, they had to return to their hometowns, where a majority of the residents still considered African Americans an inferior type of human being. Wartime deaths and sacrifices had produced little change in white supremacist attitudes.

The NAACP, which supported the war, decided that evidence of black sacrifice during the war might help reduce prejudice. The association's leaders knew that African American soldiers had confronted unequal treatment and open hostility from fellow soldiers and officers. To document the racism and prejudice black soldiers faced during the war, the NAACP sent W. E. B. DuBois to France to collect data for a history of the African American role in defeating the Germans. After interviewing hundreds of black officers and enlisted men, DuBois wrote about their bravery in the trenches, and noted that in the Jim Crow army blacks worked in largely menial positions. He also reported on the racist attitudes held by many U.S. service members, including the highest commanders in the military. They "fought more valiantly against Negroes than they did against the Germans," DuBois concluded (Schneider, 2002, 354–56).

African American soldiers returning to the South in 1919 found that little had changed. Jim Crow had not gone away or ever changed. Patriotism and bravery in the trenches had not changed racist attitudes nor moved black

Americans closer to the dream of equal rights under the law and Constitution. Military service apparently meant nothing to the white supremacists. Instead, many whites resented the presence of black veterans and saw military training as a dangerous step towards full equality. "The high wages and allotments" African Americans received in the military "have made them shiftless and irresponsible," complained the Houston *Chronicle*. Senator William Kirby of Arkansas grumbled that military service had changed the "disposition" of many black veterans, making them more "idle and arrogant" and more "troublesome" than ever before. A new breed of blacks, "the New Negro" as they called themselves in the North, was emerging from the war experience, and white Southerners needed to be on guard against their coming demands for social and political equality.

A great threat to the superiority of the "white race" came from these young African Americans, especially those who had been stationed in the North or in France during the war. These young black veterans defiantly rejected the traditional behavior of the older generation, the "good Negroes," those "old darkies," who quietly and graciously accepted the superiority of the white Anglo-Saxon race and accepted and never challenged the inferiority of their own race. Now, just because of their wartime patriotism, they actually felt worthy of demanding full equality. "Before we submit," to that ridiculous idea, an enraged white Georgian screamed, "we will kill every negro in the South" (Newby, 1965, 159–60).

Representative, and future secretary of state, James F. Byrnes of South Carolina, offered another view of the new brand of African Americans emerging in the early 1920s. "If as a result of his experience in the war he does not care to live in this land without political and social equality," he told a crowd in reference to the New Negro, "then he can depart for any other country he wishes, and his departure will be facilitated by the white people of this country, who desire no disturbing factor in their midst." Thousands of blacks had already departed the Jim Crow South during the war years; now many more considered moving away. For some blacks in Dixieland, however, the only way to defeat Jim Crow was to stay where they lived and defeat it. They had a long way to go (Newby, 1965, 158–59).

By 1920, Southern state legislatures and governors had passed more than 350 segregation laws. These Jim Crow laws separated people by race in cemeteries, churches, hospitals, labor unions, prisons, offices, factories, mines, parks, public buildings, railway trains, railway station waiting rooms, housing developments, neighborhoods, schools, stores, streetcars, theaters, funeral parlors, and any other places people could meet. Some towns excluded all people of color from residing anywhere within their boundaries, or, in the case of "sundown towns," had laws making it a crime for people of color to be found within city limits after 8:00 p.m. African Americans needed to know the local laws and customs every place they went and respect them or face the possibility of being beaten, humiliated, or arrested. Black people in the Jim Crow South knew that they could never get service in white-owned restaurants, hotels, drugstores, or department stores.

Blacks could buy Coca-Cola at some drugstore soda fountains, but only if they carried a small bucket with them. The clerk filled the bucket (if he or she felt like it) but then an African American minister, lawyer, doctor, or millionaire had to go outside in back of the store to drink it. Movie theaters sold tickets to black customers, but only for seats in the balcony, or "Nigger Heaven," as whites called it. In addition, black patrons had to enter the theater through a side or back door, or climb up the fire escape to get to the balcony—never through the front door. Parks, zoos, and golf courses had signs warning, "Negroes and dogs not allowed." Taking a streetcar or bus meant boarding at the rear in most cities, or, if the car or bus had only a front entrance, blacks had to wait until all whites had boarded before they could enter and pay their fare. On the bus, black riders had to move to the back, behind the sign attached to a seat reading "Negroes Only." If more whites entered the vehicle after the "Whites Only" area had already filled, the driver or motorman ordered blacks to get out of their seats and move farther to the rear. And in some cities, bus drivers and streetcar conductors had the authority to arrest anyone who did not move.

As long as African Americans respected the rules and stayed behind the "color line" established for them, peace reigned. Crossing that line meant trouble. In railroad depots, which required blacks to enter through separate doors, usually on the side of the building or way in the back (never in the front), it had been the law since 1881 in some states for blacks to get in line to buy their tickets, but only after all white passengers had bought theirs. African Americans paid the same fare as whites paid, but they had to wait in line until the white ticket agent felt ready to take their money— and any grumbling or complaints usually meant a longer wait. Separation on railroad cars, and every place else, served one great purpose. As Clifton Johnson, a white Northern travel writer and essayist, explained on a journey through the South at the turn of the century, "What you see on the railroad is characteristic of the whole structure of the Southern States. The Negro occupies a position of inferiority and servility, of which he is constantly reminded when traveling, by restriction, by discriminating laws, and by the attitude of his white neighbors" (Doyle, 1937, 236). Every day and in every place, Jim Crow laws reminded black Americans of their inferior status legally, politically, and socially in society. As civil rights crusader Pauli Murray explained about life in her native South when she was a child, "It was color, color, color all the time" (Murray, 1956, 270).

To get along with as little trouble as possible in Jim Crow America, black Southerners realized that they had to follow the accepted forms and patterns of behavior in the community they happened to be in or face the consequences. Sometimes, especially in unfamiliar territory, such as in moving to or travelling through a new state or city, it made good sense, if possible, to ask a new friend or neighbor how to act in particular situations. In Birmingham, Alabama, for example, black passengers entered at the rear of the streetcar, while in Atlanta, Georgia, custom and the law demanded that blacks enter from the front, after all the whites had boarded. Mistakes usually led to trouble. A black man new to Nashville got off the streetcar through the front door and received a severe beating because he was legally required to leave though the back door. (During World War I, a conductor in Birmingham threw an African American soldier from the North off of his streetcar because he refused to move further back in the Negro section as he had been ordered to do. The soldier took out his gun and shot and killed the conductor. After a quick trial he was sentenced to death and executed.) Black people never knew exactly what would happen to them if they violated a local racial custom, but the threat of death always lingered in their minds.

Whites demanded that blacks, to get along with their superiors, be humble and happy, always smiling and grinning, and ignorant, respectful, and unsuccessful. Any sign of success posed a threat to white dreams of superiority. As long as "Negroes will drink common whiskey, dance jigs, and make apes of themselves," a black college graduate acknowledged to a friend, whites applauded them as good people (Litwack, 1998, 163). Success, on the other hand, would not be accepted. Anything that challenged ideas of white superiority had to be rejected. African Americans could murder, steal, gamble, rape, get drunk, beat their children, or engage in any other criminal act and whites shrugged their shoulders and said, "What can you expect? It's part of their nature." Criminal behavior reinforced the white vision affirming the inferiority of the black race. It proved that Jim Crow laws were necessary and the best way of dealing with the "Negro problem." Northerners, Southern whites argued, did not understand that the fundamental defense of segregating people by race was that black people would never be and could never be equal to whites. They were a childish, foolish, criminally inclined group of naturally inferior beings who lacked any desire or ability to improve themselves. Jim Crow separated and protected the white race from the savages surrounding them. The biggest threat to the peace and prosperity of not only the South but of the entire United States came from the people who misunderstood that reality.

When the laws did not prove enough to contain the beast, or some over-educated, smart-alecky, black bucks rejected their inequality, the fear of beatings, burnings, and lynchings was necessary to keep African Americans in their place. After the massive nationwide outbreaks of violence in the Red Summer of 1919, lynchings reached prewar totals the next year. Early in 1920, whites in Florida lynched four black men at the same time for alleg-edly raping a white woman. On Election Day in November of that year, five blacks and two whites died in Ocoee, Florida, after African Americans attempted to vote. The white lynchers then burned the entire black commu-nity in Ocoee to the ground.

More than one hundred African Americans met their deaths at the hands of lynch mobs in 1920 and 1921. Congress debated a federal antilynching law in 1921, with no result. The bill passed the House but because of a Southern-led filibuster did not make it out of the Senate. Violence contin-ued to take its toll in July 1921, when a white girl claimed (falsely) that a black elevator operator had attempted to molest her in Tulsa, Oklahoma. (He actually stumbled and fell against her while she was getting off.) The city experienced the worst racial massacre in the United States in the twen-tieth century when whites murdered anywhere from one hundred to three hundred African Americans in a weeklong spectacle of burning and destruction. Oklahoma had not joined the Union until 1908 but quickly joined the ranks of Jim Crow states when its legislature passed a series of Jim Crow statutes. One of them required separate telephone booths for black and white callers. Just a year and a half after the Tulsa riot, during the first week of 1923, a mob of two hundred whites burned down the entire African American town of Rosewood, Florida, killing at least 8 and possibly as many as 26 residents. That mass burning followed a report (probably false) that a black man had attacked a white woman in her home.

The riots, lynchings, and bloodshed did not deter the NAACP from con-tinuing its fight against legal segregation and disfranchisement in the courts. The association lost one case challenging Jim Crow treatment but won an important victory for equality in the second, though it had little immediate impact on black lives in the Jim Crow states. The defeat came in the decision known as *Corrigan v. Buckley* (1926). It involved the ques-tion of segregated housing, while the other, *Nixon v. Herndon* (1927), con-cerned the right to vote. In the *Corrigan* case, the Supreme Court upheld a "restrictive covenant" signed by white property owners in the District of Columbia that prevented them from selling their homes to any member of "the Negro race." The court had previously declared unconstitutional a zoning ordinance passed by the Louisville, Kentucky, city council that made it a crime for either blacks or whites to buy a home on blocks where a majority of the other race already lived. The court did not base its 1915 decision, *Buchanan v. Warley*, on the issue of racial discrimination, however. Instead, it declared that the ordinance violated an American's Fourteenth Amendment right "to acquire, enjoy, and dispose of his property" whatever way he or she saw fit.

In the 1926 case, John J. Buckley sued his neighbor Irene Corrigan after she agreed to sell her house to an African American family. This agreement violated a contract all sellers had signed promising not to sell their property to nonwhites. In their unanimous 1926 decision, the nine justices of the Supreme Court ruled that the guarantee of "equal protection of the laws" applied only to government actions, not to private contracts such as the one at issue in the *Buckley* case. The court agreed that the restrictive covenant in Washington, D.C., discriminated because of race; but since it required no state or government action of any kind, and the two persons involved had signed the contract voluntarily, it did not violate the Fourteenth Amendment. In other words, governments could not mandate segregated housing, but individuals could privately agree to accomplish the same goal. The *Corrigan* decision made racially segregated housing legal. However, in 1948 in *Shelley v. Kraemer*, a case coming out of Chicago, the Supreme Court reversed its previous ruling, though it still upheld the right of individuals to agree not to sell their property to members of another race. However, because the restrictive clause required government action to enforce it, either by the police or by a judge, the contract violated the Fourteenth Amendment and was therefore unconstitutional.

Nixon v. Herndon involved the Jim Crow system that governed voting. In July 1924 Dr. Lawrence A. Nixon, a black physician in El Paso, Texas, sued in federal court after an election judge told him that he could not vote in the Democratic Party primary. Nixon had paid his $1.75 poll tax, but since 1923, Texas law allowed only whites to cast ballots in Democratic Party primaries. On appeal, the U.S. Supreme Court heard arguments on the issue in January 1927. The NAACP Legal Defense Fund provided money and legal support for the appeal. In its decision, read by Justice Oliver Wendell Holmes, the court upheld Dr. Nixon's right to vote in the primary, concluding that "color cannot be made the basis of a statutory classification affecting" the right to vote.

The NAACP declared a great victory, but Texas lawmakers found a huge loophole in the decision. The state legislature quickly passed a law giving political party leaders power "to prescribe the qualifications of its own members and in its own way determine who shall be qualified to vote." The Republican Party had not won an election in the Lone Star State since 1876 and was hardly big enough to hold a primary. Whoever won the Democratic primary ended up winning the general election. The executive committee of the Texas Democratic Party decided that only whites could join the party. The Supreme Court ruled that the government could not discriminate against voters because of their skin color, but political parties, being private institutions, could. By allowing Dr. Nixon the right to vote, the court effectively denied all other black voters that same right. The justices reaffirmed the right to deny people the right to vote because of their color, a right it first established in the 1883 *Civil Rights Cases*.

Dr. Nixon went back to court. After five years of battling and losing in state courts, the Supreme Court once again accepted his appeal. This time it decided in his favor once again. In *Nixon v. Condon* (1932) in a narrow 5 to 4 decision, the majority ruled that the party executive committee, by barring blacks from voting, was operating as an agent of the state and therefore had violated the Fifteenth Amendment provision banning the use of race in determining voting rights. Again, the decision contained a loophole quickly filled by the Lone Star State's legislature. The new primary law removed all laws concerning primary elections from the state law code, leaving primary election procedures entirely in the hands of party officials. Government was no longer involved in the process.

The private Democratic Party soon provided that only whites could participate in its activities. That rule remained in effect for 12 years before the Supreme Court acted on the issue of primary voting rights once again in *Smith v. Allwright* (1944). In this 8 to 1 decision, the majority decided that conducting elections, whether primary or general, was always a state function. Therefore, by denying blacks the right to vote in their primary, the Texas Democratic Party had done so solely on the basis of race, and the government had supported that discrimination in a function for which it alone bore responsibility. Such an action violated the constitutional rights of African Americans, which no state had the power to do. *Smith* opened the doors to black voting in a state that had denied them that right for more than half of a century. *Smith* played a major role in ending Jim Crow–style voting restrictions. It marked the beginning of the end of "white primaries." Black participation in primaries increased by wide margins in Georgia, Florida, Louisiana, South Carolina, and Texas by 1948 and two years later more than 20,000 African Americans participated in Mississippi's Democratic primary, compared to fewer than 2,500 in previous primaries (Klarman, 2004, 135–38).

Jim Crow laws kept blacks out of Southern politics, out of good public schools, and out of public places in general by the 1920s. Jim Crow attitudes even influenced how government agencies and private relief groups responded to the needs of African American citizens during times of major natural disasters and crises. The Great Mississippi Flood of 1927 began on April 16 with the collapse of a levee protecting Cairo, Illinois, from the rising waters of the Mississippi River. Within five days, raging water from the worst flood in the river's history had reached Mounds Landing, Mississippi, an all-black town at the state's northern edge, and the floodwaters easily smashed through the levees protecting it. The flood also swept away unknown numbers of African Americans who had been working day and night to reinforce the levee wall. By time the waters began to recede, the river had killed at least 247 people, according to the Red Cross, though the relief workers never could agree on the exact total. The number of deaths remains unknown because rescue crews never located all the bodies. Hundreds of black prison inmates worked in chains along the river during the flood, and when raging water crushed the levees, their bodies ended up dozens of miles away. The reaction of federal and state authorities to the plight of thousands of African American refugees provides an excellent example of racial attitudes that flourished during the Jim Crow era.

President Calvin Coolidge appointed Secretary of Commerce Herbert Hoover, who had won wide praise for his handling of Red Cross relief efforts in Europe following the Great War, to direct the federal government's relief efforts along the Mississippi. Feeding and clothing the thousands of homeless refugees became an enormous problem. Conditions in Greenville, Mississippi, deteriorated rapidly, as the floodwaters had swept away most of its business district and most of its housing, leaving behind more than 10,000 homeless men, women, and children, 75 percent of them black. They took up refuge in tents or simply on blankets on the ground. They had no food or water and no way to escape the tragedy, as roads and the railroad leading out of town had completely disappeared. Rescue boats got to the city, but only after three days of turmoil. There were enough boats to take away all of the refugees, according to African American witnesses, but when they arrived the rescuers allowed only the 33 white women and children they found in the refugee camp to board them. When the boats moved out, they left thousands of desperate African Americans behind. Apparently, the white cotton planters who dominated the region's economy and controlled its political system did not want to lose their labor force. They feared that if African Americans left the area they would never return, so they told National Guardsmen who arranged for the rescue to take away only the whites they found. (In the year after the flood, at least 50% of the black community totally abandoned Greenville and headed north to Chicago.)

The Greenville "rescue" proved to be only the first of many examples of how Jim Crow relief efforts actually worked. Food provided by the Red Cross and federal government went first and in larger quantities to white Mississippians and the white Arkansas flood victims on the other side of the river. Leftovers went to black refugees. Black refugee camps had armed guards surrounding them while the white camps had none. Herbert Hoover sent investigators into the African American camps after hearing complaints of the physical and verbal abuse the refugees received. The investigators reported on the many instances of abuse and mistreatment of African Americans they discovered committed by the all-white Mississippi National Guardsmen sent to guard and "protect" them. The future president read the reports and filed them away, never responding to them or releasing them to the public. He did not want to arouse racial antagonisms at this "critical time," he explained. Instead, Hoover created a Colored Advisory Commission to investigate in more detail conditions in the camps. Headed by Robert Russa Moton, who had succeeded Booker Washington (who had died of stress and high blood pressure in 1915) as principal of Tuskegee Institute, the commission issued its preliminary report in June. The report included recommendations for bettering conditions for the thousands of still homeless refugees in the camps—none of them ever implemented (Daniel, 1977, 170–73).

Moton included in his list of recommendations removing the guards from the camps, providing cots—not just blankets—for all refugees, allowing African Americans to occasionally have first pick in selecting clothing and food donated to the Red Cross rather than always giving whites that chance, and improving the method of giving reports on the reconstruction efforts underway. The commission sent its final report to the secretary of commerce in November. It included statements not normally found in reports written by educated, well-to-do "good" African Americans such as Moton and the rest of his advisors. In the final report, they expressed their surprise at "the fear on the part of the colored people" they found in talking with them. "They are afraid that if they tell the truth, and somehow it is discovered that they have 'talked too much,' that they would be killed," apparently a possibility conveyed to them by members of the National Guard.

The sharecroppers also seemed reluctant "to ask for the things to which they were entitled under the Red Cross." White landlords got everything they needed—food, clothing, even money, "without difficulty," while the very small number of "Negro landowners" in the flooded region "are not able to secure supplies or rations or repairs" of any kind without a long wait and a great deal of difficulty. After submitting their report, the commission heard nothing more from Secretary Hoover or anyone else in the Commerce Department, ever (Daniel, 1977, 231).

Herbert Hoover promised Moton that if he became president he would see to it that the African American flood victims received everything they needed to restart their lives. All Moton had to do to assure that promise was to keep his committee's report secret. Hoover won the presidency and Moton kept his part of the bargain, but the promised assistance never came.

The Republican Party and President Hoover adopted a policy of doing as little as possible for a still very loyal constituency. The Democratic Party maintained its "whites only" commitment and did nothing to assist African Americans. By the end of the 1920s, however, a new, very small political party in the United States emerged with the nation's "Negro problem" at the top of its agenda. The Communist Party of the United States (CPUSA), founded in 1918, launched a campaign to win the allegiance of white and black sharecroppers, tenant farmers, and workers at its April 1929 convention. It became the first U.S. party to offer a civil rights program and to directly challenge the Jim Crow system. To begin its campaign the party and its Young Communist League sent a small group of black and white field organizers into the South under orders to establish racially integrated worker's committees. The cotton mill workers in North Carolina would be the first people the CPUSA decided to recruit. Children worked in the mills, many of them under the age of 14, some of them as young as 10. "They were undersized probably because they didn't get enough to eat. And they worked the same long hours as their mothers," one of the organizers reported. Jim Crow attitudes in the South had long defended and fully supported the practice of child labor.

The National Textile Workers Union (NTWU) had been active organizing a branch in eastern Tennessee. Early in 1929 it called a strike in the region's cotton mills. Five thousand textile workers walked out of the mills calling for shorter hours and better pay. The Communist Party sent a team of organizers to join them. For the standard six-day, 55-hour workweek, textile workers received $15.81. Since mill workers saw their jobs as "white work" (which generally meant the jobs were higher paying and probably less dangerous and dirty than work reserved for African Americans), only a few blacks labored inside the cotton mills, and in separate parts of the factory. Communist Party organizers hoped to replace "race consciousness with class-consciousness"; forget skin color and concentrate on the unity of all workers became the key theme in their recruiting efforts.

After the Tennessee strike ended in a bitter defeat for the workers, Gastonia, North Carolina, became the focal point of the party's efforts in the South. The Communists wanted a union, but it had to be integrated. Social class would eventually replace race as the key factor in the lives of the South's working poor. Out of the struggle with mill owners in Gastonia, an interracial movement of the poor would emerge. About four hundred African Americans worked in the mills in Gaston County, more blacks than in any other county in the state. Albert Weisbrod, one of the Communist organizers, told white strikers to invite fellow workers "white and black" to come together to future meetings. At one of the first large rallies, white mill workers tied a rope across the meeting room to separate the audience, whites on one side and blacks on the other side. When CPUSA organizers objected, a significant number of whites went back to work rather than risk having to sit next to a black fellow worker. "Union membership," one of the whites who fled from the meeting told a reporter, "conflicted with my obligation to put the Anglo Saxon race first."

After six weeks in North Carolina, a black Communist organizer sent a letter to his colleagues in New York City, in which he complained that "the attitude of 'cracker' strikers toward the Negro has not changed a bit." They would not meet with African Americans, he sadly concluded, and probably never would. He promised, however, to try to "uphold racial equality" even if that had to be done in segregated branches. The New York Communists would have nothing to do with such a pessimistic outlook. Party leaders expelled one of the organizers because he agreed to hold a meeting in front of an all-white audience, with African Americans excluded. Workers had to be told to forget skin color; it meant nothing really. The only thing that mattered was winning the class war all workers were fighting against the ruling class.

A rival union organized by the American Federation of Labor had accepted Jim Crow customs and established separate branches for blacks and whites. Any attempt at integration would only lead to fights, in the view of AF of L leaders. Besides, every union local in the United States met in segregated union halls. Why should anything different be expected in Jim Crow country? The Communists in New York would have none of that petty racism, however, and insisted that workers had to forget their skin colors and come together as a class.

Ella Mae Wiggins, a white mill worker, and a single mother and poet with four children, became the party's most effective organizer during the Gastonia strike. After a rally in Stumptown, an all-black community, at which she made an impassioned speech, five white thugs hired by the mill owners shot and killed her. Eyewitnesses identified the murderers and they were arrested, but an all-white grand jury refused to indict them. Despite Wiggins's death, the organizing effort eventually led to a lengthy strike. It ended in complete failure because the CPUSA's campaign ran out of money and withdrew from Gaston County. The effort to create something really new in the South, an integrated union, had failed. However, the Communist Party did not give up its fight against American racism, and a trial in Alabama gave it another opportunity to recruit African American members (Gilmore, 2009, 79–80).

Nine black boys ("boys" in actuality, because their ages ranged from 13 to 20), jobless and mostly illiterate, had been arrested and charged with raping two white women on top of a boxcar on a freight train as it moved slowly across northern Alabama, close to the town of Scottsboro. Under the state law governing rape, the young blacks faced the death penalty. At their first trial, an all-white jury found them guilty after 10 minutes of deliberation and sentenced all but the 13-year-old to death. (Alabama juries decided whether or not a murderer would be electrocuted.) The jury told the judge that they could not reach a decision on the youngest defendant. One juror had refused to consider death for him, believing it sinful and un-Christian to execute someone so young. The judge declared a mistrial in his case.

Two Communist Party members who had witnessed the entire proceedings wired party headquarters in New York City suggesting that it become involved in the case. It contained many issues worthy of consideration: racism, Jim Crow justice, and Southern poverty among them. The boys' defense attorney at the trial, a real estate lawyer hired by the defendants' families, had showed up drunk the first day of the trial. The presiding judge replaced him with a local attorney who during the entire length of the court proceedings did not ask a single question of any witness nor did he call any defense witnesses. Had the CPUSA not sent a prominent attorney to prepare an appeal, the "Scottsboro Boys" would have gone to the electric chair within a few weeks and the trial would have been forgotten.

The Communists sent Samuel Leibowitz, a well-known New York defense lawyer and a noncommunist, to prepare an appeal. The NAACP received a request for help from the mother of one of the "Boys" but rejected any aid because it did not want to become involved in any way with communists. The International Labor Defense Committee (ILD) and Samuel Leibowitz presented the legal work in Alabama. The state's Supreme Court rejected the appeal and Leibowitz took it to federal court. His argument centered on the inadequate defense the "Boys" received at the trial. In *Powell v. Alabama* (1932), the U.S. Supreme Court voted 7–2 to overturn the guilty verdict and grant a new trial. Ozie Powell was one of the nine black defendants convicted by the jury. The majority concluded that the "Boys" original attorney had not presented an adequate defense, which had denied them their Fourteenth Amendment right to "due process." The justices ordered new trials for all the defendants, except for the 13-year old, who the majority decided was too young to be charged with rape. Their decision meant that in death penalty case states had to provide qualified lawyers for all impoverished defendants. *Powell v. Alabama* represented an important victory in the fight against Jim Crow justice. African Americans accused of murder now had the constitutional right to a lawyer. No longer would illiterate defendants have to face the possibility of a death sentence alone before an all-white jury and an always-white judge.

The Supreme Court's decision did not end the "Boys' ordeal," however. Alabama quickly retried the cases and another all-white jury reached a guilty verdict, even though one of the alleged rape victims testified that she had lied; no rape ever took place, she testified. The prosecutor told the jury that she had become a communist during the trial and therefore could never be trusted to tell the truth. Leibowitz appealed again and once more the U.S. Supreme Court reversed the verdict. This time Leibowitz raised the issue of jury selection, protesting that an all-white jury had denied the all-black defendants a jury of their "peers." In *Norris v. Alabama* (1935), the court by 8 to 1 challenged another long-standing element of Jim Crow justice, allowing only whites to serve on juries. The court majority held that by excluding African Americans from jury rolls, states had denied black defendants "the equal protection of laws guaranteed by the Fourteenth Amendment." It ordered a new trial. At the third trial, the NAACP took charge of the defense because the Communist Party withdrew from the case. This jury had one black member, but it still produced a guilty verdict, though the jurors recommended a 75-year prison term, not death.

In 1936, the state dropped the charges against four of the defendants, with the requirement that they leave Alabama, which they quickly did. Three other of the "Boys" spent several more years in prison before receiving a pardon from the Alabama governor in 1944. The last of the Scottsboro Boys remained in prison for six more years before he escaped from a chain gang and managed to get to Michigan. In 1976, Governor George Wallace pardoned all of the "Boys," but by this time only one of them was still alive. Jim Crow justice had taken its toll once again; it had ruined the lives of nine of its victims. The CPUSA had demonstrated its commitment to equal rights for all and the NAACP had won a great victory over Jim Crow. Chicagoan Oscar De Priest, the only African American member of Congress in the 1930s, told a black audience in Atlanta "to lend no ear to Communism, it is not good for you because the Negro depends upon the white man for a job," and whites hate communists. They would never hire black communists, he warned. The NAACP established a strong anticommunist reputation (at least in the North) during the struggle, a reputation that disappeared quickly, however, as the movement against Jim Crow gained strength after World War II (Carter, 1969, 170–73).

The association won its first important political victory in 1930 by blocking President Herbert Hoover's nomination of Federal District Judge John J. Parker to the U.S. Supreme Court. The North Carolina Republican had told a white audience during his 1920 campaign for governor, "The participation of the Negro in politics is a source of evil and danger to both races and is not desired by the wise men in either race." That statement seemed perfectly permissible in 1920, but 10 years later it proved to be very troubling to anyone on the national stage, a sign of progress. The NAACP campaign helped convince the Senate to reject the nomination (Goings, 1990, 23–24).

By 1930, the Great Depression had brought the U.S. economy to the edge of collapse. Unemployment and bank failures had reached unprecedented heights. Prices for cotton, tobacco, peanuts, and other crops grown in the South had reached new lows. The South, the poorest region of the country since the end of the Civil War, suffered even greater economic distress. The economic collapse hit sharecroppers especially hard. In Mississippi and Alabama, poor farmers, white and black, had incomes that averaged about $132 in 1931–32, making them the poorest people in all of the United States (except perhaps for Indians on reservations). The Hoover administration did nothing to provide any relief for the poorest of the poor, the farmers and sharecroppers. State governments in the Jim Crow South did even less for their most destitute citizens.

The 1932 election brought Franklin D. Roosevelt to the White House, and he seemed, at the beginning of his administration, to offer little more than Hoover had provided. However, the new administration seemed aware that some things in the economy needed changing and that many people needed help. This new attitude in the White House indicated that at least the new people in Washington cared about the struggles of the poor, the unemployed, and the destitute. Jim Crow, however, played a major role in the design and funding of the new relief agencies and job creation programs presented to Congress by the Roosevelt administration. Jim Crow's defenders made sure that African Americans would be excluded from programs such as Social Security and that Jim Crow work rules applied to construction projects throughout the South. Jim's Crow's protectors in Congress made sure that legislation aimed at reducing unemployment, helping farmers, and creating jobs did so without changing or challenging racial discrimination and inequality in the South. The fight for equal rights and equal opportunity lost out during the Depression years to the political realities of U.S. race relations in the South—white power prevailed. Not a single program passed by Congress required Jim Crow to step aside so that all Americans could have their constitutional rights.

References

Carter, Dan T. *Scottsboro: A Tragedy of the American South*. Baton Rouge: Louisiana State University Press, 1969.

Daniel, Pete. *Deep'n as It Come: The 1927 Mississippi River Flood*. New York: Oxford University Press, 1977.

Doyle, Bertram. *The Etiquette of Race Relations: A Study in Social Control*. Chicago: University of Chicago Press, 1937.

Gilmore, Glenda. *Defying Dixie: The Radical Roots of Civil Rights, 1919–1950*. New York: W. W. Norton, 2009.

Goings, Kenneth W. *"The NAACP Comes of Age": The Defeat of Judge John J. Parker*. Bloomington: Indiana University Press, 1990.

Klarman, Michael J. *From Jim Crow to Civil Rights: The Supreme Court and the Struggle for Racial Equality*. New York: Oxford University Press, 2004.

Litwack, Leon. *Trouble in Mind: Black Southerners in the Age of Jim Crow*. New York: Alfred A. Knopf, 1998.

Murray, Pauli. *Proud Shoes: The Story of an American Family*. Boston: Beacon Press, 1956.

Newby, I. A. *Jim Crow's Defense: Anti-Negro Thought in America, 1900–1930*. Baton Rouge: Louisiana State University Press, 1965.

Schneider, Mark Robert. *"We Return Fighting": Civil Rights in the Jazz Age*. Boston: Northeastern University Press, 2002.

Stockley, Grif. *Blood in Their Eyes: The Elaine Race Massacre of 1919*. Fayetteville: University of Arkansas Press, 2001.

Wilkerson, Isabel. *The Warmth of Other Suns: The Epic Story of the Great Migration*. New York: Random House, 2010.

FIVE

Jim Crow: From the New Deal to the Double "V," 1933–1945

FRANKLIN ROOSEVELT AND HIS ECONOMIC ADVISORS thought that restoring the devastated economy began with saving U.S. agriculture. Sharecroppers in the South did not fit into the picture, however. Saving agriculture meant saving family farms and big producers. The first farm program the new president sent to Congress in 1933, the Agricultural Adjustment Act (AAA), contained nothing that would help landless tenant farmers or sharecroppers directly. Instead, the AAA production program gave most of the money provided by Congress to the landowners, while the people who needed the most assistance ended up getting the least. Under the program established to help restore prices for agricultural products, landowning farmers could get money for destroying one-third of whatever crops they had already planted that year; the same supply reduction applied to farm animals. Reducing food supplies immediately would lead to increased prices in future years. As outlined in the bill passed by Congress, the Department of Agriculture would send a farmer a check for the market value of the crops or animals he destroyed in the program's first year. Farmers could only destroy one-third of whatever they produced, however. If a farmer owned 30 acres, he would plow less than 10 acres and receive a check from the government for the market value of the crop he would have planted on that land. If a farmer owned 10,000 acres, the government sent a check for the market value of 3,333 acres. This system applied to corn, wheat, sugar beets, peanuts, rice, cotton, tobacco, and livestock. Obviously, bigger farms and plantations received the most money.

In 1933, at lest 80 percent of African Americans in the Southern states made their livings as sharecroppers or tenant farmers, meaning they did not own any land. An almost equal percentage of poor whites earned their living the same way. Sharecropping developed after the Civil War and remained the dominant method of agricultural production in the South until after World War II. In this system, the landowner or plantation "boss" provided the sharecroppers with "furnish"—the housing, food, tools, and seeds they needed to survive—while the "cropper" and his family supplied the labor. The owner decided which crops to grow, usually cotton, sugar, rice, or peanuts. After harvest, the owner paid the sharecropper with 30 to 50 percent of the crop he and his family had produced, minus the cost of his "furnish." The croppers rarely had any cash when they signed their annual contract, because they bought their "furnish" on credit from a store owned by the plantation boss and it charged outrageous prices for those goods. The boss deducted the cost of the "furnish" from whatever he owed the cropper. Many times this cost exceeded the amount of money earned by the cropper, so the boss added that debt (plus interest) to the amount he deducted from whatever the croppers earned the next year. According to laws passed in Jim Crow states, sharecroppers could not leave the planta-tion they contracted to work on until they had repaid all their debts. Crop-pers who left prior to repayment faced criminal prosecution. At any time he felt like it, on the other hand, the owner could evict the cropper from his plantation.

Tenant farming allowed a farm worker to rent land from the owner. However, because tenants rarely had any cash, their "rent" came from a percentage of the crops they harvested. This "crop rent" usually meant that the landowner received one-fourth to one-third of the value of the crop produced by his tenants. Neither sharecropping nor tenant farming led to prosperity and wealth for anyone except the master of the plantation.

One section of the agricultural bill said that a farmer or landowner could not evict any sharecroppers or tenants from the land they had contracted to work. Plantation owners had to provide their laborers with land to grow food to feed their families. The law said that owners had to share some (it did not specify how much) of the money they received from the government with their sharecroppers and tenants. The program provided no enforcement procedures to make sure landowners carried out these requirements, however. Abused workers had to go to court to get some-thing of what they were entitled to receive. Southern federal judges proved to be less than friendly to sharecroppers and tenants. In 1933, a federal judge in Arkansas ruled that because sharecroppers played no role in sign-ing the contracts required by the Department of Agriculture, they lacked "legal standing" to demand their enforcement. Jim Crow demands for inequality made it into the nation's farm relief programs.

Jim Crow senators and representatives ensured that racial restrictions and inequalities limited every important government program established during the Great Depression, from the New Deal job programs to Social Security to the minimum wage legislation of 1938. Social Security excluded coverage for every category of employment in which African Americans made up a significant part of the U.S. workforce. All farm workers (which included sharecroppers and tenants), laundry workers, hospital workers, and domestic employees (maids and butlers) were prohibited from being covered. As the NAACP's Charles Houston told the House committee holding hearings on the Social Security bill, "from a Negro's point of view it looks like a sieve with the holes just big enough for the majority of Negroes to fall through." According to Houston, the job categories excluded meant that two-thirds of all African Americans would not be covered (Katznelson, 2005, 23–24).

Social Security confronted the same problem that important reform legislation always faced; it depended on state governments to implement and administer key parts of the program. Just getting enough votes for passage in the Senate required assurances that African Americans would not receive the same benefits and treatment that their fellow white citizens would get. Senator Richard Russell of Georgia assured his Southern colleagues that no matter what benefits were being debated on any legislation affecting race relations, "we are not going to yield an inch." Jim Crow inequality would be preserved or no Americans would receive anything. Congress gave states the power to set benefit levels for aid to the elderly, aid to children, and unemployment compensation. For example, Georgia provided $18.00 in unemployment compensation per month for feeding, clothing, and housing an entire family. Alabama and Mississippi set their maximum payment even lower. One state official in Mississippi explained that "these folks have been poor all their lives. They are used to living on nothing." So why should the government give them more?

In 1938, Congress applied similar rules for coverage to the minimum wage law. At first, Democratic members of Congress from Jim Crow states (along with most Republicans) fought vigorously against any minimum wage. They succeeded in removing farm workers, laundry and hospital workers, and butlers and maids from coverage, and reduced the national minimum wage standard from 50 cents to 25 cents an hour. The power of Southerners in the House and Senate came partially from the limited number of voters legally allowed to cast ballots in the districts and states they represented. Jim Crow voting laws severely limited voter registration and participation. The excluded voters included hundreds of thousands of poor blacks (and whites) who could not pay poll taxes or pass literacy tests. Only 24 percent of adults over 21 voted in the Jim Crow states in the 1940 presidential election, compared with more than 60 percent of adults in the rest of the country. Ninety-five percent of the people casting ballots in the South were white and economically middle class or above; the poll taxes, literacy requirements, and "understanding" clauses prevented most of the rest from exercising their right to vote.

True democracy and self-government was the major casualty of racist voting laws. Most of the poor and almost all of the black population in the Jim Crow states had no influence on their political leadership, at either the state or national level. According to Ralph Bunche in his 1940 study called *The Political Status of the Negro*, only 14 percent of adults voted in Texas. Only 16 percent of adults voted in Mississippi, only 18 percent in Arkansas, and 20 percent in Georgia.

Jim Crow elections were held in one-party states, and the Democratic Party candidate always won. Competition came only in the primaries, which were limited to white voters in most of the South. Southern senators and members of the House who avoided challenges in the primary expected long careers in Washington, and the longer they served the more power they accumulated. Both the Senate and the House followed the seniority rule in their selection of committee chairs, usually the most powerful person on the committee. The member of the majority party on any congressional committee who had the most years of service in the Senate or House became the chair. Most of the permanent or "standing" committees in Congress had chairpersons from Jim Crow states. They all adhered to their region's signature legislative agenda—do not back down on questions of race; make sure to maintain inequality between blacks and whites in every program created—and left it behind on every important piece of New Deal legislation they touched. Southern members of Congress frequently sided with Republicans to block any measure that even seemed to treat blacks and whites equally, or that specifically aimed at protecting African Americans from the abuses of white supremacy, such as antilynching laws. White political leaders from Jim Crow states recognized the importance of lynching in maintaining black inequality.

White Southerner racists recognized "lynch law" as their final defense against social and political equality. In the Jim Crow states, lynching and the fear of being lynched proved to be the most effective tools in maintaining white supremacy. From 1880 to 1930, white mobs lynched 3,220 African Americans in the 11 states of the Old Confederacy. In the 1920s, 385 African Americans had been tortured and killed in public lynchings; in the following decade, the number of lynchings dropped to 144, the lowest total since the 1870s. Lynching is defined as an illegal death "at the hands of a group acting under the pretext of service to justice, race, or tradition." Lynchers may have felt they were justified in performing their deed but according to the laws of every U.S. state, they had committed murder.

Under the Jim Crow definition of justice, however, members of lynch mobs had no reason to fear being arrested. State authorities rarely prosecuted anyone involved in a lynching, no matter how brutally the crime had been carried out. Opposition to lynching could cost a political leader his career. In 1927, the governor of Mississippi attributed his loss in the primary to his calling out the National Guard to prevent a lynching. In Washington, Congress had debated federal antilynching bills in 1921 and again in 1930, however filibusters by Jim Crow senators had prevented their passage. The Senate would filibuster again in 1935 and 1937, ending again with similar results. A federal law making lynching a federal crime was necessary, supporters argued, because Southern law enforcement officials were not doing their job. Between 1880 and 1930 more than three thousand African Americans had been lynched but only 54 people had ever been convicted and punished for any of those crimes. And the punishments handed out to lynch mob participants included fines of a hundred dollars and jail terms of three months for lynchers in one Alabama case and a two-year suspended sentence for a lynch mob leader in Texas in 1920. Jim Crow justice prevailed again. Something needed to be done, and Southerners were not doing it. Jim Crow leaders were not going to let it happen. Federal involvement in investigating lynchings would create a national police force that would take away the power of local officials to handle their own affairs. A federal lynch law would be a step towards creating a police state and a federal dictatorship. It would threaten white supremacy.

In 1935, debate on an antilynching bill, passed by the House, ended in the Senate when Jim Crow senators threatened to kill Social Security legislation if supporters did not withdraw a bill labeling lynching a federal crime. In 1937, the debate on lynching began during a summer marked by two particularly savage lynchings of black men in the South. In the first atrocity, a mob of more than three thousand white men, women, and even children in Florida tortured and burned alive a young African American who had allegedly murdered a white woman. The local newspaper praised the mob for its work. "What America needs today are men who are willing to defend virtue and womanhood not only against the brute Negro, but the social temptations of today that are placed around our girls." A grand jury investigated the lynching but concluded that the murder had taken place "at the hands of a small group of persons unknown to us" (McMillen, 1990, 246–48).

The following year a mob in Duck Hill, Mississippi, dragged two African Americans from their jail cells after they had been arraigned for allegedly killing a white woman. Both men swore that they were innocent, though one of them shouted out a confession while being burned with a blowtorch. The other prisoner maintained his innocence until mob members gouged out his eyes with an ice pick. The lynchers then doused their victims with gasoline and set them on fire, while other mob members laughed and cheered as they watched their black victims burn to death. A grand jury investigating the crime concluded that, even though the killings had taken place in broad daylight at the hands of unmasked men and women, the members of the mob could not be identified, so authorities arrested no one.

The extreme barbarity of the 1937 lynchings changed very few minds among the Southern members of Congress. Lynching was barbaric but necessary. The future of the white race would be threatened. Calls for national action from the NAACP and the Association of Southern Women for the Prevention of Lynching (ASWPL), organized in 1930 to fight the "shame of lynching," produced a similar lack of effect. The ASWPL became one of the first white groups in the South to fight any part of the Jim Crow system that protected the honor of white womanhood. Defenders of lynching said it was a local matter that state and local authorities should handle. If blacks just kept from raping white women, they argued, lynch mobs would disappear. Jim Crow senators filibustered successfully in 1935 and 1937 (as they had done in 1921) against what they called federal government interference in local affairs. A senator from Louisiana declared that only the fear of being lynched kept the "savages from attacking and raping our white women" (Dray, 2002, 359–60).

The filibuster in 1937 tied up the Senate for more than a month before supporters gave up the fight so they could consider other important economic legislation. The Senate never got to vote on any antilynching legislation in the 1930s, showing the power of Southern states in Washington. Jim Crow senators successfully used filibusters, which at the time required a two-thirds vote of the Senate to bring to an end, every time a proposal came up for consideration.

The number of lynchings declined significantly in the 1930s, though the mob-administered tortures handed out grew more gruesome and barbaric. Whites continued to get away with their crimes. The Jim Crow system of justice ensured, however, that African Americans arrested in the South received much harsher sentences than whites for committing the same crime. In the Southern states, the enforcement of law and order lay in the hands of the local county sheriff. Voters elected the sheriff, another example of how denying African Americans the right to vote greatly influenced their treatment at the local level. Even in counties with majority black populations, the sheriffs were white. These elected county sheriffs had their own rules to guide them. They knew how to handle troublemakers and how to punish lawbreakers. How many African Americans they abused, mistreated, tortured, and beat to death will never be known, but considering the methods authorities had used in punishing "lawbreakers" in the past, the convict lease system and chain gangs being two examples, the numbers must have been enormous.

In the states of the Old Confederacy, the sheriff and his deputies in rural areas and small towns, as well as the police chief and his patrol officers in cities, enforced two kinds of law, "negro law" and laws for everybody else. As historian Neil R. McMillen has observed, "negro law" meant that bigamy was a crime for whites but not for African Americans because blacks were just naturally promiscuous and faithless to their families. Having two or three wives would be no surprise for black men. Stealing, on the other hand, especially blacks stealing from whites, was a serious crime, while the police rarely investigated cases of blacks stealing from other blacks. The police even treated murder differently. If a white man, especially if people considered him a man of "good standing" (which meant a churchgoing family man), killed an African American man, woman, or child, he rarely faced a judge and jury. On the other hand, if a black killed a white man or woman, regardless of the circumstances, after a quick trial before an all-white jury, the killer faced almost certain death in the electric chair or life imprisonment at a minimum—if jury members had any compassion (McMillen, 1990, 202–6).

The horror stories concerning the abuse and mistreatment of black prisoners throughout the South are numerous. In Mississippi in 1930, Oscar Perkins, an African American, confessed that he had killed a white woman. However, the confession came only after three sheriff's deputies beat him over the head with their pistols, hung him over a fire where he dangled until he passed out, then threw a bucket of cold water on him and measured him for his coffin. A jury convicted him and he was executed. In another example of police brutality, Gerrard White, a black man accused of killing a white planter, confessed to the crime after the police threw him on the floor, held him down, and poured water into his nose, which made him feel that he was drowning (the "water torture"). After struggling and writhing on the floor in great pain, he confessed. A jury convicted him and sentenced him to death. On appeal, the Mississippi Supreme Court threw out White's confession, concluding that the police had attained it only by inflicting "pain and horror." He was retried, an all-white jury convicted him again—this time without the confession—and he was executed. In 1946, an all-white jury convicted a 15-year-old African American boy of killing a white man and sentenced him to death. Mississippi quickly carried out that execution.

The executions based on "confessions" or flimsy evidence continued. In 1953, the Magnolia State put a severely retarded black man to death for murder. He did not have a lawyer at his trial, nothing unusual in Jim Crow states, but neither the state supreme court nor the U.S. Supreme Court accepted his appeal. The courts somehow ignored or forgot a principal of justice set by Mississippi's top court when in 1926 it said that, "The duty of maintaining constitutional rights of a person on trial for his life rises above mere rules of procedure" (McMillen, 1990, 246–48).

Prisoner's rights in Jim Crow states received a boost from a Supreme Court decision offered in *Brown v. Mississippi* (1936). The case began with the murder of a prominent white cotton farmer in Kemper County, Mississippi, in 1934. The sheriff arrested three African American sharecroppers, Ed Brown, Henry Shields, and Arthur "Yank" Ellington, and took them to jail in Meridian, a few miles away. The men "voluntarily" confessed to the killing, the Meridian *Star* reported, and when the sheriff heard rumors that a lynch mob was gathering he ordered all his deputies to make sure no violence took place. A grand jury quickly indicted the prisoners for first-degree murder. The trial began the next day. The prisoners had court-appointed white defense attorneys. District Attorney John Stennis, a future U.S. Senator, handled the prosecution. One day later, the all-white jury returned a guilty verdict after deliberating for no more than 30 minutes. The judge ordered all three to be hanged on May 11; hangings in those days took place in the county where the crime had been committed.

The crime, the arrest, and the conviction had all taken place within one week, not unusual in Mississippi in cases involving blacks supposedly killing prominent whites. County authorities took pride in the fact that they had achieved justice without mob violence. Kemper County, which had witnessed twice as many lynchings as any other county in the state, this time demonstrated its commitment to "fundamental fairness." One of the three white defense attorneys, John Clark, had "trouble" with the evidence presented at the trial, however, and decided to file an appeal of the verdict with the Mississippi Supreme Court. During a brief talk with the defendants before the trial—the judge had given the lawyers exactly 30 minutes to interview their clients—Clark noticed numerous scars and burn marks on their arms and necks. One of the prisoners ("Yank" Ellington) had a "neck all scarred up with a ring around it that could be seen" from across the room, Clark remembered. During their time on the witness stand, all three defendants testified that deputies had severely beaten them with sticks and clubs, and whipped them—with leather straps with buckles—until they confessed. The confessions were the only evidence presented by the prosecution.

During his testimony, one of the deputies told the court that indeed the whippings had taken place, but in his view, they were "not too much for a Negro; not as much as I would have done if it were left to me." "Yank" Ellington had been so severely tortured and beaten that for the rest of his life he walked with a limp and could stand only if someone held onto him. The brutal beatings by the deputies became the basis for an appeal.

The Mississippi Supreme Court rejected the appeal, with two judges dissenting. The defendants' counsel had not raised the issue of torture at the trial, so under traditional rules of justice it could not form the basis of an appeal. One of the dissenting justices wanted to ignore the rules on what constituted proper grounds for appeal. "It is a common saying that there are exceptions to all rules," especially when lives were at stake, he insisted (Cortner, 1986, 123). The majority refused to allow any exceptions and upheld the death sentence. The court reset the execution date to February 8, 1935. Clark suggested that the three defendants had not received a fair trial because the judge had denied their attorneys enough time to prepare an adequate defense. The majority rejected this argument, too.

Upset with the court's rejection, John Clark wrote to the NAACP asking for assistance. The association had previously sent him a small check to help prepare his first appeal and now agreed to help pay for a federal appeal. To help raise funds for the long process of appeals, the NAACP placed a picture of the three Mississippi blacks on the front cover of its magazine, *The Crisis*. Most of the money for the appeal, the association explained, "must be raised outside of Mississippi" because the state's "colored citizens seem afraid to lift their voices or pool their money to fight for themselves" (Sullivan, 2009, 172). The leadership in New York seemed unaware of the danger faced by any African American in Mississippi whose support of the NAACP became public knowledge. The civil rights group had been unable to establish a branch in the state. This failure illustrated the enormous fear that filled the hearts of Mississippi's black community. However, the *Brown* case inspired the organization of the state's first NAACP branch, with a membership of 126, in Meridian. "Our people have decided to take a stand, whatever the cost may be," the branch's president courageously announced.

Attorney Clark suffered a physical and mental breakdown shortly after losing the appeal in state court. Former Mississippi governor Earl Brewer, Clark's close friend, took over the case in order to "help right a grievous wrong," he told his wife. The appeal finally made it to the Supreme Court. Brewer told the justices that the sheriff had obtained the confessions only after hours of extreme torture, making them less than trustworthy. A unanimous court agreed, overturning the guilty verdicts, and ordered a new trial for the three African Americans now on death row. No court should accept confessions gained through torture, the Supreme Court ruled. "The rack and torture chamber may not be substituted for the witness stand," Chief Justice Charles Evans Hughes, author of the decision, declared (Cortner, 1985, 134).

For white Southern racists, the *Brown* case illustrated the major problem with Supreme Court "interference" in local affairs. Outsiders, including the justices of the Supreme Court, did not understand the "race problem" the way white Southerners did. African Americans remained law-abiding only because of the continuing threat of harsh punishment. "You do not know where the beast is among them," a Texas member of Congress informed his colleagues Jim Crow justice helped keep the peace (Cortner, 1985, 123–24). If a lynch mob had killed the three blacks in Meridian, it would have acted justly, because it would have carried out the will of the people. The "savages" would have gotten what they deserved and justice would have been done. Justice would be quick, the punishment appropriate, and honor would be restored. But "outsiders" meddled in the affairs of Mississippi law enforcement and the killers got away. As one Southern newspaper explained, "A white woman's honor" was more important than any black man's life.

Slowly the Supreme Court, in cases such as *Powell v. Alabama, Norris v. Alabama*, and *Brown v. Mississippi*, established basic procedural rights that Southern courts had to grant African American citizens. All-white juries still presented a problem, as did all-white state and local law enforcement personnel. The court would tackle these problems, but not until after World War II. In most Jim Crow states, white justice still ruled.

The NAACP emerged as the largest and most important defender of constitutional rights for African Americans, though it still had difficulty building branches in the Jim Crow South. There were other groups fighting Jim Crow. The Commission on Interracial Cooperation (CIC), established in 1919 after World War I in Atlanta by a Southern white member of the clergy, Will Alexander; the Highlander Folk School, founded in 1932 in Tennessee by another clergyman, Myles Horton; and the Southern Negro Youth

Conference (SNYC) also joined the struggle. The SNYC emerged out of a 1937 conference of the Communist Party (CPUSA) in Richmond, Virginia, devoted to understanding the race problem. The meeting attracted both communists and liberals from areas throughout the South. Earl Browder, CPUSA chair, addressed the hundred or so people in attendance, declaring that the new group, the SNYC, would fight for "free and equal education," "equal pay for equal work," "the right to vote and to serve on juries," and "an end to lynching" (Gilmore, 2009, 362).

The CPUSA remained one of the two political parties—the other was the American Socialist Party—in the country that put civil rights for all Americans at the top of its agenda. The SNYC organized a voter registration drive in North Carolina and sponsored conferences on how to fight Jim Crow in several Southern cities. When its affiliation with the CPUSA was revealed during the Red Scare of the 1950s, the government placed it on the attorney general's list of illegal, un-American organizations. The CPUSA remained active in the fight for racial equality and justice until Congress made it a crime for Americans to join the Communist Party in 1954. It had played a key role in the fight against Jim Crow in the 1920s and 1930s, despite its small membership.

The CIC did not directly attack Jim Crow. Methodist minister Will Alexander, its founder, preferred to bring together the "best people," white and black, in Southern communities to discuss racial problems and work together to peacefully resolve them. By the "best people," Alexander meant elected officials, ministers, doctors, lawyers, teachers, and respected business leaders. At their meetings and discussion groups, they pledged to work together to educate the rest of the public about racial issues.

The educational approach proved to be slow and frustrating. The "best people" approach meant sitting down with members of the other race and talking about how to resolve racial problems involving housing, education, employment, law enforcement, and health care. Just getting to know something about the problems and prejudices experienced by others would help bring citizens together to work in common to find solutions. Jim Crow should not be directly challenged or confronted. People needed education on matters of race relations rather than conflict. The "best people" needed to play the role of educators.

Racial problems could be resolved peacefully once everyone had a decent job and access to a good education. Lingering in the minds of many members was the fear that good jobs and good schools would not end discrimination or remove prejudice. Jim Crow laws applied to every black American, whether they were educated, employed, prosperous, intelligent, and talented or not. The wealthiest, most highly educated, or most success-ful African American in Atlanta, Birmingham, Memphis, or Oklahoma City still had to ride in the Jim Crow car, or could still be arrested for drinking from the wrong water fountain, or shot dead for sitting at the wrong table in a restaurant, or for "looking the wrong way" at any white woman.

In 1935, Alexander took a job with the federal government, though he remained head of the CIC during his time in Washington. In Washington, he worked in the Department of Agriculture as deputy administrator of the Resettlement Administration (RA), later renamed the Farm Security Administration (FSA). In 1937, President Roosevelt chose Alexander to head the FSA. One of the most radical New Deal agencies, the FSA included programs to provide low-interest loans to sharecroppers so they could build homes and begin farming on their own land.

Another very controversial program sponsored by the RA moved several thousand impoverished sharecroppers and tenant farmers, white and black, into government-built housing on abandoned or vacant land pur-chased by the Department of Agriculture. The residents of such commun-ities in the South lived in rigidly segregated housing communities. Southern members of Congress denounced the program anyway, even though it tried to follow Jim Crow standards of segregation. Virginia sena-tor Harry Byrd labeled the program wasteful, extravagant, and an example of an unnecessary intrusion into local affairs by a "collectivist government." Thousands of people would suffer so Jim Crow could survive. When Repub-licans regained control of Congress in 1946, they eliminated the FSA and sold the 11,000 homes it had built to the highest bidders.

Though not founded directly to confront Jim Crow, the Highlander Folk School played an important role in the fight against segregation in the South. Its two white founders, Myles Horton and Don West, established the school in Monteagle, Tennessee, in 1932 to help educate "rural and industrial leaders for a new social order." The school's educational pro-grams emphasized labor history, union organizing skills, and, after 1942, how to live together in an integrated society. The school seldom had more than 12 full-time students in the 1930s. It welcomed its first African Ameri-can speaker in 1934 but had to abandon its plan to integrate all classes and workshops after receiving threats of bombings and fires from members of the surrounding communities. Students and faculty supported Horton's simple social philosophy—working people could find the solutions to what-ever problems they faced by looking within themselves. By 1944, with help from the United Auto Workers union, the school sponsored its first fully integrated workshops. This violation of Jim Crow etiquette led to charges that it had become a "Communist training school." Highlander closed its doors in 1961 after an investigation by the state legislature found that Communists had worked at the school and labor "radicals" had taken classes there. The state revoked the school's charter (Egerton, 1995, 331).

Even though New Deal reforms discriminated against black Americans, most realized they still benefited from them. In 1936, in the North and West, African Americans turned away from the Republican Party and began voting for Democrats in massive numbers. Blacks in the Jim Crow South continued to be excluded from the voting booth. The poll tax and understanding clause prevented them from voting. But President Roosevelt, who had never called for racial justice or openly supported antilynching legislation or an end to the poll tax, did have an informal group of African Americans advising him—his so-called "black cabinet." These advisors included economist Robert Weaver, educator Mary McLeod Bethune, and William H. Hastie, who later became a federal judge. They made the president aware of the needs of blacks. For black people, just the presence of African American advisors, formal or informal, meant that the government was paying attention to their problems and needs. That Eleanor Roosevelt met with Mary Bethune, daughter of an illiterate South Carolina sharecropper, meant even more. As an advisor to the National Youth Administration, Bethune advocated nondiscriminatory hiring policies, and in her meetings with the president encouraged him to become more outspoken in support of equal rights for her people.

The president met with leaders of the NAACP in the Oval Office, though he never publicly supported the association's goals or efforts. Eleanor, on the other hand, always denounced lynching and segregation, and favored equal rights for all Americans. In one of his few appearances before an all-black audience during the 1936 election, the president spoke to students at Howard University in Washington, D.C. He told them that "among Americans there should be no forgotten men and no forgotten races." The students gave him an enthusiastic response and recognized that they had a friend in the White House. Even though the president never attacked Jim Crow, never criticized the poll tax, and never supported antilynching legislation, Roosevelt remained popular in the African American community. Simply indicating that he was aware of the problems faced by blacks in Jim Crow America kept them on his side (Sullivan, 2009, 209).

During the Great Depression the NAACP was the only national organization fighting against Jim Crow laws and segregation. The National Urban League worked mostly in Northern cities and had no large presence in the South. The NAACP had branches in many areas of the South, though many of them were extremely small and inactive. In 1935 the national office decided to resume its campaign against Jim Crow in the courts. James Weldon Johnson, the famous black poet and longtime executive secretary of the NAACP, had deep ties in the South. He was born in Florida and in the 1920s made frequent trips to the South, helping to establish several new association branches in his home state and others. In 1930 he retired from his job as executive secretary, and Walter White, another black Southerner, replaced him. White, who as a young boy had witnessed the 1905 Atlanta Race Riot, also travelled widely through the South and spent much of his time investigating lynchings. White wrote a book about lynching and fought for Congress to pass a law making it a federal crime.

The NAACP had three important victories in the 1920s: the 1923 *Moore* case concerning fair trials, a 1927 Texas case—*Nixon v. Condon*—that seemingly outlawed the white primary, and blocking the nomination of Judge John Parker to the U.S. Supreme Court in 1930. At its 1932 convention, the association vowed to fight two difficult problems: that of unequal pay for white and black teachers and that of expanding access for African American students to professional and graduate programs at public universities. A new voice had joined the NAACP's fight against discrimination. Charles Houston, dean of Howard University Law School, began working part-time for the NAACP in 1933 and encouraged all African American lawyers to join him in a campaign "to reconstruct the entire southern picture." Within 25 years, he believed, the entire Jim Crow legal structure could be broken down through federal court action. With that goal accomplished, blacks could finally enjoy their full constitutional rights as Americans.

One of Houston's colleagues at Howard, William Hastie, saw a further benefit to the legal campaign for equal rights: victories in carefully selected legal cases provided the NAACP with "an opportunity to rally dispirited and discouraged Negroes to fight again for that equality and human dignity" (Sullivan, 2009, 184–89). Hastie advocated a campaign that appealed to the sense of fairness possessed by white Americans. Victories in court advancing the ideals of equality and justice would find wide support across the United States, and America at last would live up to its democratic promise.

The first important case involving graduate and professional school access came out of Maryland in 1935. The law school at the University of Maryland had denied entry to an African American applicant, Donald Murray, a graduate of Amherst College. In a letter explaining that decision, the university president cited a state law requiring that an African American student, regardless of his or her course of study, had to attend all-black

Morgan Academy or all-black Princess Anne Academy. Black law students could also receive state aid if they enrolled in an out-of-state law school. In April, Murray filed suit in Baltimore City Court against the University of Maryland, charging it with discrimination. In his first major case for the NAACP, Thurgood Marshall, a 1933 graduate of Howard University Law School, argued in Murray's favor. He pointed out that neither all-black college had a law school, nor had they any plans to build one.

In June, in a major victory, a city court judge ordered the University of Maryland Law School to admit Murray. The state appealed. Maryland did not have funds to pay for an out-of-state program, but as the case progressed through the appeals process, the legislature quickly provided some money. Maryland took the case to the state court of appeals, which also overturned the university's rejection of Murray. "Compliance with the [state] Constitution cannot be deferred at the will of the state," the justices explained. "Whatever system is adopted for legal education now must furnish equality of treatment now." Maryland decided not to appeal this decision. Being a border state, Maryland never had the rigid Jim Crow system found in Deep South states, so *Murray v. Maryland* proved to be a victory, but a narrow one, since no other Jim Crow state followed Maryland's example. Donald Murray entered the law school of his home state in the fall of 1936.

The most significant case concerning education that the NAACP won in the thirties involved Lloyd L. Gaines, an African American student from St. Louis. He had graduated from Missouri's all-black Lincoln University and wanted to study law. The University of Missouri Law School rejected his application; however, it offered to pay his tuition to law school in any other state of his choice. Gaines refused to accept that offer, however, and with the support of the NAACP filed suit in federal court charging the University of Missouri with racial discrimination. Lincoln University did not have a law school. The state legislature discussed and agreed to build a law school at Lincoln shortly after Gaines filed his suit, but he did not want to wait until construction was completed. The case of *Missouri ex rel. Gaines v. Canada* reached the U.S. Supreme Court in 1938. The unanimous decision offered by the court held that Missouri had denied Gaines and other black citizens of the state equal access to higher education in violation of the Fourteenth Amendment. It ordered the state university's law school to admit Gaines or to build a "separate but equal" law school for blacks.

Missouri responded by building an all-black one-room law school at Lincoln. Lloyd Gaines did not enter the new law school, however; he had mysteriously disappeared. His family did not know what had happened to him. According to rumors, he had died in Chicago from pneumonia. Whatever the truth might be, the Supreme Court in *Gaines* provided its first ruling on the question of segregated higher education, and it became an important step towards 1954 and *Brown v. Topeka.*

World War II gave African Americans another opportunity to display their bravery, patriotism, and fighting abilities. But those traits still had to be demonstrated in a segregated, Jim Crow military. The Nazi persecution of Jews in Germany seemed very similar to the white supremacist system that existed in the Jim Crow South. Nazis recognized the connection between U.S. and German racist thinking. Julius Streicher, editor of *Der Sturmer*, a militant anti-Jewish magazine in Germany, told an audience of Nazi Party members in 1936, "We do not kill Jews in Germany. . . . We have other and more civilized methods of punishing them"—apparently he was referring to making noncitizens of Jews, which the 1935 Nuremberg Laws had accomplished. "In America," he reported, "Negroes are killed by mobs without fear of punishment and for the most trivial reason(s)."

Adolf Hitler expressed his great admiration for the Jim Crow system of laws and governing and his admiration for the slave-owning American South on several occasions. He told one Nazi that the North's victory in the Civil War "was a perversion of history that left the United States structurally damaged." When the Confederacy surrendered, he continued, it destroyed true historical destiny of the United States. The German chancellor took comfort in the fact that several U.S. states had adopted laws that "worked to keep the races separate and minority groups pure" (Gilmore, 2009, 171).

Members of lynch mobs in the Jim Crow South may not have been fascists (they probably did not even know what that word meant), but they shared with Hitler's legions certain feelings and attitudes—for instance, the significance of race in human history, the superiority of the white race (the "Aryan race," in Hitler's terms), and the inferiority of certain peoples, especially people of color. Nazis and Southern white supremacists also shared bitterness and rage toward people who had defeated them in a war. Nazis believed Jews had betrayed them during the Great War and were no better than bacteria and bugs. Southerners believed that black people were a dirty, nasty, criminal race of savages. A German newspaper informed its readers that thirty U.S. states had laws forbidding marriages between whites and blacks. In 1939, a Nazi Party newspaper published an article informing its readers that the United States did not live up to its claim of equal rights for all. The U.S. Senate had recently defeated an antilynching bill, the paper reported, and a lynch mob would be something German Jews never had to encounter. Another Nazi newspaper marveled at the fact that Americans were "outraged at the elimination of Jews from German universities" yet they did not "even consider the exclusion of Negroes from many American universities" (Kuhl, 1994, 98–99).

Race riots had never marred Germany, but they seemed to be a common theme in U.S. history, according to some Nazi scholars. In 1934 a Nazi historian concluded that Americans had always treated blacks much more brutally than Germans treated Jews. By November 1938, however, the Nazis were catching up. Nazi mobs slaughtered more than four hundred Jews and hung their bodies from lampposts during the anti-Semitic riots that took place during *Kristallnacht* "the Night of the Broken Glass," as the Germans called it (although the violence actually lasted for almost an entire week). The deadly destruction during that week of anti-Jewish brutality mirrored the antiblack savagery of race riots in Atlanta, Houston, East St. Louis, Chicago, Tulsa, Rosewood, and all the other cities and towns across the United States where racial violence had exploded.

After Congress declared war against Japan and Germany, more than 2.5 million black men registered for the draft (out of a total of 12 million draftees), and 1 million eventually saw duty in the U.S. military. They all fought in segregated units. The navy, which fought intensely against accepting any African Americans, finally backed down under intense pressure from President Roosevelt and civil rights groups, and began training some black sailors in the spring of 1942. Yet the navy remained the service branch with the smallest number of African Americans in its ranks. Blacks never accounted for more than 4 percent of navy personnel. The U.S. military had followed Jim Crow rules and customs since the Civil War, and that practice remained unchanged during World War II. The World War I experience, when the army assigned its all-black units to mostly noncombat roles in construction and transportation battalions, did not change either. Even though all-black units had fought bravely in the trenches of the Great War, white officers reported that African Americans had not performed well in combat and many had run away.

The NAACP saw the war as another opportunity to push for equality at home as well as abroad. African Americans could fight two enemies at once during the war. The editors of *The Crisis* outlined a program to fight Jim Crow and racial discrimination in the military and the Jim Crow states. The editors expressed the NAACP's deep sorrow for the "brutality, blood, and death among the peoples of Europe, just as we were sorry for China. But the hysterical cries of preachers of democracy for Europe leave us cold. We want democracy in Alabama, Arkansas, in Mississippi and Michigan, in the District of Columbia and in *the Senate of the United States*" (Sullivan, 2009, 207–8; emphasis in the original).

In 1941, A. Philip Randolph, head of the Brotherhood of Sleeping Car Porters, started a determined campaign to end U.S. racism when he launched the March on Washington Movement (MOWM). Joined by Walter White of the NAACP and many others, the march leaders demanded that President Roosevelt issue an immediate executive order banning discrimination in the defense industry. Though the planned march never took place, the march movement achieved a major victory when the president issued Executive Order 8802, which banned discriminatory hiring practices in government agencies and the defense industry. The order also created a temporary Fair Employment Practices Committee (FEPC), which had authority to investigate all charges of racial discrimination by military contractors. MOWM leaders recognized the importance of this order and cancelled the march. The order marked the first time in U.S. history that a government agency had the power to take action against any form of discrimination.

President Roosevelt appointed a white Southern newspaper editor, Mark Ethridge of Louisville, Kentucky, to head the FEPC. In one of his first speeches, much to the despair of African American leaders, Ethridge assured business leaders in Alabama that they had nothing to fear from his committee. Executive Order 8802 did not require desegregation. Neither did it threaten the Jim Crow labor system nor did it challenge the system of unequal pay that had kept many black and white workers in poverty for most of their lives, though whites always received higher wages than were paid to African Americans. Ethridge concluded his address to Southern corporate executives by reassuring them that "There is no power in the world—not even in all the mechanized armies of the Earth, Allied and Axis—which could now force the Southern white people to the abandonment of the principle of social segregation." Jim Crow would survive in the United States even after the victory over Nazi racism. Despite the weaknesses of the FEPC, its tiny budget, its reluctant chairperson, and its lack of enforcement authority, it showed black Americans that the president of the United States recognized that the problem of discrimination existed and that the federal government had to do something to end it (Gilmore, 2009, 362).

Early in 1942, the *Pittsburgh Courier* announced a campaign to fight for what it called the "Double V," a victory over Jim Crow racism at home along with the defeat of fascist racism overseas. The *Courier* and other black-owned newspapers kept up the campaign to defeat segregation until the war ended. The Double V crusade could count no significant victories, yet it kept the fight against Jim Crow alive. The victory over Nazi racist doctrine played an important role in weakening the racial theories used to defend Jim Crow inequality and to kill Jews in Europe. A black soldier who helped liberate the Nazi death camps in Europe and buried the corpses of the thousands of victims he and his fellow soldiers discovered within the gates of the Buchenwald death camp said the experience reinforced his commitment to "fight for my freedom and rights" at home. Another black soldier wrote that the mangled and battered bodies he saw reminded him of "how many times my people were lynched and mistreated across [my] country and nobody raised a voice."

Richard Wright, reflecting on a series of letters from black soldiers in Europe he read, letters describing the racist attacks and humiliations they had faced almost daily, concluded that "each and every Negro, during the last 300 years, possesses from that heritage a greater burden of hate for America than they themselves know." He thought it beneficial that blacks tried not to think about the experience of their race, "for if they ever started thinking about what happened to them they'd go wild." If whites ever thought that black Americans remembered what happened to them in the United States, the whites "would start out to shoot them all in sheer self-defense" (Litwack, 2009, 88–89).

Racist doctrines were weakened. Jim Crow laws and attitudes were not. One black veteran from Georgia, realizing the difficulties he and other African Americans faced upon returning home to Dixie, wrote to his father, "Now we are coming home, Sir. What are we coming to? We feel ashamed and hurt when we look around and see everybody that comes to the South treated with all the courtesy of American citizens. . . . Anybody, yes anybody as long as they are not Colored" (Litwack, 2009, 91).

The army, navy, army air force, marines, and coast guard did nothing to change their long-held racist structure or attitudes during the war. Every military unit remained segregated, black soldiers continued to serve only in transportation and construction units, and they faced racist hostility and hate in their training camps and in military bases throughout the entire war. Of the one million African Americans who served in the military during the four years of war, not one served in an integrated unit. The NAACP thought the war against German and Japanese racism would widen the war against Jim Crow at home. In 1934, Charles Houston had called for making the army an example to the world of what "a more united nation of free citizens" could accomplish, but Army Chief of Staff General Douglas MacArthur rejected that idea.

Winning equal rights at home seemed equally as important as defeating "master race" ideology in Europe and Asia, the NAACP insisted, but Jim Crow military traditions barely changed. During debate on the Selective Service (Draft) Act, Southern senators opposed an amendment that would have allowed African Americans to volunteer for the armed services, because it could lead to racially "mixed units," and that would encourage dangerous ideas of equal rights and interracial marriage. Any mention of equality in any way or any form always raised the notion of interracial marriage in the eyes of any Southern whites, and that was forbidden—for the honor of white men, marriages between black men and white women could never be allowed. The decision on whether to accept black volunteers for combat should be "left to the Army," according to Senator Lister Hill of Alabama. The army and all the armed services would have answered with a loud "No," the senator realized, because the military assigned soldiers to jobs based on reports from First World War commanders insisting that black troops had never fought well when given a chance on the front lines (MacGregor, 1985, 4, 8–9).

Segregation, according to the military, was not discrimination. Instead, it meant efficiency and improved morale. Separate units based on skin color promoted strength and unity among the troops. In accord with that reasoning, when the military opened training bases in the South, it sent whites and blacks to separate facilities. The armed forces even mandated Jim Crow conditions at their Northern training posts. In the U.S. armed forces, Jim Crow was not something regional; it was military practice everywhere. General George C. Marshall summarized the army's attitude on integration when he told a group of black newspaper publishers, "The Army is not a sociological laboratory; to be effective it must be organized and trained according to the principles, which will insure success. Experiments to meet the wishes and demands of the champions of every race and creed for the solution of their problems are a danger to efficiency, discipline, and morale and would result in ultimate defeat." Jim Crow was a necessary racial policy to follow to ensure victory over Nazi racism (MacGregor, 1985, 30–31).

This commitment to military "efficiency" came at a high cost. In 1943, racial violence broke out at military bases in Mississippi, Georgia, Texas, and Kentucky. In response, the War Department created the Advisory Committee on Negro Troop Policies. The committee recommended sending African American troops into combat rather than continuing the policy of relegating them to construction projects, digging, truck driving, and burial details. In March 1944, the first black combat units landed in Italy and African Americans fought German troops for the first time. The commitment of black soldiers to combat helped reduce racial tensions, because white troops no longer could argue that the army kept African Americans away from the front lines because they were too cowardly to fight and that they would run away rather than face Nazi soldiers. However, that no evidence existed to prove those charges did not change military policy concerning black troops. Military leaders stood as solidly in defense of racial segregation in combat as Jim Crow senators and members of Congress stood in opposition to the Double V.

When the war ended, little had changed in U.S. race relations either in the military or in the South. Jim Crow still ruled in both places. Racial violence had flared in U.S. cities and on military bases during the war against Hitler. Less than six weeks after the Japanese attack on Pearl Harbor, a mob in Sikeston, Missouri, dragged Cleo Wright, an African American accused of stabbing a white woman, out of his jail cell in the middle of the afternoon. They tied him to the back of an automobile and dragged him through the streets to the black side of town, where they poured gasoline over his severely mangled but still living body, set him on fire, and cheered as he slowly burned to death. The authorities made no arrests in the aftermath of Wright's murder, though it had taken place during broad daylight, perpetrated by unmasked killers.

In the summer of 1943, 34 people died before a race riot in Detroit, Michigan, ended. Many of the participants in the killings and bloodshed, both white and black, were migrants from Mississippi, Alabama, and other Dixie states, who had come North to find jobs in the war industries. Jim Crow attitudes made the journey with the migrants. The fighting began on a Sunday afternoon in a picnic grove, which both races claimed "belonged to them." President Roosevelt had to send the army's 101st Airborne Division into the city to restore order. The all-white Detroit police force killed 17 rioters, all of whom were black. Thirteen other African Americans had been beaten or shot to death by "persons unknown." Hundreds of other African American men, women, and children suffered broken bones and smashed heads and filled hospital emergency rooms before the army restored peace. A short time after the Detroit riot, violence in New York City left six blacks dead and hundreds more injured after police shot and wounded an African American soldier who tried to keep them from arresting his mother. When rumors that the soldier had actually been killed swept through Harlem, rioting broke out immediately as people rushed into the streets.

The defeat of fascism ended Nazi plans to build a master white race. But U.S. white supremacists did not give up and continued to battle for their dream of Anglo-Saxon domination long after the war ended. Black poet Langston Hughes compared white Southerners, or "Dixie Nordics," as he called them, to Nazis, pointing out that as the Hitlerites treated "the Jews, so they treat the Negroes, in varying degrees of viciousness ranging from denial of educational opportunities to the denial of employment, from buses that pass Negroes by, to jailers who beat and torture Negro prisoners, from the denial of the ballot to the denial of the right to live" (Winkler, 2000, 142). White racism still lived in the hearts of many white Americans, and they refused to give it up. The dream of building the true master race continued to burn in their hearts.

When World War II ended, six million European Jews lay dead. For African American troops, albeit in the rigidly segregated U.S. military, the defeat of Nazi racism had offered them another opportunity to demonstrate their patriotism and valor. They had accomplished that goal with great distinction. Once white Americans recognized their willingness to make the ultimate sacrifice for democracy, African American veterans hoped, they would bring an end to Jim Crow and allow African Americans to gain their full constitutional rights. In reality, however, despite their many wartime sacrifices, black Americans still faced a long, bitter struggle to reach that goal.

References

Cortner, Richard. *A "Scottsboro" Case in Mississippi: The Supreme Court and Brown v. Mississippi*. Jackson: University Press of Mississippi, 1986.

Dray, Philip. *At the Hands of Persons Unknown: The Lynching of Black America*. New York: Modern Library, 2002.

Egerton, John. *Speak Now Against the Day: The Generation Before the Civil Rights Movement in the South*. Chapel Hill: University of North Carolina Press, 1995.

Gilmore, Glenda E. *Defying Dixie: The Radical Roots of Civil Rights, 1919–1950*. New York: W. W. Norton, 2009.

Katznelson, Ira. *When Affirmative Action Was White: An Untold History of Racial Inequality in Twentieth-Century America*. New York: W. W. Norton, 2005.

Kuhl, Stephan. *The Nazi Connection: Eugenics, American Racism, and German National Socialism*. New York: Oxford University Press, 1994.

Litwack, Leon. *How Free Is Free? The Long Death of Jim Crow*. Cambridge, MA: Harvard University Press, 2009.

MacGregor, Morris J. *Integration of the Armed Forces: 1940–1965*. Washington, D.C.: Department of the Army, 1985.

McMillen, Neil. *Dark Journey: Black Mississippians in the Age of Jim Crow*. Urbana: University of Illinois Press, 1990.

Sullivan, Patricia. *Lift Every Voice: The NAACP and the Making of the Civil Rights Movement*. New York: The New Press, 2009.

Winkler, Alan. *Home Front U.S.A.: America During World War II*. Arlington Heights, IL: Harlan Davidson, 2000.

SIX

The Long, Slow Decline of Jim Crow, 1945–1954

WHEN AFRICAN AMERICAN SOLDIERS came home from World War II they could not send their children to the same school as white children in Alabama, Arizona, Florida, Georgia, Kansas, Kentucky, Louisiana, Mississippi, Missouri, New Mexico, North Carolina, Oklahoma, South Carolina, Tennessee, Texas, Virginia, West Virginia, or Wyoming. Laws governing education continued to require separate schools for African American and white students in these states. Eleven states in this group were in the American South. In Jim Crow America, the states generally imposed a $20 per day fine on any white parents sending their children to a "colored school," or any black parents sending their kids to a "white school." Teachers who violated the segregation laws, a white teacher teaching in a "colored school," for instance, would lose their teaching certificates. Black veterans could not marry a white person in 29 states, including all 11 former Confederate states. Violating the ban on interracial marriage called for a penalty of up to a year in prison, although in Texas and Virginia violators could get up to five years.

In Alabama, Florida, Georgia, Kentucky, Louisiana, Mississippi, Missouri, North Carolina, South Carolina, Texas, Virginia, and West Virginia, the law required that railroad companies provide "separate but equal accommodations" for black and white passengers. Railroad stations needed separate waiting rooms and ticket windows for people of color. Laws in Jim Crow America required streetcar companies to designate separate seating areas for black riders (always in the back). Other states and local governments demanded that librarians maintain separate branches for the use of black patrons, and that state prison officials provide separate penitentiaries or segregated cells, eating facilities, and recreation areas for black prisoners. Alabama, as did other Jim Crow states, prohibited white and black prisoners from being kept in the same cells or chained together on chain gangs. Some states prohibited white female nurses from taking care of "black male" patients; several required that circuses provide separate entrances and two ticket takers to divide black patrons from whites. Other state legislatures made it a crime for homes for blacks to be built in white communities; demanded that coal mining companies build separate restrooms for black employees; or required that movie theaters, opera houses, and all places of public entertainment separate black customers from white.

In 1931, the South Carolina legislature tried to keep the white race pure (the goal of all Jim Crow laws) when it made it a crime for black and white employees to "work together within the same room, or to use the same doors of entrance and exit at the same time ... or to use the same stairway and windows at the same time, or to use at any time the same lavatories, toilets, drinking water buckets, pails, cups, dippers, or glasses." A short time later the state mandated segregation in cemeteries, public parks, recreation centers, amusement centers, and beaches. It even required that all school bus drivers be of the same race as the children they transported.

All of these Jim Crow laws in all of these Jim Crow states remained on the books when the war against Nazi racism ended.

During the war, the Supreme Court offered one decision that substantially increased African American voting in the Jim Crow states. Most Southern states had primary elections, a system that allowed voters to choose candidates for the general election in the fall. Overruling two previous decisions that had found the practice of allowing only white participation in political party primaries legitimate—because according to the court, political parties were private institutions not subject to state regulation, and they should be allowed to make their own decisions concerning who could vote in the primaries they sponsored—in a case coming out of Texas, *Smith v. Allwright* (1944), the 8–1 majority ruled that white primaries violated the Constitution. Primary elections, in which voters chose their party's candidate in the general election, were an "integral part" of a state's election procedures. State law authorized those elections and regulated the procedures of primaries. Therefore, political parties became agents of the state, which meant that they were governmental institutions subject to regulation by the federal government and the protections offered by the Fifteenth Amendment. Race could not be used to bar a person from voting in a primary election or a general one. After this decision, black voting registration in Texas increased from 750,000 to more than a million.

Alabama, Georgia, Louisiana, Mississippi, and South Carolina, the five states referred to as the "Deep South," had the largest African American populations in the United States, and refused to make any changes in their election laws. A senator from Louisiana assured fellow whites that "the South at all costs will maintain the rule of white supremacy," no matter what the Supreme Court said (Klarman, 2004, 246). Alabama quickly passed a law that required voters "to understand the Constitution to the satisfaction of" the always-white voting registrars.

A 1946 Supreme Court ruling in *Morgan v. Virginia* outlawed a Virginia law that required all buses travelling in the state, including those that crossed through Virginia on their way to other destinations, to be racially segregated—whites in front, blacks in the back. The case began in 1944 when Irene Morgan, a 27-year-old African American who had boarded the bus in Maryland and was on her way to visit relatives in another state, refused to obey the bus driver's order to give up her seat to a white passenger when it entered Virginia. The driver called the state police and they arrested Morgan and took her to jail. At her trial and conviction, she was fined $10, which she refused to pay. She took her case first through Virginia's court system, where the judges on the local, appellate, and state supreme court upheld her fine and conviction. Then, with the help of the NAACP, she took her case to federal court.

In early 1946 the U.S. Supreme Court heard Morgan's appeal, and issued its verdict in June. With only one dissent, the court ruled that Virginia's law mandating segregated seating on interstate buses, and similar laws in other states, violated the constitutional rights of Americans. The law required seating arrangements based on race on all buses, and that requirement "hampers freedom of choice in selecting accommodations," the majority decided. The decision applied only to buses (and other forms of public transportation) travelling across state lines, however. Jim Crow rules remained safe within states. Buses and trains whose routes remained entirely within one state could still require segregated seating, but if the bus or train crossed state lines they could not.

In early 1947, sixteen interracial passengers (eight blacks, eight whites) began a bus trip in Richmond, Virginia, aimed at testing the court's ruling in *Morgan* in other areas of the South. They called it "the Journey of Reconciliation." Their trip would take them through Virginia, North Carolina, and Tennessee. At their first stop, in Durham, North Carolina, police arrested and released two members for violating the state's segregation law. In Asheville, North Carolina, police arrested the entire group, and charged them with breaking local Jim Crow ordinances. When they were released they headed for Chapel Hill, where a white mob stopped the bus, dragged the protestors onto the street, and beat them severely. But they did not fight back. The police arrested all 16 members of the nonviolent group and took them to jail. A judge convicted two "Freedom Riders," one black, one white, of violating North Carolina's law requiring segregated buses and sentenced them to 30 days on a chain gang. However, he then convicted two white men of engaging in mob action and sentenced them to 90 days in jail. He had a final message for the Freedom Riders. "It's about time you Jews from New York learned that you can't come down here bringing your niggers with you to upset the customs of the South," he advised as deputies led the prisoners from the courtroom. Two weeks later the Journey of Reconciliation ended, unable to complete its goal. The protestors had maintained their nonviolent commitment despite the mob hatred, violence, and beatings they endured. Fourteen years later, another interracial group called the "Freedom Riders" took a similar journey with a similar pledge of nonviolent resistance to any attacks through the Deep South, and it provoked even more violence than the Journey of Reconciliation had inspired, and it too ended unsuccessfully.

During the war, racial violence in the United States continued to cast a dark shadow on the American dream of equal rights for all, and 1943 witnessed the most deadly rioting of the war years. Beaumont, Texas, erupted in racial violence in June 1943 after a white woman accused a black man of raping her. Twenty-one deaths (twenty blacks, one white) were recorded during the three days of violence that followed. The deadliest rioting of the year took place in Detroit, Michigan, in July. Twenty-nine people were killed and hundreds more wounded in the Motor City. The blood began to flow in the auto plants, where black and white workers fought each other with hammers and screwdrivers. Fighting quickly spread to the streets, parks, and picnic groves. Thousands of Southerners, white and black, had come to Detroit looking for jobs in the defense industry. They brought their racial attitudes with them. President Roosevelt had to send the army into Detroit to restore peace. New York City; Mobile, Alabama; Indianapolis, Indiana; Baltimore, Maryland; St. Louis, Missouri; and Washington, D.C., all experienced smaller racial conflicts that same summer.

Congress's attempt to extend the life of the Fair Employment Practices Commission came to an abrupt end even before the war against fascism ended. Southern senators successfully blocked an attempt to extend the life of the FEPC in February 1945 with a lengthy Senate filibuster. The filibuster was becoming the main weapon used by the Jim Crow senators in their fight against equal rights. Senators had used filibusters successfully to prevent passage of legislation that could have ended some of the more un-American Jim Crow practices, such as the antilynching bills introduced

between 1935 and 1942. Senate rules required only 32 votes to keep a filibuster going, and Jim Crow states already had 22 of those votes on hand.
They needed only 10 more votes to keep the Senate tied up and unable to
act on any other measures as long as the filibuster lasted. Those votes
proved easily available from conservative Republicans and western Democrats concerned about race relations in their own states.

Under Senate rules of debate, members could hold the floor as long as
they kept talking. Because their speeches did not have to be related to the
bill under discussion, the Bible, articles in an encyclopedia, law books, or
newspaper stories—and sometimes the entire newspaper—were permissible and frequently used sources of words to kill time. When a speaker
tired—and some speakers held the floor for 10 or 12 hours—they simply
turned the floor over to a friendly colleague, who began his own multi-
hour oration. When six, twelve, or twenty senators joined together, they
could hold up Senate business for days and weeks. Only one measure could
be voted on during a filibuster: a cloture petition could be voted on, but
introducing it required the support of at least 20 senators. Once the petition
was successfully introduced, it required a two-thirds vote of a Senate
quorum—which was the number of senators required to be present to conduct business (49 out of 96 since 1912). Two-thirds of that quorum (32 out
of 49) were required to impose cloture on debate or it continued.

Ending a filibuster became even more difficult because of a rules change
in 1949. The change demanded by Jim Crow senators before the beginning
of debate on the poll tax increased the number of votes required to pass a
cloture petition to two-thirds of all 96 Senators (64 out of 96), rather than
the usual quorum. The Jim Crow senators used that change to successfully
filibuster against a bill that would have made poll taxes illegal. Southern
senators now had more than enough votes, with a little help from
conservative Republicans, to defeat a cloture petition and maintain the
filibuster. They used the filibuster to block the passage of all civil rights
legislation introduced in Congress between 1949 and 1957.

A few legal victories in the Jim Crow states encouraged the feeling
among NAACP leaders that white attitudes towards the African Americans
had changed, if only slightly, for the better during the war. Early in 1946,
Thurgood Marshall successfully defended 27 black residents of Columbia,
Tennessee, charged with attempted murder during a race riot. The town
40 miles south of Nashville had experienced three days of bloody racial
violence in late February 1946. The riot began after a fistfight between a
black World War II veteran and a white businessman, also a veteran. When
the police arrived, they arrested the black veteran and charged him with

"attempted murder" because he had hit the storekeeper. The white sheriff let the black veteran return home that evening when he found out that a lynch mob was gathering. By this time both black and white communities were getting out their guns and preparing for a fight. When a group of armed whites entered the black section of town, they began shooting randomly into homes and businesses. Black Columbians responded by returning fire. A black schoolteacher explained this African American reaction to a white journalist, "We got tired of getting kicked around. We just got tired of it . . . [We decided] we'd rather die than take it anymore." The shooting went on all night. By sunrise, four black men had been killed.

During the fighting, dozens of state and local police rushed into the black community and arrested hundreds of black men, apparently at random. Twenty-seven of those arrested were charged with attempted murder. When their trial began three months later, Thurgood Marshall led the defense team, which included several white lawyers. Marshall, who now headed the NAACP Legal Defense and Education Fund, came to Tennessee in response to a letter he received from relatives of the defendants. The trial judge accepted a defense motion and moved the trial to Lawrenceburg, a small town 20 miles south of Columbia. The new judge interviewed more than seven hundred potential jurors (all of them white) before accepting twelve of them, and the trial began. After considering the evidence, the jury surprised everyone and acquitted 26 of the defendants of all charges against them. The jury found one of the Columbia defendants guilty of attempted murder, but he received a pardon from the governor after serving a brief part of his sentence.

After his successful courtroom appearance in Lawrenceburg, Marshall headed back to New York City, but he did not get very far. While driving out of Columbia, police arrested him and charged him with drunken driving. He protested, but the police ignored him and took him to jail. On the way, they drove Marshall to a river where hundreds of white men, many in KKK regalia, had gathered. The future Supreme Court justice thought the mob was ready to lynch him. After a few minutes the white deputies sped away, however, and probably saved his life. A magistrate released Marshall the next morning after determining that the NAACP's top attorney had not been drunk. That a Southern white jury listened to a black attorney defending twenty-seven black Americans charged with attempted murder and found all but one of them innocent offered him some hope that attitudes might be changing even in Jim Crow America.

Important changes were underway in attitudes toward race in the United States outside the South. For the first time since the Civil War, guaranteeing equal rights for all became a major political issue in a U.S. election. In 1946, President Harry Truman established a Committee on Civil Rights, chaired by Charles E. Wilson, chief executive of the General Electric Corporation. Truman said that he created the 25-member committee, composed of business, religious, educational, and labor leaders, to study the race problem in the United States and then recommend "more adequate and effective means and procedures for the protection of the civil rights of the people of the United States." The lynchings of nine black veterans in the South in 1945–46 had appalled the president, and he decided to do something to improve the racial climate. Truman and his advisors also apparently recognized the growing importance of the black vote in key Northern states, especially New York, Michigan, and Illinois. In any close election, they told the president, African American voters could hold the key to winning the popular and electoral votes in those states.

The purpose of the Committee on Civil Rights was to propose ways to ensure that "our Bill of Rights were implemented in fact" for everybody in the United States, according to the president. He gave the committee a year to complete its job. After hearings and discussions across the country, the committee issued its finding in a report called "To Secure These Rights." Many of its recommendations eventually became part of Harry Truman's civil rights program that he presented to Congress, the first civil rights program it considered since the end of Reconstruction. In its report, the committee rejected the "equal facilities," or "separate but equal" doctrine established in *Plessy v. Ferguson.* Instead, it acquainted readers with the bloody history of the lynchings, police brutality, and riots that African Americans faced in Jim Crow America. It called for legislation that would end discrimination and segregation in housing, employment, health care, the military, and education. Thurgood Marshall and the NAACP praised the president's commitment to equal rights for all Americans and recognized the importance of "To Secure These Rights" in the battle against Jim Crow. "The problem of the Negro and other minority groups is now before the public in a manner never equaled before," in the future Supreme Court justice's words.

Harry Truman, grandson of slave owners, became the first president to champion full racial equality. In a speech to members of the NAACP attending the group's national convention in the nation's capital, he declared that the United States had the responsibility to protect "equal rights" for all Americans. "We must make the Federal Government a friendly, vigilant defender of the rights and equalities of all Americans," he told the delegates, and "when I say all Americans, I mean all Americans."

The president had changed his views on race dramatically since the beginning of his political career. During his first political campaign in Missouri in 1922, when he was running for county judge, the future president had followed the advice of his campaign manager and joined the Ku Klux Klan because it would help him win more white votes. He quit the Klan after only a few weeks, however, when he found out that the KKK was not only antiblack but also violently anti-Catholic. As an officer during the First World War he had commanded many Catholics in his unit in France and had been impressed with their patriotism and fighting abilities. He did not openly repudiate the Klan, but he won the election.

The president took dramatic direct action in the summer of 1948. He issued two executive orders, the first ordering fair employment practices in all federal government jobs and hiring practices and the second demanding the integration of all military units. The government would now follow "a policy of fair employment throughout the federal establishment without discrimination because of race, color, religion, or national origins." Both orders helped the president surprise all the pollsters and experts who had predicted his defeat by the Republican candidate Thomas Dewey. Truman carried more than two-thirds of the African American vote in the North, which helped him carry by narrow margins important states such as Illinois, New York, and Pennsylvania. In the South, various voter registration laws accomplished their goal by keeping the black vote extremely low. The fight against Jim Crow voting registration laws in the South had yet to be won.

Truman's support for civil rights during the campaign had driven white Southerners out of the Democratic Party. Southern Democrats walked out of their party's convention and organized the States' Rights Party, or "Dixiecrats." The Dixiecrats chose Strom Thurmond, governor of South Carolina, to lead their ticket. He carried four Deep South states in the election— Alabama, Louisiana, Mississippi, and South Carolina—and received more than a million votes nationwide. Jim Crow senators from outside the Deep South did not support Thurmond's campaign. They did not want to leave the Democratic Party where many of them, because of their long years in Washington, held leadership positions in Congress. They realized that they could use their powers as committee chairmen to block any legislation concerning civil rights that might be introduced. The power they possessed in Washington seemed more significant than support for a candidate who had absolutely no possibility of winning the White House. In their choice they proved to be absolutely correct. They managed to block or significantly weaken every civil rights bill introduced in Congress for the next 15 years.

The Dixiecrats' break with the Democratic Party in 1948 had little impact on the power accumulated by Southern senators. As South Carolina senator Olin Johnston told a constituent, "we have enough southerners in the Senate—good southerners—to vote down or talk down any attempt at passage of the antilynch, anti–Jim Crow, or other anti-southern legislation" that comes to the floor (Finley, 2008, 221). When President Harry Truman's civil rights proposals were introduced in Congress in 1949, Southerners showed their power. Before the Senate debate on civil rights, it considered a proposed change in its rules governing filibusters. Northern liberals had proposed a new procedure for ending filibusters. The new rule would have required a simple majority vote, rather than the traditional two-thirds vote, to impose "cloture," the word used for the procedure ending the debate.

Jim Crow senators, led by Richard Russell of Georgia, launched a filibuster against the proposed change in filibuster rules. The suggested change threatened "minority rights," Southern senators, a true minority—there were only 22 senators from Southern states—warned. Passing the rule would lead to a "dictatorship of the majority." The rule change was not accepted. With assistance from some Republicans, the South won the battle to protect filibusters. Their victory ensured the defeat of Truman's civil rights proposals—a call for a federal antilynching law, an end to the poll tax, and creation of a permanent Fair Employment Practices Commission (FEPC) were all successfully filibustered. The president's entire civil rights agenda went down to defeat.

As the filibuster in Washington ended in a victory for the segregationists, a brutal murder in Florida reminded the nation of the violence often associated with living in Jim Crow America. On Christmas Day, 1951, Harry T. Moore, head of the Florida chapter of the NAACP, and his wife Harriette died when a bomb exploded directly under their bed. Moore had been a longtime civil rights activist, having organized a branch of the NAACP in 1934. In 1941, he established the Florida State Conference of the NAACP and became its unpaid executive secretary. Beginning in 1943 Moore took it upon himself to investigate and report on every lynching in his home state. Between 1944 and 1950 he helped 116,000 African Americans register in the Florida Democratic Party. In 1946, Moore and his wife were both fired from their teaching jobs in Brevard County in retaliation for his political activity. He then became a paid, full-time organizer for the NAACP.

In July 1949, four young black men were arrested for allegedly raping a white woman in Groveland. A white mob destroyed most of the black community in that town, burning homes and businesses to the ground. At their trial, in typical fashion, an all-white jury convicted the four blacks of rape and sentenced them to death. The U.S. Supreme Court overturned the convictions in 1951 and Florida prepared for a new trial. On November 6, County Sheriff Willis McCall, a notoriously brutal racist, was driving two of the defendants to court for a pretrial hearing. The car suddenly stopped and the sheriff ordered his two handcuffed prisoners to get out of the car, pulled out his pistol, and shot them. He killed one prisoner and nearly killed the other. McCall claimed that the prisoners had tried to assault him while trying to escape. The wounded prisoner testified that he and his friend had done nothing. McCall just stopped the police car and started shooting. Harry Moore became involved and called for McCall's indictment for murder. But, in typical fashion, when a white sheriff killed a black "rapist" and wounded his accomplice in a county with white district attorneys and a majority white population, nothing happened.

Six weeks after the killing of the prisoner, Moore and his wife were killed by a bomb placed in their bedroom under their bed. The FBI conducted three extensive investigations, but the murders were never solved. Moore was the first NAACP official killed in the fight against Jim Crow. He and his wife were the only husband and wife killed in the struggle against Jim Crow segregation.

The bombing and deaths in Florida—or any place else, for that matter—had little influence on the debate over civil rights in Washington. In Congress, Southern opponents of legislation that threatened local control of race relations continued their so far successful strategy of block, delay, and filibuster. Because of Senate filibusters, Congress could not pass any meaningful civil rights legislation during the remainder of Truman's presidency. In the federal courts, however, the results were different, and federal judges established a record of overturning Jim Crow segregation in many areas of U.S. life. In 1948, the Supreme Court in *Shelley v. Kraemer* outlawed restrictive covenants (contracts forbidding the sale of property to members of specific racial or religious groups). That same year, in *Sipuel v. Board of Regents,* the court struck down an Oklahoma law forbidding African Americans from attending graduate school at the state university. Two years later, in two separate decisions, *McLaurin v. Oklahoma State Regents* and *Sweatt v. Painter* (1950), the Supreme Court ruled for equality in higher education. In the first, the Supreme Court ordered the University of Oklahoma to admit George W. McLaurin, a 68-year-old black teacher, to its graduate program in education. After admission, McLaurin found himself alone in a row of desks "reserved for Negroes." In the library he was given a separate desk and in the cafeteria he ate alone at a separate table. He went back to federal court, where Kentucky-born Chief Justice Fred

Vinson ordered Oklahoma to end separating McLaurin from the rest of the students, because such treatment denied him "his personal and present rights to equal protection of the laws." The Fourteenth Amendment, according to the chief justice, demanded that McLaurin "must receive the same treatment . . . as students of other races."

The second 1950 case affecting race and higher education involved Heman Sweatt, a black mailman in Texas who wanted to become a lawyer. However, the University of Texas Law School denied his application strictly because of his color. The NAACP provided legal assistance and Thurgood Marshall argued Sweatt's case all the way to the U.S. Supreme Court. Texas had hastily created a law school for African Americans during the court fight, as Missouri had done in 1938 for Lloyd Gaines. However, Chief Justice Vinson ruled that the new school lacked the requirements that would make it equal to the state school. It did not have a distinguished faculty, a sufficient library, or a proud tradition such as that of the University of Texas Law School. Therefore Sweatt would have been at a great disadvantage when seeking employment after graduating from the segregated black school. Vinson ordered that Sweatt be admitted to the all-white state school.

In these decisions the Supreme Court ruled in favor of integrated schooling, but only at the university or graduate school level. Several court cases aimed at ending Jim Crow segregation in elementary and high schools were launched in 1947 and 1948, however, and after making their way through state and federal courts reached the Supreme Court in 1951. In the fall of 1947, Reverend J. A. DeLaine, a public school teacher as well as a minister in rural South Carolina, went to the Clarendon County School Board and asked if they would provide school buses for the county's black students. None had ever been provided by the county before, even though 90 percent of the students in the county were African American and some of them had to walk eight miles or more each way to get to their school. The all-white board, in a county with 2,800 black school-age children and just 300 white children, refused Reverend DeLaine's request. According to board members, African American parents had never paid enough in taxes to support a bus program. It would be unfair to white parents to ask them to pay for the transportation of black students. State educational officials also refused to provide funds for buses. Black parents in the county raised enough of their own money to buy an old bus, though it broke down so often they ran out of funds for repairs and the school bus stopped running.

DeLaine decided to take legal action, and the South Carolina NAACP along with the NAACP Legal Defense and Education Fund in New York City agreed to support the case. Thurgood Marshall filed the first brief in federal court in Charleston but the judge, Southern-born, threw out the case on a technicality. DeLaine refused to give up and in 1950 presented a petition to the school board signed by 20 African American parents in Clarendon County asking for bus transportation for their children. Harry Briggs, a gas station attendant, and his wife Eliza, a maid, had been the first to sign their names to the petition. Both lost their jobs within days after the board received the petition, and the school board fired Reverend DeLaine at its next meeting. He continued the legal battle despite losing his job. NAACP lawyers returned to federal court in South Carolina, this time asking not just for buses but for a complete end to segregated schools in the state.

The trial began on May 28, 1951. Hundreds of African Americans filled the courthouse, and others stood on the lawn waiting for news from the trial. Thurgood Marshall and his team of lawyers planned to provide evidence depicting the inequality of education in the state's schools. One witness described the unequal facilities in black schools throughout the state, including a description of the four outdoor toilets provided for the 694 students enrolled in one elementary school. But the most important evidence came from a group of social scientists, mostly psychologists, called by Marshall to describe the impact of segregated education in dismal surroundings on the minds of black students; in particular from Kenneth Clark, a social psychologist from Columbia University in New York City, who described a series of interviews he had conducted with 16 black students in Clarendon County.

Dr. Clark and his wife, Mamie, had developed a test using white and black dolls as one method of showing the effects of racism and discrimination on young children. When asked to choose which doll, white or brown, they found most able and attractive, African American children almost always chose the white doll. This demonstrated the negative influence of race on their perceptions, Clark concluded. Though some NAACP lawyers felt this evidence was too weak to present in court, Marshall convinced a majority of his staff that the doll test "was a way of showing injury to these youngsters" (Sullivan, 2009, 404). Marshall's chief assistant, Robert Carter, a future federal judge, presented other expert witnesses, including psychologists from Harvard and Vassar, to support Clark's conclusion that segregation harmed black children. Segregated education in terribly unequal facilities made students feel inferior, they all agreed, and that attitude stayed with them for the rest of their lives. More than that, the experts testified, when separating students by race, even in school systems that provided relatively equal educational courses of study, black children still emerged feeling psychologically inferior.

The three-judge panel hearing the case, known as *Briggs v. Elliott*, dismissed the evidence presented by the psychologists and ruled 2–1 that segregation was constitutional. The majority opinion told South Carolina, however, to begin building and establishing more equal educational facilities for black students within six months. The one dissenting judge concluded that "segregation is *per se* inequality," but his opinion angered so many whites that he had to retire shortly after presenting his dissent and move out of South Carolina due to many threats against his life. The NAACP decided to appeal the *Briggs* decision, and it became one of the five cases included in the 1954 *Brown v. Topeka Board of Education* decision.

One of the five cases covered by *Brown* included suits filed by two African American families in Delaware—the Beltons and the Bulahs. Eventually, the two separate cases were combined into one, *Belton v. Gebhart*. Both families had been denied permission to send their children to all-white schools close to their homes. In *Belton v. Gebhart*, the African American parents sued because they had to send their children to a dilapidated and segregated high school rather than to the almost-new all-white school much closer to their home. The other case, *Bulah v. Gebhart*, involved the transportation issue, specifically the refusal of Delaware to provide bus transportation for black children. Sarah Bulah, a black single mother, was angry because a bus carrying white children passed her house twice a day, but refused to stop to pick up her daughter. Both the Beltons and Bulah petitioned their local white schools to admit their children, but both requests were denied. The NAACP joined with the parents charging discrimination and filed suit in the Delaware Court of Chancery. The court ruled that the black parents had been denied equal protection of the law and ordered that their children be admitted to the white schools. The school boards involved filed an appeal of that decision in federal court, and both Delaware cases eventually were included in the *Brown* ruling.

Another of the cases decided along with *Brown* emerged from the segregated school system in Washington, D.C. A group of African American parents sued the District of Columbia school board after their children were denied admission to the newly constructed John Phillips Sousa Junior High School. The parents, one of them named Spottswood Bolling, filed suit in federal court with the assistance of the NAACP. In *Bolling v. Sharpe*, NAACP attorney James Nabrit did not raise the issue of inequality in the education of black students, even though conditions in the district's all-black schools were appallingly inferior to those in white neighborhoods.

Instead Nabrit argued that segregation itself denied black students equal protection of the law, because there was no legitimate reason to assign them to schools simply because of the color of their skin. Simply separating people by race, he asserted, violated their constitutional rights as U.S. citizens. The district court judge hearing the case did not agree, noting that segregation in the nation's capital had recently been ruled constitutional by the District of Columbia Court of Appeals. Nabrit filed an appeal, and the U.S. Supreme Court accepted the case.

The fourth case named in the *Brown* decision, *Davis v. County School Board of Prince Edward County, Virginia*, began with a student-led protest of the terrible conditions faced by African American students in the Farmville, Virginia, all-black high school. An African American student, Barbara Rose Johns, led 456 fellow students (the entire student body) out of Robert Russa Moton High School on April 23, 1951, to protest the terrible physical and educational conditions found in the county's black high school. The students declared a boycott until conditions improved, and it lasted for two weeks. Unlike the white high school, Moton had no cafeteria, no gymnasium, no showers or dressing rooms for athletes, no teachers' restrooms, inadequate classrooms for teaching science, and no industrial arts shop. Along with these physical and equipment shortcomings, students at Moton were offered no classes in physics, world history, foreign languages, wood- or metalworking, art, drawing, or physical education. White students could take classes in all of those areas. The striking black students demanded the same courses offered to the white students. Though almost half of the residents (45%) of Prince Edward County were black, the school board was all white.

After the board refused to accept the students' petition asking for an end to segregation in the county's schools, the NAACP filed a suit in federal court in Richmond on behalf of the black students, challenging Virginia's school segregation law. A three-judge panel heard the proceedings. During the trial, NAACP attorneys Spottswood Robinson and Robert Carter presented anthropologists, psychologists, educators, and psychiatrists who testified that the act of segregation, separating young black students because of their race, created a sense of inferiority in their minds that affected their ability to learn and had a negative impact on their entire lives. Separating elementary school children and high school students by color made African Americans feel unwanted and hopeless. Because the laws imposed segregation, the feelings of inferiority were "deeper and more indelible," Carter said. Because the law mirrored the values and customs of an entire nation and established the rules by which its citizens lived their lives, legal segregation (*de jure*) was particularly harmful. Singling a person out simply because of the color of his or her skin; or treating those individuals differently by providing them with inferior, second-class schools (when they paid the same taxes as other members of society); or offering those same people inadequate and frequently nonexistent medical care; or subjecting that segregated community to brutal and unjust treatment by the police and courts; and denying them basic human rights including the right to vote, the right to serve on juries, or even the right to sit where they please on a bus, "implanted unjustly" in members of that population "a sense of inferiority as a human being to other human beings," and seeded their minds "with hopeless frustration," one of the social scientists told the court (Kluger, 2004, 627–44).

Attorneys for the school board presented the long-held white Southern defense of Jim Crow. The three-judge panel of white Southerners summarized that defense in their unanimous opinion. First, the judges wrote that "the separation provision" of the Virginia constitution "rests neither upon prejudice, nor caprice, nor upon any other measureless foundation." It simply "declares one of the ways of life in Virginia." Echoing William Graham Sumner, the jurists asserted that segregation in public schools "has for generations been a part of the *mores* of her [Virginia's] people." Then they explained "the greater opportunities for the Negro" that segregation offered. Leaving out the vast disparity in pay that existed between African American and white educators, they noted that "Virginia alone employs as many Negro teachers . . . as are employed in all of the thirty-one non-segregating states." Most white residents would have agreed with the federal judges' boasting that in "29 of the 100 counties in Virginia, the schools and facilities for the colored are equal to the white schools, in 17 more they are now superior, and upon completion of the work authorized or in progress [the state had recently increased its yearly appropriation for 'colored schools'], another 5 will be superior." With these facts in mind, African American parents had no reason to complain about the quality of education provided for their children in Virginia.

The court then addressed the problems that would result if they ordered schools to be integrated. "So ingrained and wrought in the texture of their life is the principle of separate schools," the judges warned, "involuntary" elimination of segregation "would severely lessen the interest of the people of the state in the public schools, lessen the financial support, and so injure both races." Separating black students and white students in the public schools caused "no hurt or harm to either race," the judges concluded. They ordered the Prince Edward School Board to do more to equalize education for all students in the county with "dispatch" (United States District Court Eastern District of Virginia, at Richmond, *Davis et al. v. County School Board of Prince Edward County, Va., et al.*, 103 F. Supp. 337 Civ. A No. 1333). The NAACP filed an appeal to this lower court decision.

The case that gave its name to the famous 1954 decision declaring Jim Crow public schools unconstitutional was filed in the summer of 1950. The case began when 13 African American parents, all members of the local NAACP branch in Topeka, Kansas, took their children to the public schools in their integrated neighborhoods and tried to enroll them. School authorities refused to admit any of the black students, and told their parents to take them to one of the city's four schools established for blacks. The parents filed a discrimination suit in state court against the city board of education on behalf of their children. Oliver Brown, a minister, was the first parent listed in the suit, and the case became *Brown v. Board of Education of Topeka, Kansas.*

Pastor Brown's eight-year-old daughter Linda had attended a segregated school in Topeka for four years before he decided to challenge the Kansas segregation statute. The law allowed elementary school boards, but not high school boards—Kansas high schools were integrated—to decide whether or not they would be segregated. The schools established for black students were funded equally with white schools, and teachers were paid equally. The Browns did not challenge the quality of the education Linda received. They challenged the fact that she had to take a bus past an all-white school a few blocks from her home to get to her school far from home. Thurgood Marshall and NAACP officers thought the Browns' case presented an opportunity to challenge the whole idea of segregated education. Equality of education was not the key issue; separating people by race was the issue. Because of the nature of the Browns' argument, many African American teachers in Topeka opposed their challenge to segregation. If schools were integrated, many black teachers would lose their jobs.

The *Brown* case, and the other cases which joined with it, reached the Supreme Court in December 1952 and was argued again one year later because of the unexpected death of Chief Justice Fred Vinson on September 8, 1953. President Dwight Eisenhower now had the opportunity to nominate a new chief justice. He chose former California governor Earl Warren to replace Vinson, and the Senate gave its consent. During the reargument of *Brown*, John W. Davis, head of the legal team defending Jim Crow, cited Southern history, custom, and legal precedent in support of racial segregation. He assured the justices that it had always been the intention of the South "to produce equality for all of its children."

Responding for the Browns and the NAACP, Thurgood Marshall told the court that they could uphold Jim Crow segregation only by finding that "for some reason Negroes are inferior to all other human beings," since they were not considered worthy of being educated alongside whites and received one-fifth to one-tenth the money the legislature appropriated for white students. Jim Crow laws were simply an attempt by white Southerners to keep blacks in an inferior position in society, separate and unequal (Kluger, 2004, 667–78).

In his discussions with the other justices, Warren let them know that racial segregation, in his view, could not be defended unless one assumed that blacks were inferior to whites. During their discussions of the case in the late winter and early spring of 1954, the chief justice gradually convinced all of his colleagues that he was right. In its unanimous opinion issued on May 5, 1954, written by the chief justice in a simple style that could be understood by all Americans as he insisted, the court ruled that state-imposed racial segregation in public schools violated the constitutional rights of minority group Americans. "To separate [children] from others of similar age and qualification solely because of their race," Warren insisted, "generates a feeling of inferiority as to their status in the community that may effect their hearts and minds in ways unlikely ever to be undone" (Kluger, 2004, 706–8).

The chief justice referred to evidence from Dr. Kenneth Clark's research to defend his conclusion. This marked perhaps the first time the Supreme Court cited social science research, rather than simply "the law" or "the Constitution" in one of its opinions. Under "the law" as understood in Southern states, Jim Crow laws imposing racial separation in areas outside of school segregation remained constitutional. The *Brown* decision applied only to public school segregation. It did not apply to Jim Crow discrimination in courtrooms, jury boxes, voting booths, hotels, motels, restaurants, libraries, swimming pools, or anywhere else. Despite its limited area of application, the *Brown* ruling was a major step forward in the move toward equal rights for all Americans.

The *Brown* ruling did not include something most Supreme Court decisions usually contained—a "remedy" to correct unconstitutional actions or a method of resolving the problem presented by the case. In *Brown*, the court declined to order any immediate action to end segregation. The justices thought that such an order would lead to racial violence and riots. Instead, they invited the lawyers to attend a second hearing a year later at which remedies would be offered. On May 31, 1955, in what became known as *"Brown II,"* the justices ruled that the interests of African American students, which demanded an immediate end to segregation, "had to be balanced against the public interest," meaning the reactions of white Southerners. (A poll taken at the time found that less than 20 percent of whites in the South supported school integration.) The justices presented a "go slow" remedy. It gave local school boards responsibility for developing plans to desegregate and gave federal judges power to oversee implementation of those plans. The court did not set a deadline by which schools had to be integrated or plans had to be accepted. It required only that school districts "make a prompt and reasonable start" towards eliminating Jim Crow education. Thurgood Marshall told the court that only when "Negroes are involved" did it delay the granting of constitutional rights to citizens. The "go slow" approach encouraged white resistance. A majority of Jim Crow school districts in the South were not integrated until 1970.

The first year after the court's ruling offered some hope that white Southerners might obey the Supreme Court. The NAACP announced that in 1955 more than five hundred school districts in the South and other states with legally segregated schools, including Kansas, Maryland, Missouri, and West Virginia, had begun to or developed plans to desegregate. These districts included Washington, D.C., and the two districts in Delaware covered in the original *Brown* decision. By 1956, the pace of desegregation slowed down dramatically. Organized opposition from groups such as the White Citizens' Council (founded in Sunflower County, Mississippi, in 1954) and the Defenders of State Sovereignty and Individual Liberties (created in Petersburg, Virginia, in 1954) emerged to lead the movement to resist integration. Mississippi established a State Sovereignty Commission to fight "all elements antagonistic to the state's way of life" in 1956.

The commission hired investigators and informants (including several African Americans) across the state, whose main job was to keep watch over people leading desegregation efforts. A member of the Sovereignty Commission explained its responsibility to a newspaper reporter; the South, he claimed, was "under threat of being overrun by an alien force led by communists." The commissioners had stopped "the radicals and communist-led marchers from taking over Mississippi," he bragged to a radio reporter.

The White Citizens' Council in Mississippi, which worked closely with and received funds from the commission, distributed thousands of copies of a book called *The Cult of Equality* to all the white public schools in the state, informing students that "Negroes are lazy. It is difficult to tell when they are telling the truth. They will steal chickens, food, and small sums of money.... There is also a resemblance between a great ape and pure-blooded Negroes." The WCC launched "an educational campaign" against *Brown* and in support of "Racial Integrity," sending speakers to schools in every county. They lectured on topics from "white supremacy" to Confederate history (Kennedy, 1990, 35–36). The money for printing and distributing the book came from the State Sovereignty Commission.

Jim Crow states resorted to many different tactics to fight "communists" and outside agitators, and "un-American civil rights activists" spreading the "vicious lie" of equality to the youth of the South. Georgia, Louisiana, Mississippi, and South Carolina had laws forbidding members of the NAACP from teaching in public schools. Many Jim Crow states passed laws requiring the NAACP to publish its membership lists (so employers could fire any of their employees whose names appeared on those lists). The laws impacted the NAACP's membership, by 1958 more than 245 branches in the South closed their doors as thousands of members quit the organization. An Alabama judge fined the NAACP's state branch for failing to make its list public, and the state shut it down until the U.S. Supreme Court declared in *NAACP v. Alabama* (1964) that the association had a constitutional right to operate in the state and did not have to turn over a list of its members to state authorities.

Southern governors, senators, representatives, mayors, school board officials, library boards, and other officials responded to *Brown* by declaring it unconstitutional and vowing to oppose it with every means available. They initiated a campaign of "massive resistance" to fight school integration. One of the more effective methods of avoiding integration was to let school principals select students on the basis of their academic aptitude and their conduct and behavior in the classroom. More than four hundred school districts adopted "pupil placement" laws to avoid complying with *Brown*. The laws forbid racial discrimination in selecting students but allowed school authorities to reject anyone if they concluded that his or her attendance threatened "the morals, conduct, health, and personal standards" of other pupils in the school.

The Virginia legislature created a model law, establishing a Pupil Placement Board for the state and giving it sole power to assign students to public schools. The board, with members appointed by the always pro-segregation governor, determined which school students would attend based on their health, aptitude, and "sociological, psychological, and like intangible social scientific factors." Parents unhappy with their child's placement could appeal, a process that normally took more than a year to complete. The parents had to sue in court and had a better chance of having their child's placement overturned if they hired a lawyer, which very few black or white parents could afford. The lengthy and expensive appeals process discouraged most black parents from pursuing the appeals process. Virginia schools remained heavily segregated.

"Pupil placement" laws proved very valuable in preserving Jim Crow education. In 1957 in North Carolina only 12 black students in the entire state attended "integrated" schools. A federal district court rejected a black family's discrimination lawsuit based on the slow pace of integration, however, maintaining that "enough race mixing" had taken place to meet the standard established by *Brown*. The U.S. Supreme Court refused to declare placement laws unconstitutional.

Southerners in Congress did everything they could to denounce *Brown* and support segregation. In the spring of 1956, 19 senators and 77 members of the House of Representatives signed a "Declaration of Constitutional Principles," which became known as the "Southern Manifesto." (Albert Gore Sr. and Estes Kefauver of Tennessee and Lyndon Johnson of Texas did not sign.) Issued on March 12, 1956, the manifesto condemned the Supreme Court's "clear abuse of judicial power" in issuing its *Brown* decision. The ruling violated the Constitution and the Supreme Court had exceeded its powers, because the subject of education was not mentioned in the Constitution or in the Fourteenth Amendment. The court had no business interfering in an area of American life not mentioned by the Founding Fathers in the great document they had produced.

The manifesto asserted that the justices on the current court had "substituted their personal political and social ideas for the established law of the land." In fact, they had abandoned the law and substituted sociological and psychological theories in its place. *Brown*, the signers of the manifesto concluded, encouraged "agitators" to enter the South and try to destroy the peaceful relations between black and white citizens that had always existed. The declaration included a pledge "to use all lawful means to bring about a reversal of this decision which is contrary to the Constitution and to prevent the use of force in its implementation." It ended by urging white Southerners to "refrain from disorder and lawless acts."

The Southern Manifesto's call for peaceful resistance failed to stop the violence. Many Southern political leaders and organizations simply ignored the pledge to use "all lawful means" in resisting the court's call for desegregation. Senator James Eastland, one of the loudest congressional voices urging resistance to *Brown*, explained to the people of his home state, Mississippi, that "there is no law that says a free people must submit to a flagrant invasion of their personal liberty." The "personal liberty" Eastland referred to included his constituents' right to send their children to all-white schools and to treat other Americans as second-class citizens. Governor Herman Talmadge promised his fellow white Georgians that he would "fight integration even if" he was the only governor to do so, which he was not. Governors in Virginia, South Carolina, Florida, Alabama, Mississippi, Louisiana, and Texas joined him in the fight for white supremacy. The most widespread reaction to *Brown* among whites was to refuse to accept it.

The newly organized White Citizens' Council (WCC) became the largest group—by 1956 it claimed over 300,000 members—in the South fighting integration. Born in July 1954, just two months after the Supreme Court issued its *Brown* ruling, in Indianola, Mississippi, the council grew rapidly across the entire South, attracting business leaders, bank presidents, plantation owners, doctors, lawyers, and many local judges and politicians. Members prided themselves in not being Klansmen (civil rights activists referred to them as "Klansmen in suits"), because they pledged to defend and support white supremacy with peaceful means. The WCC criticized the Klan for using violent methods in defense of Jim Crow. Council members preferred to use their economic power in the fight against equal rights. Coming from the economic elite in counties, towns, and cities throughout the South, council members followed a simple philosophy, "to make it difficult, if not impossible, for a Negro who advocates desegregation to find and hold a job, get credit, or receive a mortgage." African American teachers were fired, tenant farmers lost their land, and workers lost their jobs whenever they tried to register to vote or advocated school integration.

The WCC newsletter insisted that supporters of equal rights belonged to a communist conspiracy that wanted to "mongrelize" the white race and destroy the United States. Council members promised to avoid violence, yet Senator Eastland, owner of the largest cotton plantation in Sunflower County, handed out leaflets at his campaign rallies proclaiming, "When in the course of human events it becomes necessary to abolish the Negro race, proper methods should be used. Among these are guns, bows and arrows, sling shots and knives" (Cobb, 1992, 134–35).

Brown did not end Jim Crow, but it was the beginning of the end. The *Brown* decision had reversed the Supreme Court's century-long support for segregated elementary and high schools and encouraged African Americans to push for even more of the constitutional rights they had never enjoyed. The lesson they had learned since the end of slavery was that those rights could be won, but only through struggle, perseverance, and bloodshed. Jim Crow would not die a quiet death.

References

Cobb, James C. *The Most Southern Place on Earth: The Mississippi Delta and the Roots of Regional Identity.* New York: Oxford University Press, 1992.

Finley, Keith. *Delaying the Dream: Southern Senators and the Fight Against Civil Rights, 1938–1965.* Baton Rouge: Louisiana State University Press, 2008.

Kennedy, Stetson. *Jim Crow Guide: The Way It Was.* Boca Raton: Florida Atlantic University Press, 1990.

Klarman, Michael J. *From Jim Crow to Civil Rights: The Supreme Court and the Struggle for Racial Equality.* New York: Oxford University Press, 2004.

Kluger, Richard. *Simple Justice: The History of* Brown v. Board of Education *and Black America's Struggle for Equality.* New York: Vintage Books, 2004.

Sullivan, Patricia. *Lift Every Voice: The NAACP and the Making of the Civil Rights Movement.* New York: The New Press, 2009.

SEVEN

After *Brown*: Jim Crow Is Overcome

THE SUPREME COURT HAD RULED that separating students by race violated the constitutional rights of U.S. citizens and created serious psychological problems for the victims of segregation. It was now up to the president of the United States to enforce the court's mandate. Unlike Harry Truman, President Dwight Eisenhower had never challenged or spoken out against Jim Crow segregation. He responded to *Brown* by suggesting that racial attitudes could not be changed by court decision. He did not agree with the court's decision and he did not believe in integration. "I don't believe you can change the hearts of men with law or decisions," he told a reporter. (As a lifelong military man, he had spent much of his career on army bases in the South and had always served in a segregated army.) He announced his support for a bill that would expand the ability of African Americans to register to vote, however, believing that the right to vote was the key to safeguarding the other rights "of the American Negro." The president's call for voting rights protection became part of the civil rights bill he sent to Congress in 1956.

Other Jim Crow laws were being successfully challenged in federal courts in the early fifties. In July 1955, the U.S. Court of Appeals for the Fourth Circuit (located in Atlanta) upheld a challenge to Columbia, South Carolina's segregated bus system. The appellate judges ruled that the standard of "separate but equal" facilities could no longer be applied in the states under its jurisdiction, though that ruling never seems to have been enforced. Five months later, Rosa Parks, secretary of the Montgomery, Alabama, branch of the NAACP, refused to give up her seat on a bus when a white passenger asked her to move to the back. The bus driver had Mrs. Parks arrested. "I had decided that I would have to find out what rights I had as a human being and a citizen," she explained (Sullivan, 2009, 424). Following her arrest and release from jail, she and other activists against segregation organized a 381-day bus boycott in the city. Reverend Martin Luther King Jr. played a prominent role in the Montgomery Bus Boycott and emerged as a leader in the fight against Jim Crow. In 1957 he organized the Southern Christian Leadership Congress (SCLC), which played a major role in the battle against Jim Crow.

During the bus boycott, the NAACP filed a challenge in federal court to the Alabama law mandating bus segregation and came away with a victory over racial segregation. After an appeal all the way to the U.S. Supreme Court, it ruled the Alabama law unconstitutional, ending the boycott. When the boycott ended, the bus company in Montgomery hired its first two African American drivers (Bartley, 1969, 217–18).

Violence played a major role in determining the outcome of the antisegregationist campaign—not black violence but white violence against blacks, including lynchings, riots, and murders of black children. The lynchings that had angered President Truman after the war ended included the brutal killing of four blacks, two war veterans and their wives, in Monroe, Georgia, in July 1946. The killings took place after a fight between one of the men and the son of his white employer. The murderers were never discovered, though they make have included the local sheriff. Four years later, an all-white jury in Virginia sentenced seven young black men to death for the alleged rape of a white woman. (Ten states—all in the South—allowed the death penalty in cases of rape. In Mississippi, all prisoners executed for rape in the twentieth century were black; the same was true in Georgia —the one white sentenced to death had his sentence commuted by the governor.) The presiding judge announced that the case would be tried "in such a way as not to disturb the kindly feeling now locally existing between the races." The all-white jury quickly convicted all seven, despite less than convincing evidence—the alleged victim was the only witness, and she had difficulty identifying any of the men she said had raped her.

Defense attorneys argued that the Virginia law allowing the death penalty in rape cases was biased, pointing out that of the 45 men sentenced to death for rape since execution was allowed in 1908, not one of them had been white. The Virginia Supreme Court maintained that statistical evidence did not prove bias. The court also refused to consider the fact that two white police officers in Richmond recently convicted of raping a black woman had received seven years in prison. The Virginia justices criticized the defense lawyers for even raising the issue of race in their appeal. The U.S. Supreme Court rejected a final appeal, and the seven blacks were put to death in Virginia's electric chair early in 1951. The Virginia case served as another example of what the NAACP referred to as "legal lynchings."

Another case of Jim Crow justice involved Willie McGee, a young Mississippi African American executed for allegedly raping a white woman. An all-white jury in Laurel took less than three minutes to reach its verdict. The only testimony linking McGee to the crime came from the alleged victim. McGee told the court that he had been having an affair with the woman for several years. When he broke it off she raised the rape charge. The Mississippi Supreme Court overturned the original verdict, however, because, it said, the strong public feeling aroused by the rape had prevented McGee from having a fair trial. The same court overturned a second conviction because blacks had been excluded from the jury—the first time any Mississippi court had ever come to that conclusion. After a third trial and conviction, McGee was sentenced to death a final time.

In their appeal of the third verdict, McGee's lawyers argued that no rape had taken place because the relationship had been consensual. The Supreme Court of Mississippi refused to consider that possibility. The chief justice spoke for all white Southern men when he loudly told the defense team what all whites in the South took as a matter of faith: "If you believe, or are implying, that any white woman in the South, who was not completely down and out, degenerate, degraded and corrupt, could have anything to do with a Negro man, you not only do not know what you are talking about, but you are insulting the whole South." The concept of interracial sex appalled whites so much, "that we could not even consider it in court." On May 7 McGee was executed in Mississippi's portable electric chair. A few hours before his death, McGee had written his wife a short letter asking her never to forget that "the real reason they are going to take my life is to keep the Negro down in the South" (Dray, 2002, 398, 404–6). McGee became the 109th person executed in Mississippi since 1930. Ninety of the prisoners executed were African American, another statistical measure of Jim Crow "justice."

The Tuskegee Institute reported that no lynchings of blacks took place in the United States in 1952, the first time that could be reported since it had started keeping a record of them in 1882. No lynchings were reported over the next two years either. However, in 1955 three lynchings of African Americans were counted. The murder of Emmett Till in Mississippi in the summer of that year received the most attention. Till, a 14-year-old Chicagoan, was spending the summer visiting his great-uncle Moses Wright in the small town of Money, Mississippi. Despite warnings from his mother before his first visit to Jim Crow territory, who told him that he should never talk to a white lady and always say "Yes sir," when talking to a white man, Emmett decided to impress his friends by doing just those things.

After buying a candy bar in a store he said "Bye babe," to the white clerk and according to her trial testimony whistled at her as he walked out the door. At 2:00 a.m. the next morning two white men came to Mose Wright's cabin and asked to see "the boy" who had "done all that talk to the white lady in the store." They dragged the seventh grader out of his bed and took him to their car, where according to Mose Wright a voice asked, "Is this the one?" A woman's voice replied, "That's him," and Till was pushed into the back seat and never seen alive again. A few days later a fisherman found his badly mutilated body in the Tallahatchie River with a 125-pound cotton mill wheel tied around his neck.

The sheriff eventually arrested two white men, one of them the husband of the store clerk. At their trial, Moses Wright identified the two as the men who had come to his cabin and taken his nephew away. (Wright left Mississippi after his testimony and never returned, fearing for his life.) The all-white jury took less than 30 minutes to find the men "not guilty." The foreman explained later that the jury came to that decision because the body taken from the river had been so badly disfigured, the 12 white men could not determine that it was really Emmett Till. The killing and trial gained wide attention because it was one of the first times a trial in Mississippi had been covered by national news networks. Mamie Till, Emmett's mother, decided to bring her son's body back to Chicago, and thousands of African Americans walked passed his open casket and saw his mutilated face. A picture of the badly disfigured face appeared on the cover of the next issue of *Jet* magazine, a widely distributed African American journal, bearing further witness to white brutality. Mrs. Till explained that she wanted as many people as possible "to see what they had done to her son." A few months later the two killers sold their story to a white journalist for $3,000. They described how they had severely beaten young Emmett with their fists and battered his face with rocks before throwing his body into the river. Till's killing was not the only incident demonstrating racial hatred in the Magnolia State that summer. The same month Till was murdered, a white Mississippi state representative shot and killed a black voting rights activist in broad daylight on the courthouse lawn in Brookhaven. That killer, too—like so many others—got away with it.

In 1956, Congress began consideration of what became the Civil Rights Act of 1957. In his State of the Union Address of 1957, President Eisenhower (who had received almost half of the black vote in his 1956 reelection campaign) asked Congress to create a bipartisan commission to investigate complaints alleging racial discrimination in government hiring practices. He also asked for a Civil Rights Division in the Department of

Justice to handle charges of discrimination in government contract work and cases involving denial of the right to vote. The president's suggested civil rights agenda included provisions that allowed "aggrieved individuals" to sue in federal court if they felt they had been denied their right to vote. Voting rights cases would be heard without juries, because (as the bill's supporters argued), juries in the South would be all-white, and they would never convict white election officials of denying blacks their right to vote. The House passed a bill containing all of the president's provisions by a relatively wide margin, but Senate action faced major obstacles.

Led by Senator Richard Russell of Georgia, Jim Crow senators launched an all-out campaign to prevent passage of any of the president's recommendations. First, they defeated an attempt to make it easier to break filibusters by requiring only a three-fifths majority of the Senate, rather than the two-thirds majority demanded by the rules. After that victory, Russell led off debate on the House-passed civil rights bill by asserting that the section prohibiting a jury trial in voting rights cases threatened every American's precious constitutional rights. Federal judges would hear voting rights cases without the presence of juries. Majority Leader Lyndon Johnson of Texas, who had his eyes on the White House and recognized the importance of African American votes, wanted the bill to pass so he agreed to a compromise that dropped the no-jury provision from the legislation. The "fundamental rights" of all Americans were therefore protected, and no white registrar in Jim Crow states or counties would ever be convicted of preventing blacks from voting. With that accomplished, the Senate passed the final bill, but only after Senator Strom Thurmond completed a 24-hour, 18-minute speech. During his rambling address he read all of the voting rights laws in effect in all 48 states, plus much more. A few minutes after Thurmond stopped talking, the Senate passed the Civil Rights Act of 1957 and President Eisenhower signed it into law—the first civil rights bill coming out of Congress since 1875.

During Senate debate on the civil rights bill, white supremacists in Arkansas rioted against a federal judge's order to desegregate Little Rock Central High School. The judge ordered the school administration to begin desegregating in the fall. The school board decided to integrate the senior class in high school first and work backward; the junior class would be desegregated in 1958, the sophomore class in 1959, and so forth until all grades were integrated. On the first day of the fall semester, nine African American students arrived at Central High School to register for classes. An angry, hostile, shouting and screaming mob of white parents, some teachers, and most students greeted them. Governor Orville Faubus, a bitter opponent of integration, had sent units of the Arkansas National Guard to maintain order, and dozens of guardsmen surrounded the school. When one of the African American students, Elizabeth Eckford, approached the front door, the mob screamed and yelled and would not let her enter. The National Guard did nothing to protect her, and the black students turned away. That night white students set fire to several police cars, threw rocks through windows, and refused to go home.

The next morning the Little Rock Nine returned and another mob greeted them. This time the African American students entered the building—where they found themselves virtually alone—but were quickly removed after the Little Rock police chief told them he could not guarantee their safety. City authorities called the White House, telling President Eisenhower that they could not control the situation without federal help. The president ordered one thousand troops from the 101st Airborne Division into the city to prevent a riot. He went on television that evening, and in what would become a major theme in the battle against Jim Crow, asked white parents in Little Rock to consider how newsreel scenes of white Americans yelling, beating, and punching young African Americans looked to people in Africa, Asia, and Latin America. Fighting and racially motivated violence aimed at preventing integration would only help the Russian Communists in the war for the hearts and minds of the people of the world. If we wanted freedom for all peoples in the world, we as a nation had to support freedom at home.

The Little Rock Nine finally entered the school and classes began with a few white students and teachers in attendance. Throughout the school year they endured beatings, shoving, racial insults, and many death threats. White students set their lockers on fire and one of the Nine was stabbed and had acid thrown in her face. Only five of the nine original students completed the year at Central High. The next year Arkansas closed its entire public school system and leased the buildings to "private" corporations to administer. Only white students were accepted. In a referendum on the privatization plan, voters approved it 130,000 to 7,500. (Few blacks took part in that election because of the state's restrictive Jim Crow registration laws. They still could not vote.) Public schools in Arkansas remained closed until the U.S. Supreme Court ordered them reopened in a 1959 ruling. "An evasive scheme" such as that of making public schools private, the unanimous court announced, could not be used to avoid desegregation. In 1972, 15 years after the riots at Central High (and 18 years after *Brown*), all public schools in Little Rock were integrated without riots.

Opponents of integration planted so many bombs at public schools, from Virginia to Florida to Texas, that Congress took action. The 1960 civil rights law made it a crime to cross carry explosives across state lines with the intention to use them to blow up "any vehicle or building." It also established that if "any Negro" living in an area which showed a historical "pattern or practice" of denying African Americans the right to vote, he or she could request a federal judge to issue an order declaring him or her "qualified to vote." Blacks granted such an order would be allowed to vote. The method for gaining the order for getting the right to vote proved too complicated for many African Americans to pursue. Even if a judge issued the order, the state could appeal that decision and challenge the voter's credentials again. Each potential voter had to file an individual request in federal court to get the right to vote, which proved very dangerous in many counties in Jim Crow states. So, the 1960 law did not gain voting rights for many blacks in the South. Election judges disobeying the order would face contempt charges in federal court. Registered black voters in Mississippi totaled 6.1 percent of the eligible population; in 1964 that number had risen but barely, to 6.7 percent. Alabama did better; African American registration increased from 13.7 percent to 23.0 percent.

Two provisions of the original bill faced loud criticism from Southerners and were removed. One would have created a Commission on Job Opportunity Under Government Contracts to investigate charges of discrimination in companies with government contracts. The other objectionable section of the bill offered federal "technical assistance" to schools undergoing desegregation. Jim Crow senators claimed that both provisions "victimized the South" to help liberals win Northern black votes in the upcoming election. In eliminating these provisions, Southern Democrats received needed support from Senate Republicans. As in 1957, Majority Leader Lyndon Johnson steered what remained of the bill through the Senate. As of 1960 only 6 percent of school districts in the Jim Crow states had been integrated, mostly in rural counties and small towns with very small numbers of African Americans.

The fight for equal rights entered a new phase in February 1960 when four African American students at North Carolina Agricultural and Technical College—the state's four-year black college—in Greensboro sat down at the "whites only" counter in the local Woolworth's dime store. They asked for coffee and doughnuts, which the white waitress refused to serve them. They sat without service until the store closed. Returning the next day, they sat for four hours without service. The four had been reading an essay on "nonviolent resistance to evil" by Mahatma Gandhi, the Indian leader of the fight to get the British out of India, before engaging in what they called their "sit down" protest, which soon became "sit-ins." They pledged not to fight back if hit by anyone, and they kept their word. The sit-ins spread to other stores in the city and included white students from the local Women's College of North Carolina. Despite harassment by Klansmen and members of the White Citizens' Council, the protests continued until late July, when the Woolworth Company agreed to serve all "properly dressed and well behaved people," whatever their race.

The sit-in movement spread to cities and towns across the entire South, with the goal being to get service for African Americans in every store and at every lunch counter from Greensboro to Nashville to Richmond to New Orleans and Oklahoma City. In many places the protests were met with arrests, violence, and beatings. In April 1961, with a few hundred dollars donated by the Southern Christian Leadership Conference (SCLC), the group's executive secretary 55-year-old Ella Baker, a longtime field director of the NAACP, and James Lawson, leader of the sit-in movement in Nashville, joined in a meeting in Raleigh, North Carolina, with other leaders of the emerging civil rights movement. They established a group called the Student Nonviolent Coordinating Committee (SNCC) and elected Fisk University student Marion Barry (a future mayor of Washington, D.C.) as its first chairman. Ella Baker became an "adult advisor." One student at the conference said that SNCC would fight for equal rights under the law but that "the greatest progress of the American Negro in the future will not be made in Congress or the Supreme Court; it will come in the jails."

Jim Crow played a key role in John Kennedy's narrow victory over Richard Nixon in the presidential election of 1960. Events in the South had a major impact on African American voting decisions in the North. Early in May, Dr. Martin Luther King Jr. received a traffic ticket in Georgia, receiving a $25 fine and 12 months' probation. In October police arrested him during a sit-in demonstration in Atlanta. The sit-in charges were dropped but the judge sentenced him to four months in prison for violating his probation. Refusing to let him out on bail (the normal practice granted whites in similar circumstances), the judge ordered him immediately sent to jail. In the middle of the night and without notifying his family or attorney, Dr. King was secretly taken to a Georgia state prison, which had a notorious reputation for mistreating African American prisoners.

Dr. King's family, concerned about his disappearance, contacted both the Kennedy and Nixon campaign staffs asking if they could help them find their husband and father. Richard Nixon did nothing, but John Kennedy called Mrs. King, offering his assistance. The future president's brother, who knew Georgia's Democratic governor, contacted the governor, who telephoned the judge and asked him how he could deny bail in a misdemeanor case. The judge granted bail the next morning and Dr. King was freed two weeks before the election. News of his involvement in getting the civil rights leader released helped John Kennedy, who had never been known for his support of equal rights while in the Senate, gather more than 70 percent of African American votes in the election, up significantly from the slightly more than 50 percent the Democrats had won four years before. Those black votes proved especially important in the critical states of New York, which Kennedy narrowly won, and Illinois, which the Democrats carried by less than five thousand votes. Kennedy's narrow victory in 1960 demonstrated that Jim Crow had become a powerful national issue.

The year 1961 began with a dramatic confrontation on the campus of the University of Georgia. On January 6, a federal judge ordered the school to admit Charlayne Hunter and Hamilton Holmes, two African Americans, for the upcoming quarter. When they tried to register, a white student mob welcomed them with jeers and angry shouting. "Two, four, six, eight," the whites shouted, "We don't want to integrate." A few days after they enrolled, another white mob surrounded Hunter's dormitory and had to be driven away by tear gas. The university then suspended the black students "for their own safety and the safety of other students." A majority of the university faculty surprised the administration by signing a petition condemning the violence and demanding the return of the two black students. Four years later Hunter and Holmes become the first African American students to earn bachelor's degrees from the University of Georgia.

In December of 1960 the Supreme Court declared in *Boynton v. Virginia* that segregation in bus terminals serving passengers travelling across state lines violated the Interstate Commerce Act of 1887. That decision set off a second round of "Freedom Rides" modeled after the 1947 "Journey of Reconciliation." Segregation in public transportation had been a long-time aggravation for African Americans in Jim Crow states. The first Jim Crow laws separated people on trains by race onto separate cars. African Americans paid the same fare as whites on buses, streetcars, and trains. They waited for transportation in the same place (though in segregated seating facilities). Why could they not sit wherever they pleased? The journey of a bus from Washington, D.C., to New Orleans signaled the difficulty many civil rights campaigns would face over the next three years, 1961 to 1964.

In May 1961, thirteen Freedom Riders (seven black and six white) rode out of Washington, D.C., on a Greyhound bus intending to travel through Virginia, the Carolinas, Georgia, Alabama, and Mississippi on the way to

New Orleans. Eleven of the Riders were from the Congress of Racial Equality (CORE) and two were members of the Student Nonviolent Coordinating Committee (SNCC). The Riders encountered no trouble in Virginia or North Carolina, but several were beaten and arrested when they reached Rock Hill, South Carolina, in violation of the Supreme Court's ruling. The bus crossed Georgia safely, but one hundred Ku Klux Klansmen attacked the bus as it approached Anniston, Alabama—smashing windows, slashing tires, and setting it on fire. As the passengers escaped the bus, the Klansmen beat them with baseball bats. In Anniston, a mob at the bus station beat them again, but the bus managed to drive away. In Birmingham another mob attacked the Riders, beating one so severely he required more than 50 stitches to close the wounds to his head. Federal Bureau of Investigation agents had been informed of the attack in the Alabama capital, but they did nothing to protect the nonviolent Freedom Riders.

Attorney General Robert Kennedy called upon CORE to end the Freedom Rides, blaming "extremists on both sides" for the bloodshed. The bus driver refused to drive the Freedom Riders any further. So, they decided to fly from Birmingham to New Orleans. When bomb threats delayed their takeoff, Klansmen circled the plane for several hours before it left the ground. Diane Nash, leader of the Nashville Student Movement, announced that she and other students would continue the Freedom Ride. Ten students (eight blacks and two whites) took a bus to Birmingham. When they got off the bus, Sheriff Eugene "Bull" Connor arrested them and had them driven back to the Tennessee border, where they were left in the middle of the night. The ten made their way back to Birmingham, where nine students from Atlanta joined them at the Greyhound terminal, where another Klan-led mob surrounded them. The new Riders could not find a driver willing to carry them anywhere.

During the bus terminal confrontation, Robert Kennedy called the Alabama governor and persuaded him to protect the students as they continued their journey. He also called the Greyhound Corporation and demanded that it send a driver, which it did. When the Freedom Ride resumed, the bus drove 90 miles an hour towards the state line, escorted by several Alabama Highway Patrol cars. When the bus reached the Montgomery city limit, the highway patrol drove away. When the bus reached the terminal, more than a thousand Klansmen attacked it, making sure to smash the cameras of any photographers in the area. When Alabama Public Safety Director Floyd Mann saw Klansmen beating three bleeding, nonviolent Riders with bats and chains, he pulled his pistol and ordered them to stop, saving their lives.

When the bloody attack ended, the injured Riders were taken to the only hospital in the city willing to treat them, St. Jude's Catholic. In the emergency room, they promised to continue their journey. "We are prepared to die," Jim Zwerg, the most severely wounded of the Riders, informed reporters. Robert Kennedy ordered federal marshals in Alabama to enforce the Supreme Court decision. That evening, May 21, more than 1,200 African Americans filled Montgomery's First Baptist Church to honor the Freedom Riders. A much larger, hostile crowd of three thousand whites stood outside the church, shouting and screaming racial insults at Martin Luther King Jr. when he arrived to give his speech. No police or National Guard troops patrolled the streets; only a small group of federal marshals stood in front of the church door. The white mob set fire to a car as the people inside the church sang freedom songs. Rocks smashed through the windows and the mob rushed toward the church, ready to burn it to the ground along with everybody inside. The National Guard finally showed up and used tear gas to break up the white mob. The Alabama Guardsmen refused to let the African Americans assembled inside out of the church, however, forcing them to remain inside—at bayonet point—the entire night.

The next day President Kennedy received a promise from the governors of Alabama and Mississippi that they would protect the Freedom Riders from further mob violence when their journey continued. When, after three days of absolute terror, the bus with the 12 Freedom Riders—protected by 40 state police cars—left Montgomery, it headed for Jackson, Mississippi, without making any more stops. In the Mississippi capital, the Riders used the "whites only" restrooms and sat at the "whites only" lunch counter until they were arrested. They were tried and convicted but refused to pay the fines ordered by the judge and spent the next 39 days in jail. They served their sentence on Parchman Farm, one of the most violent prisons in the United States. When they entered the prison both male and female prisoners were stripped of their clothing, which was replaced by black-and-white-striped uniforms. When two white Riders refused to undress, guards took them inside the administration building and shocked them with cattle prods until they removed their clothes.

Two protestors were put into each eight by ten cell. The cells were segregated by race. The Freedom Riders ate bug-ridden food, slept in windowless jail cells, had no exercise or reading material, and were allowed two showers per week. The Riders kept up their morale by singing freedom songs, even after the guards took away their beds when they refused to stop and they had to sleep on the cement floors. When they protested, a deputy brought in a fire hose and blasted them with water until their cells were flooded. They kept singing. They were released after 39 days, and the Riders found they had awakened many Americans to the horrors of racist justice. They had experienced real Jim Crow–style brutality and taught many others the real meaning of Jim Crow justice.

President Kennedy called for a "cooling off period." Attorney General Robert Kennedy, after much criticism for not offering more protection for the Riders, said that he did not believe that the Department of Justice could "side with one group or the other in disputes over Constitutional rights." CORE and SNCC rejected the president's call and established the Freedom Riders Coordinating Committee to organize more rides. During the remaining days of summer more than 60 buses carrying newly recruited Freedom Riders came to Jackson from every part of the South. Police arrested more than three hundred Riders in the Mississippi capital, and they all ended up at Parchman Penitentiary, where they received even more inhumane treatment than the original group of Riders had been subjected to. Guards put eight of them, not two, in each cell and gave them no soap, toilet paper, or mattresses. The single toilet in each cell quickly backed up onto the floor. One black Rider described her treatment by the guards: "They made me take medicine, which made me run to the toilet. They tore my blouse off. We nearly froze to death. We only had one meal on Sunday. It was terrible. I never thought people could be so mean" (Oshinsky, 1996, 238).

The Freedom Riders never reached New Orleans, but the bloody attacks by white racists against the nonviolent protestors brought the reality of "the southern way of life" to the attention of other Americans. The Riders and their nonviolent acts of civil disobedience led to some changes. The Interstate Commerce Commission (ICC) issued an order for bus companies to desegregate by November 1 or face fines. Most obeyed the ICC order. Beginning on the established date, passengers could sit where they pleased on a bus, and "white" and "colored" signs were removed from all buses, bathrooms, and waiting rooms. The Freedom Rides had broken through the "color line" that separated white and black citizens in one area of Southern life for generations. The bloody attacks on the Riders revealed the intense hatred that challengers to Jim Crow would have to face if they wanted to change the system.

Bloodshed marked many protests against segregation between 1962 and 1964. In 1962, a riot erupted on the campus of the University of Mississippi when James Meredith, the first black student admitted to the university, under the order of a federal judge, arrived on campus. Meredith, guarded by U.S. marshals, tried to enroll for classes, but white students and outside agitators rioted, preventing him from registering. That evening President

Kennedy made a nationally televised address, pleading with students to remain calm. He asked them to think of what images of the violence would look like to the people of Africa and Asia. If Mississippi students wanted the United States to win the hearts and minds of those people, they would return to their dorm rooms and stop the violence. Some students went home but many others, including the entire football team, did not. The violence continued throughout most of the night, and by morning two rioters were dead and fifty others were badly wounded.

After Governor Ross Barnett refused to act, the president placed three thousand Mississippi National Guardsmen under his own control and ordered them onto the University of Mississippi campus to restore calm and clear it of troublemakers. Within two days of the president's order, 16,000 additional military personnel patrolled the streets of Oxford, slowly restoring order. Meredith, a political science major, had served for nine years in the U.S. Air Force prior to beginning his college career. He first attended the all-black Jackson State College before transferring to the University of Mississippi. Because of frequent death threats and daily racial slurs, federal troops had to remain on campus to protect Meredith's life. They stayed until 1963, when he became the first African American to graduate from the university.

The next racial violence that attracted national news coverage began on April 2, 1963, when Martin Luther King Jr. and the SCLC launched an antisegregation campaign in Birmingham, Alabama, the city most civil rights leaders considered "the most segregated city in America." Dr. King, along with Ralph Abernathy and Fred Shuttlesworth, two local ministers who had organized the local SCLC branch, led the first march, which attracted fewer than one hundred people, mainly fellow ministers, to protest against the city's Jim Crow laws. The three leaders were quickly arrested and sentenced to jail for marching without a permit. Those arrests led to a violent confrontation that evening between two thousand African Americans and the city's racist all-white police force. Hundreds of blacks and even a few policemen were injured.

While serving his term, Dr. King received a letter from a group of white clergymen in Alabama accusing him of being an agitator who came into the state only to stir up trouble and encourage violence. Dr. King responded to the ministers by sending them his famous "Letter from Birmingham Jail." In it he rejected the charge of being an "outside" agitator and troublemaker. Then he outlined his philosophy of nonviolent resistance to evil, which he based on the teachings of Mahatma Gandhi, the leader of the protests against British colonialism in India. The British had left India in 1948 largely because of Gandhi's nonviolent demonstrations and marches in the 1930s and 1940s. The key to victory was never to respond to violence with more violence, no matter how badly you were beaten, shot at, kicked, or abused. Never bring yourself down to the level of your oppressor and abuser by responding with violence and abuse was the message Gandhi had taught Dr. King, whether he was a British colonial administrator or the Birmingham police chief. By refusing to resort to violence, protestors demonstrated the moral superiority of their cause. "The means we use must be as pure as the ends we seek," Dr. King asserted.

The letter included a defense of a protest strategy based on deliberately breaking the law. Dr. King based this strategy on early Christian philosophy. "An unjust law," according to St. Augustine, the fourth century Catholic philosopher, "is no law at all." Unjust laws, in his view, included any laws that "degraded human personality," or were inflicted on a minority that "as a result of being denied the right to vote, had no part in enacting or devising the law." Jim Crow laws fell directly under that definition. Segregation laws "distort the soul and damage the personality." The Jim Crow system of laws gave the majority "a false sense of superiority" and in return the minority acquired "a false sense of inferiority." "Direct action" challenged laws that were unjust and forced a community, or a state, or a nation to confront the issues of inequality and discrimination resulting from those laws. Dr. King's response to the Alabama clergymen received no answer or reply but became famous for its explanation and defense of the tactics and goals of the civil rights movement.

The day after the confrontation with Birmingham police, thousands of African American men, women, and schoolchildren marched to protest "police brutality." Marches continued for five days even though the police tried to break up the demonstrations with fire hoses, police dogs, and electric cattle prods. Birmingham police, who had been instructed by "Bull" Connor to use whatever means they felt necessary, including attack dogs and water cannons, to disrupt the marches, arrested more than 1,500 marchers during the first few days of protests, while hundreds more of the peaceful demonstrators were seriously injured by police dogs and police clubs. When the SCLC organized marches of thousands of African American schoolchildren, Bull Connor's police arrested hundreds of them, using dogs and water cannons to disperse the rest of the young marchers. Pictures of the children being abused by the police and threatened by snarling dogs appeared in newspapers and on television screens across the country. The brutality employed by Birmingham's police disgusted many Americans and bore witness to the intense hatred that divided white and African Americans in the Alabama capital.

Eight days after the children's marches began Martin Luther King announced that an agreement had been reached with an all-white committee of political and business leaders in the city. Under prodding from President Kennedy, the businessmen promised that within 90 days all public accommodations in the city, including hotels, motels, restaurants, lunch counters, government offices and buildings, courtrooms, parks, and many other places where people could meet, would desegregate. The businessmen also promised to provide more job opportunities for African Americans.

Murders in Mississippi and Alabama added to the long record of racial violence that bloodied the history of Jim Crow America. On June 23, 1963, William Moore, a white postman from Baltimore, died from bullet wounds he suffered after unknown gunmen shot him on a road in northeast Alabama. Moore was marching for peace and racial justice. He began his protest in eastern Tennessee intent on getting to Mississippi carrying a sign that read "Equal Rights for All—Mississippi or Bust." Police never found his killers. On June 12, that same year, a sniper killed Medgar Evers, head of the Mississippi branch of the NAACP, as Evers got out of his car in front of his home. Evers had been leading a series of sit-ins protesting segregation in downtown Jackson when he was murdered. Police arrested white supremacist Byron De La Beckwith and charged him with the crime. Tried twice before all-white juries in Jackson in 1964, both trials of De La Beckwith ended in not guilty verdicts. (In 1994, 31 years after the crime, a jury of eight African Americans and four whites convicted Beckwith of first-degree murder based on new evidence and testimony from a witness who had heard him boast of the killing at a Klan rally in 1964. Sentenced to life imprisonment, he died in a prison hospital from heart disease in 2001.)

In June 1963, Alabama governor George C. Wallace, elected the year before on a slogan promising "Segregation now! Segregation tomorrow! Segregation forever!" stood in the University of Alabama's registrar's office to block the registration of Vivian Malone and James Hood, two black students. The governor read a statement charging that a federal judge's order to enroll the students was "a frightful example of the oppression of the rights, privileges and sovereignty of this state by the Federal Government." Later that day, a federal judge ordered that the students be allowed to register, and the governor, in a scene shown on national television, stepped aside as they approached the registration office accompanied by federal marshals and a deputy U.S. attorney general. The voters of Alabama elected

Wallace governor three more times before turning the office over to his wife. He also ran for the presidency four times and became a popular national spokesman in defense of Jim Crow.

On August 28, more than 250,000 Americans attended a march on Washington to protest the lack of jobs for African Americans and the discriminatory treatment of black citizens in the United States. It was the largest protest demonstration in U.S. history. They gathered at the Lincoln Memorial to hear speeches calling for jobs and equal rights for all. The demonstrators carried thousands of signs calling for "Jobs and Freedom Now" and Martin Luther King delivered his famous "I Have a Dream" speech. A few days after the march, President Kennedy sent a civil rights bill to Congress.

By September 1963 just one Jim Crow state, Mississippi, still had a completely segregated school system—not a single black student had entered an all-white public school anywhere in the state. Even neighboring Alabama school districts had a few integrated elementary and high school districts; but the state capital, Birmingham, was not one of them. A federal judge ordered the city to begin desegregation in the fall. The city closed most of its schools rather than following the judge's order. Governor Wallace told the *New York Times* that only "a few first-class funerals" would stop integration in his state. On September 15, a Sunday morning, a bomb killed four young African American girls—Addie Mae Collins, Denise McNair, Cynthia Wesley, and Carole Robertson—attending Sunday school in the Sixteenth Street Baptist Church, the 21st time since 1955 that blacks in the city had been killed in bombings. A riot in which two more African Americans died broke out that evening.

A witness told police that he saw a white man place a box under the steps of the church earlier that morning. Later identified as Robert Chambliss of the KKK, known to fellow Klansmen as "Bomber Bob, " police arrested him and charged him with the murders. An all-white jury found Chambliss not guilty later that year, though he received a six-month jail sentence and a $100 fine for having 122 sticks of dynamite in his truck when taken into custody. (In 1977, at a second trial 14 years after the crime had been committed, another jury—with eight blacks and four whites—found Chambliss guilty of murder and sentenced him to life imprisonment. He died in prison in 1985.)

President Kennedy had submitted a civil rights proposal to Congress two months before the March on Washington, but then he offered a revised bill after Dr. King's speech. The new legislation called for federal authority to file suit to desegregate "public accommodations," financial aid for schools that were beginning to desegregate, and a cutoff of all federal funds for school districts that refused to begin desegregation programs. The bill cleared a major obstacle in October when the House Judiciary Committee approved a bipartisan measure after lengthy and intense negotiations between Republican and Democratic leaders. The House bill went much further than the president's proposal, providing money for desegregation of public facilities (parks, playgrounds, swimming pools, etc.) and creation of an Equal Employment Opportunity Commission (EEOC), with power to end discrimination in businesses and unions.

After President Kennedy's assassination on November 22, new president Lyndon Baines Johnson asked Congress for "the earliest passage of the civil rights bill" for which President Kennedy "had fought so long." The House passed the bill by a wide margin in February 1964. The House bill contained 10 sections, or "articles" as Congress calls them. The most important parts of the bill included Title I, which called for uniform voter tests and provided that a sixth-grade education would be accepted as proof of literacy. Title II provided that "discrimination based on race, color, religion, or national origin in all public places," defined as "restaurants, cafeterias, gasoline stations, motion picture houses, theaters, concert halls, sports arenas, stadiums, or any hotel, motel, or lodging house" was no longer legal. The only exceptions were owner-occupied hotels or motels with five rooms or less.

Title III gave the attorney general authority to file suit in federal court on behalf of "individuals aggrieved," under Article II. Title IV gave the Justice Department authority to bring suit in federal court to bring about desegregation in districts that delayed or failed to take action to move forward on integration. Title V made the Commission on Civil Rights a permanent federal agency. Title VI prohibited discrimination in any programs or activities that received money from the federal government. Title VII established the Equal Employment Opportunity Commission (EEOC) and gave it power to eliminate illegal employment practices. Title VIII authorized the Census Bureau to compile voter registration statistics in counties found by the Commission on Civil Rights to have practiced discrimination. Titles IX and X created the Community Relations Service to assist in resolving disputes involving discrimination.

The House passed the bill by a wide margin in February 1964; the Senate spent a much longer time considering the proposal. Senators had debated civil rights legislation in 1938 and defeated an antilynching measure, and defeated similar bills again in 1942 and 1944. In 1946 when it considered and defeated an anti–poll tax bill, then in 1949 and 1950 when considering extensions for the Fair Employment Practices Commission and other parts of President Truman's civil rights agenda, Southern senators joined with conservative Republicans to block passage of both measures. In 1957 and 1960 Congress passed civil rights bills for the first time since Reconstruction, but in 1962 the Senate struggled over and failed to pass a measure to outlaw literacy tests.

The major weapon used by opponents of civil rights in the Senate was the filibuster. Senate rules continued to protect the right to filibuster a bill to death. A filibuster had been ended by cloture during consideration of the 1957 Civil Rights Act. A 1960 Civil Rights Act was passed without a filibuster. Both laws were very weak attempts to protect constitutional rights. Neither law required federal assistance to help communities integrate their schools, or federal help in protecting a citizen's right to vote. Nor did they create a federal agency or a commission with power to investigate and take action against discriminatory employment practices. The Commission on Civil Rights (created in the 1957 bill) had power only to investigate and report on charges of discrimination; it had no authority to end it or to punish those guilty of discriminatory practices.

The 1964 bill passed by the House contained those necessary powers and much more. So, if American "freedom" was to be preserved, the Southerner senators and members of Congress decided they had to mount an all-out, full-scale effort to block the bill's passage. A long filibuster, or "educational campaign," as Southern senators preferred to call it, was required. Senator Russell Long of Louisiana said he would lead the fight against the proposed legislation "till hell freezes over and then I propose to start fighting it on the ice" (Finley, 2008, 242).

Senator Richard Russell of Georgia, the highly respected chairman of the Armed Services Committee and longtime friend of Lyndon Johnson, emerged as leader of the filibuster. He led off the speech marathon by calling the bill "a monstrosity." He warned that the Civil Rights Act had one obvious objective, "the mixing of races in the schools of the South." If "agitators" and un-American "radicals" achieved that goal, the "stability" produced by segregation that had protected whites from black "barbarism" for generations would disappear. Soon black "criminals" would unleash a "wave of violence" unlike any seen before in the United States. The senator produced page after page of statistical evidence supposedly showing that blacks were far more likely to commit crimes, especially violent crimes, than whites. He concluded by stating a fundamental white Southern belief about blacks: they were biologically inferior to whites and would remain in a state of degraded savagery for generations to come (Finley, 2008, 209).

Another theme stressed by opponents of equal rights emphasized the bill's alleged threat to "the constitutional rights of all Americans." One Jim

Crow senator suggested that if the bill passed the "country would be run by tyrannical federal bureaucrats" who would "destroy all individual liberties." The proposed civil rights act "trampled on the Constitution" and threatened "the highest ideals of the nation," according to Herman Talmadge of Georgia. It gave federal bureaucrats authority "over private property rights" and an individual business owner's right to decide whom he or she would or would not serve. In other words, the right to discriminate on the basis of race was a right guaranteed by the U.S. Constitution. To take that right away was "un-American," "socialistic," and "dangerous to liberty." Richard Russell identified another constitutional problem raised by the bill—it directly threatened the most basic safeguard of freedom established by the Founding Fathers and a right dear to the hearts of white supremacists in and out of Congress, the principal of "states' rights." To "preserve states' rights" and to "stem the tide toward an all-powerful centralized government" in Washington, the bill could not be allowed to pass (Finley, 2008, 209–12).

Other Southern senators spent endless hours warning of the inevitability of a "race war" in the United States if the bill became law. Olin Johnston of South Carolina predicted that the law "would never be enforced without cost of bloodshed and violence." Strom Thurmond complained that "Negroes have us by the throat"; their leaders threatened violence and death for whites should the bill not pass. Allen Ellender of Louisiana took time to tell Americans that racial separation in the South was "99 percent voluntary" and approved of by Southerners of all races. Segregation was natural; just as oil separated from water, "whites separated from Negroes," the 74-year-old Ellender concluded. The filibuster continued for 74 days before a compromise ended it (Finley, 2008, 264, 276–77).

A substitute bill presented by the leader of Senate Republicans, Everett Dirksen of Illinois, was brought to the floor with the goal of ending the filibuster. The Senate accepted the substitute because it satisfied concerns of moderate and conservative senators from Northern and Western states who did not want its antidiscrimination provisions applied to the racial problems existing in their states. Dirksen's substitute exempted states with fair employment and nondiscriminatory public accommodation provisions in their constitutions and laws from federal intervention. It also barred federal courts from ordering "busing of students" to correct "racial imbalance" that might (and usually did) exist in public schools. These provisions satisfied Northern and Western senators who worried that court-ordered desegregation in their states might break down age-old patterns of neighborhood and school segregation. (Southern senators saw these changes in the House bill as proof that Northerners supported school integration—as long as it applied only to the South. Northern cities had schools as segregated as those in the South, they knew, though no laws required that white and black students attend separate schools.)

In the North segregation existed as a matter of fact (*de facto*)—people just lived that way—not because the law commanded it (*de jure*). Attitudes and housing patterns, not laws, accounted for segregated school systems in Northern cities and suburbs. Governor George Wallace's success in Northern presidential primaries proved that Northern whites were just as prejudiced as white Southerners, Thurmond and other Jim Crow defenders gleefully pointed out. (Wallace captured 33.8% of the vote in the Wisconsin Democratic primary and 29.8% in the Indiana primary.)

Dirksen's compromise took *de facto* segregation out of the hands of the courts and produced enough Republican votes to pass a cloture petition that ended the filibuster. A few days later the full Senate adopted the final version of the legislation 73–27. The House passed the Senate version shortly thereafter, and the Civil Rights Act of 1964 was sent to the White House for the president's signature. When the president acted, Jim Crow was dead and the battle to end "the southern way of life" (segregation by race), which began with the opening shots of the Civil War in April 1861, had finally ended.

President Johnson signed the bill on July 2, only a few hours after final passage by the House of Representatives. At the signing ceremony he told his listeners, "We believe that all men are created equal—yet many are denied equal treatment. . . . The reasons are deeply embedded in history and tradition and the nature of man. We can understand without rancor or hatred how all this happens. But it cannot continue. Our Constitution, the foundation of our Republic, forbids it. The principles of freedom forbid it. Morality forbids it. And the law I sign tonight forbids it." *De jure* segregation (Jim Crow segregation) had entered its final days.

Richard Russell advised his fellow Southern senators to accept their defeat as gracefully as possible. "All we can do now is swallow hard and hold our heads high," he told them, "knowing that we did everything humanly possible to further the cause of constitutional government." From the perspective of Jim Crow senators like Russell, "constitutional government" meant the right to prevent U.S. citizens from voting and to keep them out of the U.S. political process. Limits on voting participation and laws prohibiting interracial marriages were now all that protected white Christian civilization—and their famed "southern way of life"—from black "barbarism." For supporters of civil and equal rights for all

Americans, two battles still remained—the fight for voting rights and the fight to be allowed to marry a person of a different color were yet to be won (Finley, 2008, 278–79).

The victory over discriminatory voting practices, poll taxes, literacy tests, and outright intimidation (including threats against a person's job or life) came more easily than many civil rights advocates expected. Poll taxes had been abolished by the Twenty-Fourth Amendment, ratified in January 1964. Only five states, all in the South, still used that tax to discourage African American voting, the main reason the amendment was added to the Constitution with little difficulty. On March 17, 1965, President Johnson submitted the Voting Rights Act to Congress. It provided for direct federal involvement in registering voters rather than demanding that individuals file their own legal suits to get their right to vote. Individual filings had little impact on expanding black voter registration. In 1964, only 6.7 percent of eligible African Americans in Mississippi had registered to vote, and fewer than 24 percent of blacks in Alabama were legally registered. Across the South the numbers were higher, yet only 43.3 percent of black Southerners had registered while white registration reached 73.2 percent of those over 21 years of age, according to a report by the Southern Regional Council.

The 1965 Voting Rights Act as originally presented to Congress by the president gave the attorney general power to appoint federal examiners to supervise voter registration in states or voting districts where a literacy test was in force. And as of November 1, 1964, in any county where fewer than 50 percent of voting-age residents were registered or had cast ballots in the 1964 presidential election, federal examiners would also have power to register voters. Seven states, including six in the South—Alabama, Georgia, Louisiana, Mississippi, South Carolina, and Virginia—met this standard, along with Alaska, which had provisions that discriminated against Indians and Inuit (Eskimos). Another section of the law prohibited states from imposing new voter registration requirements without approval from a federal court.

Congressional debate on voting rights began just as Martin Luther King Jr. opened a voter registration drive in Selma, Alabama. Selma police, led by Sheriff Jim Clark, arrested more than seven hundred demonstrators, including Dr. King, during the first month of marches and protest rallies. In March, state police—sent to preserve order by Governor Wallace—used billy clubs, chains, rubber tubing wrapped around barbed wire, tear gas, whips, and electric cattle prods to break up one historic march as it headed across the Edmund Pettus Bridge over the Alabama River. As they crossed, the police attacked. Fifty marchers ended up in the hospital, and pictures of police brutality were broadcast across the country on evening newscasts. Three unknown white men beat a white minister participating in the march, the Reverend James Reeb, so viciously he died. Members of Congress jammed switchboards as thousands of Americans demanded federal action to end the violence.

On March 15, President Johnson made a televised address asking Congress to pass his voting rights proposal. He also said that there would be another march across the bridge and that he would federalize Alabama National Guard troops to provide protection. More than three thousand marchers led by Dr. King crossed the now famous Edmund Pettus Bridge and continued their march until they reached the state capital in Montgomery. The violence and marches in Selma, especially the arrests of hundreds of African American children marching for equality one afternoon, had great influence on the outcome of the voting rights debate in Washington. Images of police brutality in Alabama—and the nonviolent resistance of the demonstrators—helped convince many members of Congress that the time for equal voting rights for African Americans in the Jim Crow South had come.

In the Senate, the supporters of the voting rights measure expected another long filibuster, but three weeks after the debate began it ended as senators adopted a cloture motion for only the second time in its history—the first having been in 1964. The bill then passed with bipartisan support; 30 Republicans and 47 Democrats voted in its favor. In the House, numerous amendments offered by opponents were rejected and the bill passed by a wide margin, 333–85. Supporters of the bill included 33 Southern Democrats. They received standing ovations from their colleagues for their bravery in voting for the bill. In addition to the two measures in the original bill, the final version suspended literacy tests used as devices to prevent people from registering to vote. The most evidence that states could demand for any person to establish literacy would be proof of a sixth-grade education.

Jim Crow was now legally dead. Laws segregating Americans by race no longer had constitutional protection. The right to vote was now guaranteed for African Americans. Then, in June 1967 the Supreme Court declared unconstitutional the last remaining Jim Crow statutes still on the books in 16 states, the laws forbidding interracial marriage (miscegenation, as it was sometimes called). The colonial legislature had passed the first law banning interracial marriage in Virginia in 1661. By the 1920s, 38 states banned miscegenation. In the 1967 case, Richard Loving, a white male, married Mildred Jeter, who was part African American and part Native

American. In 1958, they were married in Washington, D. C., where the practice was legal. With their marriage license in hand the couple returned to their home state. But under Virginia law interracial marriages between state residents that took place outside the state were illegal. Only a few days after the Lovings returned from Washington, three policemen entered their unlocked home in the middle of the night and took them to jail. They were charged with violating the state's "unlawful cohabitation" statute along with the section of the code that made it a crime for couples to cross state lines for the purpose of evading the antimiscegenation law. They were convicted after a brief trial before a judge. Instead of giving the couple the maximum five-year sentence provided by the law, the judge fined each of them court costs of $36.29 and ordered them to immediately leave the state or go to prison for five years. The Lovings moved to Washington, D.C., where they were quite unhappy.

When they moved back to Virginia five years later, Richard and Mildred Loving decided to challenge the state's discriminatory marriage law. After it had worked its way through the state and federal court systems, the Supreme Court accepted their appeal, and heard arguments in *Loving v. Virginia* in April 1967. Chief Justice Earl Warren presented the court's unanimous decision two months later. In it he declared the law unconstitutional (reversing the court's 1883 decision in *Pace v. Alabama*). "Under our Constitution," the chief justice declared, "the freedom to marry, or not to marry, a person of another race, resides with the individual and cannot be infringed by the State" (*Loving v. Virginia*, 388 U.S. 1 (1967)). The *Loving* decision made the interracial marriage legal in all states.

The victory over Jim Crow did not mean the final defeat of racism, prejudice, and inequality in the United States. The laws were gone and the signs disappeared but white supremacist attitudes still dominated the thinking of many Americans. But their racist ideas were no longer legally allowed in the laws of U.S. states. Voting rights could no longer be denied to Americans because of the color of their skin, public buildings and schools could no longer be segregated, and African Americans could not be denied the right to serve on a jury because they were black. Since passage of the civil rights law, however, other methods aimed at preventing African Americans from registering to vote, including permanently denying the right to vote to anyone convicted of a felony, even after they had completed serving their sentences. Thousands and thousands of African Americans have lost their right to vote forever because of such laws, a policy found in no other country in the world. The United Nations Human Rights

Commission called this practice a "violation of human rights and international law" (Alexander, 2010, 187–88).

Public schools can no longer be legally segregated, but numerous all-white "Christian academies" opened in many white communities across the South, attracting thousands of white students. Job discrimination had obviously not ended, but victims of discriminatory employment policies could plead their case before the Equal Employment Opportunity Commission, which had power to investigate complaints and bring action, including imposing fines, against the offending employer. Police brutality continues to be a major problem for African Americans, but it is no longer accepted practice on many police forces as was true for so long in the past. Victims of police misconduct and prejudice can now bring their complaint to the attention of a court or a police review board in many areas of the country and have their view of events taken into consideration. And any laws that discriminate against citizens because of their race can no longer be enforced. Second-class citizenship based on race is no longer acceptable or protected by the Constitution of the United States. The era of Jim Crow segregation was over.

References

Alexander, Michelle. *The New Jim Crow: Mass Incarceration in the Age of Colorblindness*. New York: The New Press, 2010.

Bartley, Numan V. *The Rise of Massive Resistance: Race and Politics in the South During the 1950s*. Baton Rouge: Louisiana State University Press, 1969.

Dray, Philip. *At the Hands of Persons Unknown: The Lynching of Black America*. New York: Modern Library, 2002.

Finley, Keith. *Delaying the Dream: Southern Senators and the Fight Against Civil Rights, 1938–1965*. Baton Rouge: Louisiana State University Press, 2008.

Oshinsky, David M. *"Worse Than Slavery": Parchman Farm and the Ordeal Of Jim Crow Justice*. New York: Free Press, 1996.

Sullivan, Patricia. *Lift Every Voice: The NAACP and the Making of the Civil Rights Movement*. New York: The New Press, 2009.

Biographies

Booker Taliaferro Washington
(April 5, 1856–November 14, 1915)

Born on April 5, 1856, to a slave mother, Jane, a cook, and white father whom he never knew, on a small plantation in Franklin County, Virginia. Booker Taliaferro Washington moved with his mother to Malden, a small town near Charleston, after the Civil War ended in 1865. His mother, as was true with all slaves, was illiterate, but she wanted her son to be educated. Booker got a job during the day working in a salt furnace, then in a coal mine, and shortly after that as a houseboy for General Louis Ruffner, who owned the mine. While working as houseboy, Booker came under the influence of the general's wife, Viola, who taught him how to be clean, orderly, and efficient. At night, despite opposition from the general, he attended an elementary school established for freed slaves, where he learned to read and write. While at school he adopted his last name Washington, after learning about the first U.S. president.

In 1872, Booker left Malden and enrolled at Hampton Institute, a school opened a few years earlier for freed slaves by Northern missionaries. Its white principal, General Samuel Chapman Armstrong, had commanded African American troops during the war. The Hampton philosophy stressed practical, work-based education that would instill its students with character and Christian principles of morality. Classes at the Institute trained students in the nobility of hard work and self-discipline. The school prided itself on producing farmers trained in the best scientific methods and teachers. While at Hampton, Washington worked as a janitor to pay for his room and board. After graduating with honors from Hampton, he briefly attended a Baptist seminary for black students in Washington, D.C. In 1878, he returned to Hampton as a member of the faculty, where he supervised one hundred American Indian students brought to Hampton as an experiment in Americanizing Native Americans.

In 1881, the state of Alabama appropriated a few thousand dollars to build a new school for blacks in Tuskegee. The state asked General Armstrong to suggest the name of a white principal to head the school, but he instead recommended Washington. Alabama officials agreed to offer the position to the young black teacher, and Washington accepted the appointment. The school received less than $2,000 a year from the state, so most of the money for building and maintaining the campus was raised from Northern white missionary societies and philanthropists. For the next 42 years Washington headed the school and guided its growth into an institution with more than 1,500 students and more than 200 faculty.

Washington built his school on the Hampton model, offering a job-training course of study in trades such as carpentry, printing, shoemaking, and farming for boys. Girls took classes in cooking and sewing. To calm down hostile whites in areas surrounding Tuskegee, he explained that his students learned to become economically successful and they were not interested in political activity. They learned how to become successful businessmen rather than how to demand equal rights or voting rights. Andrew Carnegie, the wealthy steel industrialist, became a key financial supporter of Tuskegee and called Washington "one of the most wonderful men who ever lived." The success of his school made him very popular among African Americans, especially Southern blacks struggling through the daily fears of living in a Jim Crow society. For many black Southerners, Washington's way offered the best hope for the survival of the African American community in the violently racist, white supremacist world they lived in.

While building his school and becoming the major spokesman for the African American community, at least in the view of whites, Washington faced some major tragedies in his personal life. His first wife, Fanny, a graduate of Hampton and Washington's girlfriend since leaving Malden, was killed by a fall in 1884 only two years after they were married. His second wife, Olivia, also a Hampton graduate, suffered from poor health most of her life, and died in 1889. His third wife, Margaret, had graduated from Fisk University in Nashville and helped her husband as "lady principal of Tuskegee" for the rest of his life and became a national leader in various black women's federations.

After his September 1895 speech at the Cotton States and International Exposition in Atlanta, Georgia, Washington became recognized as the one African American voice that might replace Frederick Douglass, the great antislavery crusader and postwar U.S. diplomat who had died earlier that year. In his famous speech, Washington advocated a policy of "accommodationism." Blacks should accept Jim Crow discrimination for the time being and commit themselves to achieving economic success. He argued that blacks had to sacrifice their desire civil rights and political equality in exchange for economic gains. Once whites saw that blacks could work as hard as they did, and could run their own farms and businesses as honestly and successfully as they did, improvement in political and civil rights would surely follow.

In public, Washington said that gaining political power was not important for him or other blacks. Behind the scenes, however, he pursued a policy that expanded his own power and prestige, building what some called "the Tuskegee machine." He became the acknowledged leader of the small, mostly black, Republican Party in the South. Presidents McKinley, Roosevelt, and Taft consulted him on political appointments in Southern states, and he became very active in the National Negro Business League. He also became very influential in deciding who would receive money donated by Northern philanthropic foundations, including the Rosenwald Fund, which granted money to build schools in poor black communities throughout the South.

Washington was not an advocate of the immediate full equality and constitutional rights favored by his critics, such as W. E. B. DuBois, but argued instead for a common sense, practical approach that required a bargain with the white supremacists. Blacks would be allowed to pursue lives of modest economic well-being (even though most whites felt they would never be able to achieve it), as long as they did not demand political rights, social equality, or the right to marry their sisters and daughters. Washington conveyed this approach in his autobiography, *Up from Slavery*, which appeared in 1903. Other works by Washington include *The Future of the American Negro* (1899), *Sowing and Reaping* (1900), and *My Higher Education* (1911). Booker T. Washington died of arteriosclerosis and high blood pressure on November 14, 1915, at the age of 59. When he died, his monument, Tuskegee Institute, had a larger endowment than any other African American institution of higher education in the United States. He is buried on the campus.

William Edward Burghardt DuBois (February 23, 1868–August 27, 1963)

W. E. B. DuBois was born in Great Barrington, a small town in western Massachusetts, on February 23, 1868. DuBois's father left the family when he was a young child, leaving William and his mother as one of the few

African American families in the community. In 1884 he graduated from high school as the valedictorian. He then attended historically black Fisk University in Nashville, Tennessee. During his summers in Tennessee DuBois taught in several different African American elementary schools in the rural areas surrounding Nashville. In 1888, he enrolled as a junior in Harvard University and received a bachelor of arts degree upon graduation in 1890. The next year he received a master of arts from Harvard. For the next two years, 1892 to 1894, he studied history and economics at the University of Berlin. Upon returning to the United States, he returned to Harvard and in 1895 he completed his dissertation, "The Suppression of the African Slave Trade to the United States of America, 1638–1870," and was granted his doctorate in history from Harvard. While working on his dissertation, he spent two years teaching Latin and Greek at Wilberforce College, a small African American school in Ohio. In 1896 he married Nina Gomer, his former student, with whom he had two children.

The same year he got married DuBois began teaching as an assistant instructor in sociology at the University of Pennsylvania. Here he conducted research for his next book, a sociological study called *The Philadelphia Negro* (1899). This, along with his previous book, *The Study of the Negro Problems* (1898), placed DuBois among the leading voices in sociology in the United States. In 1897 he moved his wife and family to Atlanta, Georgia, where he had been appointed a professor of history and economics at an all-black institution, Atlanta University. He remained in Atlanta until 1909, when he helped organize the National Association for the Advancement of Colored People (NAACP) and became editor of its monthly magazine, *The Crisis: A Record of the Darker Races*. He remained in that position until 1934.

As editor, DuBois kept up a constant stream of protest in his editorials condemning the lynchings, the disfranchisement, and the Jim Crow segregation that had become the defining principles of "the southern way of life." He became recognized as the leading critic of Booker T. Washington's philosophy of "accommodationism," a policy holding that African Americans should accept inequality and second-class citizenship while working hard, producing wealth, and showing whites that they were worthy human beings who deserved the right to vote and the right to send their children to the same schools as whites. DuBois argued instead that African Americans had to fight to overthrow Jim Crow and push—through political action—for the same rights held by every other American.

The court system was the place to fight Jim Crow discrimination, he believed, not the vocational education classroom or your bankbook.

Racism could not be overcome by waiting for the "good whites" to recognize the intelligence and work ethic of "the Negroes." Not even the "good whites," favored by the "Wizard of Tuskegee," would support full equality for blacks. The U.S. Constitution was the best guardian of equal rights and liberty, not the Ku Klux Klan, or the Mississippi Constitution of 1890 or any similar documents authored by whites in Jim Crow states. The racist culture in Jim Crow country forbid any white from accepting or acknowledging the equality of all people. The rule of law in the 11 states of the Old Confederacy legalized inequality for African Americans and second-class schools for their children.

DuBois's fight for equal rights in the United States continued throughout his entire life until his death in Africa at age 93. DuBois published or edited 34 books on the lives of African Americans and their history. In 1903, he published his classic collection of essays, *The Souls of Black Folk*. It included descriptions of his teaching in a Jim Crow elementary school; a critical essay on Booker T. Washington and his negative impact on African Americans; and essays on African American literature, church music and hymns sung in the black church, and other areas of daily life. In the book's most famous passage, he defines the "double consciousness" that blacks in the United States are burdened to live with. Every day they face "this sense of always looking at one's self through the eyes of others, of measuring one's soul by the tape of a world that looks on in amused contempt and pity." Black Americans feel the "two-ness—an American, a Negro, two souls, two thoughts, two unrecognized strivings; two warring ideals in one dark body, whose dogged strength alone keeps it from being torn asunder."

DuBois quit the NAACP in 1934 over a disagreement he had with its board of directors. By the early 1930s, he had become a supporter of a black nationalist approach to solving the race problem in the United States. African Americans should control their own communities, their own schools, their own banks and businesses and hospitals. The NAACP remained committed to an integrated United States. DuBois returned to Atlanta, where he became chair of the department of sociology at Atlanta University in 1934, a position he retained until 1944. While head of the department he founded a new journal, *Phylon*, a quarterly that published articles on African American history and sociological studies of the black community. He also published an important history, *Black Reconstruction in America, 1860–1880* (1940). Here DuBois challenged the then dominant view among historians that Northern whites were responsible for most of the violence in the South. They used their congressional power to humiliate white Southerners and destroy the Southern economy in a foolish attempt to establish equality for the freed slaves.

Politically, DuBois joined the American Socialist Party in 1911 but resigned from it in 1912. By the 1940s he had become a communist, though he did not join the party until 1961. He remained committed to the party until his death in 1963. By that time he had abandoned the United States and moved to Ghana, a newly independent West African nation. In 1959 he accepted the Lenin Peace Prize offered by the Soviet Union. His main contributions to U.S. history include his lifelong commitment to human rights and freedom and his powerful attacks upon the Jim Crow laws, violence, and prejudice that dominated Southern politics for much of the twentieth century.

Martin Luther King Jr.
(January 15, 1929–April 4, 1968)

Martin Luther King Jr. was born in Atlanta, Georgia, on January 15, 1929. His father, Martin Luther King Sr., served as pastor of Ebenezer Baptist Church. His mother, Alberta Williams King, was the daughter of the church's founder. The future civil rights leader attended Atlanta's segregated public school system and at age 15 he enrolled at all-black Morehouse College. He graduated four years later with a bachelor's degree in sociology. He then attended Crozer Theological Seminary in Pennsylvania, from where he received a divinity degree in 1951. King then entered Boston University and graduated in 1955 with a doctoral degree in systematic theology. While in Boston, he met and married Coretta Scott, a music student from Alabama.

At the three institutions he attended, he studied the nonviolent philosophy of Mohandas Gandhi, the leader of the independence movement in India. A year before receiving his doctorate, King became pastor of Dexter Avenue Baptist Church in Montgomery, Alabama. On December 1, 1955, police arrested Rosa Parks, secretary of the local branch of the National Association for the Advancement of Colored People, after she violated Alabama's Jim Crow law by refusing to give up her bus seat to a white passenger. Her arrest set off a boycott of Montgomery's buses organized by the Montgomery Improvement Association. Leaders of the association asked Dr. King to lead the protest, a position he accepted even though terrorists bombed his house in January 1956, nearly killing his children. King used the nonviolent strategy of passive resistance advocated by Gandhi. Boycott participants, who included the entire African American community, pledged not to use violence even if they were attacked and beaten by the police. The boycott lasted until November 1956, when the bus company backed down and agreed to remove all signs restricting the areas where African Americans could sit.

In 1957, King helped form the Southern Christian Leadership Conference (SCLC) to coordinate civil rights campaigns. Two years later he visited India, where he learned more about nonviolent persuasion and civil disobedience. Upon returning he gave up his position in Montgomery and returned home to his father's church, becoming copastor. In 1959, while visiting Harlem in New York City on a national tour promoting his book, *Stride toward Freedom*, a disturbed African American woman stabbed King, but he survived.

Dr. King led the SCLC in several civil rights campaigns in the early 1960s. His first efforts in Albany, Georgia, ended in failure. The protests lasted for most of the summer in 1961 as Albany police arrested thousands of peaceful demonstrators. The white leadership refused to back down on any of the city's Jim Crow ordinances, so the city remained segregated. The next campaign, in Birmingham, Alabama, proved much more successful, despite the violent efforts of the city's police commissioner, Eugene "Bull" Connor, to drive the demonstrators out of the city. Scenes of police dogs attacking young marchers (many of them schoolchildren) as they were pinned against walls by water cannons filled newspapers and television screens around the world. During the Birmingham campaign, police arrested Dr. King and took him to jail. While in his jail cell, he wrote his "Letter from Birmingham Jail." In it he argued that people had the right to disobey unjust laws, which King defined as those that treated people differently because of the color of their skin. The police violence associated with the Birmingham demonstrations encouraged many Americans to support the civil rights legislation being presented to Congress by President John Kennedy in Washington, D.C.

Later in 1963 Dr. King delivered his "I Have a Dream" speech in the nation's capital to thousands of demonstrators attending the March on Washington for Jobs and Freedom. The march and the speech helped get the landmark Civil Rights Act of 1964 through Congress. Then in 1964 he received the Nobel Peace Prize in honor of his commitment to nonviolence and effectiveness in leading the civil rights movement in the United States. The next year Dr. King joined a voting rights march from Selma to Montgomery, Alabama, the state capital. More than 20,000 demonstrators joined the march, which helped gain support for the 1965 Voting Rights Act.

In 1965 Dr. King and his supporters shifted their attention to combating racism in the North. He rented an apartment in the heart of Chicago's South Side ghetto and announced plans to lead demonstrations against housing and job discrimination in the city. The protest marches into white neighborhoods were met with violence as rocks, stones, and bricks were thrown at the demonstrators. King left Chicago with little changed in the city's racist attitudes. According to Dr. King, the visit to Chicago demonstrated that racial hostility seemed more violent among Northern whites than he had ever seen in Alabama or Mississippi.

In the last two years of his life, the SCLC leader turned his attention from civil rights issues to economic inequality throughout the United States. He also made several speeches opposing the war in Vietnam. In 1967 he began planning a Poor People's Campaign for economic justice. In late March 1968 Dr. King went to Memphis, Tennessee, to support a strike by black garbage workers who were demanding higher pay. On April 4, he was shot and killed by white supremacist James Earl Ray, who had recently been released from prison in Missouri. News of the assassination sparked race riots in more than one hundred U.S. cities. Ray, who had made his way all the way to England before being arrested, was returned to Tennessee. In order to avoid the death penalty he entered a guilty plea and received a 99-year sentence for his crime, although many observers think that he might not have acted alone. Nothing has ever come of the questions and doubts surrounding the assassination, because no accomplices have ever been identified. The assassin said he would tell the whole story concerning the killing, but only if he was released from prison. Tennessee authorities never agreed to such a deal, and Ray died in prison in 1986.

Thurgood Marshall
(July 2, 1908–January 24, 1993)

Thurgood Marshall, the great-grandson of a slave, became the first African American justice of the U.S. Supreme Court when President Lyndon Johnson nominated him for that position and the Senate gave its consent in 1967. He was born in Baltimore, Maryland, on July 2, 1908, to William, a waiter at an all-white private club, and Norma, an elementary school teacher. His mother named him after one of his great-grandfather's uncles, a slave named Thoroughgood. He shortened that name because it was too long, he explained, while in school. At Baltimore's Frederick Douglass High School, he frequently got into trouble. One of his teachers punished him quite regularly by sending him to the school's basement to copy parts of the U.S. Constitution. By the time he graduated Marshall said he knew the entire Constitution by heart. After graduation he attended Lincoln University in Pennsylvania, where he joined the debate team and graduated with honors in 1930. He applied to the University of Maryland Law School but was denied entrance because of his race. He then attended Howard University Law School in Washington, D.C. He and the law school's vice dean, Charles Houston, became friends. In 1933, Marshall received his law degree from Howard, where he graduated first in his class. Marshall and Houston worked together at the NAACP in the 1930s, Houston as chief counsel and Marshall as lead attorney in most of the civil rights cases filed by the group. When because of poor health Houston stepped down as chief counsel in 1938, Marshall replaced him.

Marshall gradually developed a new legal strategy for the NAACP. Marshall decided to challenge the basic defense of segregation established by the Supreme Court in *Plessy v. Ferguson* (1896). In that case the justices decided that separating students by race in public schools was constitutional as long as the education received by each student was equal in quality. In Marshall's view, separate schools for whites and African Americans could never be made equal if students were separated by race. Racial separation and oppression caused the problems the United States faced in education, housing, transportation, electoral politics, and criminal justice, he decided, problems that "separate and equal" facilities would not resolve. Marshall achieved 28 Supreme Court victories, including the court's 1944 ruling outlawing "white primaries" (*Smith v. Allwright*) and its rejection of restrictive covenants in *Shelley v. Kraemer* (1948). But his greatest victory came in 1954 in *Brown v. Board of Education*, when the court declared that segregated schools were unconstitutional even if the education they provided was equal for all students in every school. Schools segregated by race were "inherently unequal and unconstitutional" no matter what quality of education they provided. In the *Brown* case, the court accepted evidence presented by psychologists and sociologists showing that just the act of separating children by the color of their skin was harmful to their development and their opinion of their selves. Most of the black students they tested and interviewed had very low levels of self-esteem, which harmed their ability to learn and left them unprepared to face the challenges of modern life. The social scientists traced that low evaluation of self-worth to the discriminatory effects of racial separation. Segregation by race violated the constitutional rights of African Americans because it treated them as an inferior people relegated to inferior schools. *Brown* was clearly Thurgood Marshall's greatest achievement.

In 1961, President John Kennedy appointed Marshall judge of the Circuit
Court of Appeals in New York. Marshall had a remarkable record as an
appeals court judge, writing 112 opinions, not one of which was overruled
by the Supreme Court. In 1965, President Lyndon Johnson named him
solicitor general of the United States, making him America's chief council.
The solicitor general generally argued the government side in cases
brought before the Supreme Court. Two years later, Marshall became the
first African American justice ever to sit on the U.S. Supreme Court. On
the court he became known as "the Great Dissenter." In one of his most
famous dissents, Marshall argued that using property taxes to finance
public education discriminated against African American and other minority students on the basis of wealth. Because white families owned almost
nine times more wealth and property than the average minority family,
largely a result of a long history of prejudice and discrimination, property
taxes were discriminatory and should be replaced with other, fairer sources of revenue. Rich districts would always have more money for schools
than poor districts, and poor districts were far more likely to contain large
numbers of minority students than rich ones (*San Antonio School District
v. Rodriguez*, 1973). The court majority disagreed, and property taxes
continued to be used as a major source of school financing.

Marshall also fought a long campaign against the death penalty. In his
view, it was unconstitutional in all cases. He presented statistical evidence
showing that African Americans convicted of murder were far more likely
to receive the death penalty, especially in Southern states such as Georgia,
Louisiana, Mississippi, and Texas, than whites convicted of murder. The
court refused to accept such evidence, however, arguing that each case
should be judged solely on its merits and not on statistics. The court outlawed the death penalty for a short time in the 1970s, but reinstated it in
1978. Marshall served on the court until July 1991, when he retired a few
days before his 83rd birthday. A few months before he died a reporter
asked Marshall how he wished to be remembered. He said he wanted
people to say simply, "He did the best he could with what he had." Justice
Marshall died on January 24, 1993, in his home state of Maryland.

Rosa Louise McCauley Parks
(February 4, 1913–October 24, 2005)

Rosa Parks, the granddaughter of former slaves, was born in Tuskegee,
Alabama, but grew up in Montgomery, the state capital. Her parents were
James McCauley, a carpenter, and Leona McCauley, a schoolteacher in a

small rural elementary school outside of Montgomery. Educated in Montgomery's segregated school system, she then attended all-black Alabama State College. She married Raymond Parks, a barber, in 1932. Rosa and her husband became active in the Montgomery branch of the National Association for the Advancement of Colored People (NAACP), volunteering to help free the nine young African Americans convicted of raping two white women on a train near Scottsboro in 1931. During the "Scottsboro Boys" controversy, Rosa became the NAACP's youth advisor in Montgomery, and her husband raised money in the city's black community to help pay for the many court appeals raised by the "Boys" defense team. During World War II, Rosa Parks worked with E. D. Nixon, the president of the Alabama NAACP, on a voter registration drive. In 1943, she became the secretary of the Montgomery branch.

After the war, Rosa Parks worked as a seamstress at the Montgomery Fair department store and part-time in the home of Virginia and Clifford Durr, white liberals who supported her efforts with the NAACP. In early 1955, Parks received a scholarship to attend the Highlander Folk School in Monteagle, Tennessee, spending several weeks attending a seminar on how to promote school integration in the Jim Crow South. Upon returning to Montgomery, she went back to her job at the department store. She rode the same segregated bus every morning and evening, following the rules for black passengers. She boarded the bus and paid her fare in the front like other African Americans. After paying their fare, however, blacks had to leave the bus and go to the rear door, where they could enter again and find a seat in the "colored section." White bus drivers frequently harassed black passengers, many times driving past a stop where African Americans were waiting rather than letting them board. Bus drivers in Alabama had the power to arrest riders who they considered unruly or potential troublemakers. During rush hours, drivers could also tell black customers to move further to the rear if there were not enough seats for white riders. The rear of the buses frequently became overcrowded and overheated as blacks continued to be pushed towards the back of the bus.

On December 1, 1955, on her way home Parks took her seat in the "colored section" with other black passengers. When the driver came back and asked Parks and three other blacks to get up and move further toward the rear so white passengers could sit down, she refused. The other three blacks got up and obeyed the driver's order. (Parks later explained that she was really too tired that day to move. She had not planned to deliberately violate the segregation law.) The driver called the police and had her taken to jail. Later that night E. D. Nixon and the Durrs paid her $100 bond and she was released.

The NAACP in Montgomery had been looking for an opportunity to challenge the law mandating segregated seating on public transportation. Once before in 1955 a black woman had been arrested for refusing to relinquish her seat, but NAACP leaders did not feel she was of high enough personal character to sponsor in court. (She had recently given birth to a child out of wedlock.) Rosa Parks was different: a hard-working, married, churchgoing woman, who was a model for her community. The day after her arrest Parks agreed to let the NAACP represent her in court. On December 5, a judge in the city court convicted her of breaking the law and fined her $14, which she refused to pay. Instead her lawyer appealed her conviction to the county circuit court.

While Parks was in court that December morning, a one-day bus boycott sponsored by the Women's Political Council (WPC) had begun. WPC leader Jo Ann Robinson had organized the boycott and felt overwhelmed by its unexpected success. The normally crowded city buses rode through the streets virtually empty. That evening, several thousand Montgomery blacks met at the Holt Street Baptist Church to discuss what further action to take. They created the Montgomery Improvement Association (MIA) and elected Reverend Dr. Martin Luther King as its president. They also decided to continue the boycott until the bus company ended segregation. Three hundred and eighty-one days later the MIA achieved its goal. The bus company backed down and removed its "colored section" signs from all of its buses and even hired its first two African American drivers. During the boycott more than 42,000 African Americans walked, shared cars, were picked up by their white employers, or took taxis rather than ride the segregated buses. Rosa Parks's defiant act had begun a successful protest that ended Jim Crow transportation in Montgomery.

Because of the threats and harassment she and her husband received during the boycott, they moved to Detroit, Michigan. The couple struggled financially for several years until African American congressman John Conyers Jr. hired Rosa Parks to work on his staff in his Detroit office. In 2004, she was diagnosed with progressive dementia. She died in Detroit in 2005. Her courageous action in 1955 earned her the title of "the mother of the civil rights movement." When she refused to give up her seat, one civil rights leader suggested, "somewhere in the universe a gear in the machinery had shifted."

Primary Documents

Booker T. Washington's "Atlanta Compromise Speech"
Source: Booker T. Washington, "Atlanta Exposition Speech," September 18, 1895.
Booker T. Washington Papers, Manuscript Division, Library of Congress, Washington, D.C.

On September 18, 1895, Booker T. Washington delivered his famous "Atlanta Compromise" speech at the Cotton States and International Exposition in Atlanta, Georgia. Washington, principal of the Tuskegee Institute in Alabama, was the only African American asked to address the exposition. Its goals were to increase trade between the cotton-growing states of the United States and the nations of South America and Europe. There were exhibits demonstrating the latest developments in agriculture, manufacturing, and mining along with special buildings devoted to the accomplishments of Southern women and African Americans. The three-month exposition attracted almost 800,000 visitors, despite many financial problems.

Washington discussed what many Southerners referred to as the "Negro problem" in the United States, specifically the relationships between blacks and whites in the economically depressed South. He ignored the lynching epidemic that afflicted the Jim Crow states—at least 113 African Americans died at the hands of lynch mobs in the South the year he spoke—and chose not to address the movement to deny African Americans the right to vote in the region because he did not want to offend the "good whites" in his audience. Instead he focused on developing a black business community and promoting industrial education for black youth as the best methods of improving race relations in the region. If African Americans devoted their lives to hard work and economic advancement, instead of demanding political rights, as many other black leaders seemed to advocate, good whites would recognize their abilities, and they would eventually be granted social and political equality. It was a message perfectly attuned to the expectations and attitudes of the white audience listening to his speech. To many members of the African American community, it seemed to be a surrender rather than a compromise. Washington's audience in Atlanta gave him a standing ovation when he completed his speech.

Mr. President, Gentlemen of the Board of Directors and Citizens:

One third of the population of the South is of the Negro race. No enterprise seeking the material, civil or moral welfare of this section can disregard this element of our population and reach the highest success. I but convey to you, Mr. President and Directors, the sentiment of the masses of my race, when I say that in no way have the value and [manhood] of the America Negro been more fittingly and generously recognized, than by the managers of this magnificent Exposition at every stage of its progress. It is a recognition which will do more to cement the friendship of the two races than any occurrence since the dawn of our freedom.

Not only this, but the opportunity here afforded will awaken among us a new era of industrial progress. Ignorant and inexperienced, it is not strange that in the first years of our new life we began at the top instead of the bottom, that a seat in Congress or the State Legislature was more sought than real-estate or industrial skill, that the political convention or stump speaking had more attractions [than] starting a dairy farm or truck garden.

A ship lost at sea for many days suddenly sighted a friendly vessel. From the mast of the unfortunate vessel was seen the signal: "Water, water, we die of thirst." The answer from the friendly vessel at once came back, "Cast down your bucket where you are." . . . The captain of the distressed vessel, at last heeding the injunction, cast down his bucket and it came up full of fresh, sparkling water from the mouth of the Amazon River. To those of my race who depend on bettering their condition in a foreign land, or who underestimate the importance of cultivating friendly relations with the Southern white man who is their next door neighbor, I would say cast down your bucket where you are[;] cast it down in making friends in every manly way of the people of all races by whom we are surrounded.

Cast it down in agriculture, in mechanics, in commerce, in domestic service and in the professions. And in this connection it is well to bear in mind that whatever other sins the South may be called upon to bear, that when it comes to business pure and simple, it is in the South that the Negro is given a man's chance in the commercial world, and in nothing is this Exposition more eloquent than in emphasizing this chance.

Our greatest danger is that in the great leap from slavery to freedom we may overlook the fact that the masses of us are to live by the productions of our hands, and fail to keep in mind that we shall prosper in proportion as we learn to dignify and glorify common labor and put brains and skill into the common occupations of life . . . No race can prosper till it learns that there is as much dignity in tilling a field as in writing a poem. It is at the bottom of life we must begin and not the top. Nor should we permit our grievances to overshadow our opportunities.

To those of the white race who look to the incoming of those of foreign birth and strange tongue and habits for the prosperity of the South, were I permitted, I would repeat what I say to my own race. "Cast down your bucket where you are." Cast it down among the 8,000,000 Negroes whose habits you know, whose loyalty and love you have tested in days when to have proved treacherous [meant] the ruin of your firesides.

Cast it down among these people who have without strikes and labor wars tilled your fields, cleared your forests, built your railroads and cities, and brought forth treasures from the bowels of the earth and helped make possible this magnificent representation of the progress of the South. Casting down your bucket [among] my people, helping and encouraging them as you are doing on these grounds, and to [the] education of head, hand, and heart, you will find that they will buy your surplus land, make blossom the waste places in your fields, and run your factories.

While doing this you can be sure in the future, as you have been in the past, that you and your families will be surrounded by the most patient, faithful, law-abiding and unresentful people that the world has seen. As we have proven our loyalty to you in the past, in nursing your children, watching by the sick bed of your mothers and fathers, and often following them with tear dimmed eyes to their graves, so in the future in our humble way, we shall stand by you with a devotion that no foreigner can approach, ready to lay down our lives, if need be, in defense of yours, interlacing our industrial, commercial, civil and religious life with yours in a way that shall make the interests of both races one. In all things that are purely social we can be as separate as the fingers, yet one as the hand in all things essential to mutual progress.

There is no defense or security for any of us except in the highest intelligence and development of all. If anywhere there are efforts tending to curtail the fullest growth of the Negro, let these efforts be turned into stimulating, encouraging and making him the most useful and intelligent citizen. Effort or means so invested will pay a thousand per cent interest. These efforts will be twice blessed—"Blessing him that gives and him that takes."

Nearly sixteen millions of hands will aid you [in] pulling the load upwards, or they will pull against you the load downwards. We shall constitute one third and much more of the ignorance and crime of the South or one third [of] its intelligence and progress, we shall contribute one third to the business and industrial prosperity of the South, or we shall prove a veritable body of death, stagnating, depressing, retarding every effort to advance the body politic.

The wisest among my race understand that the agitation of questions of social equality is the [extremist] folly and that progress in the enjoyment of all the privileges that will come to us, must be the result of severe and [constant] struggle, rather than of artificial forcing. . . . It is important and right that all privileges of the law be ours, but it is vastly more important that we be prepared for the exercise of these privileges. The opportunity to earn a dollar in a factory just now is worth infinitely more than the opportunity to spend a dollar in an opera house.

Jim Crow Laws: A Sampling from Various Southern States

Source: National Park Service, Martin Luther King Jr. National Historic Site. http://www.nps.gov/malu/forteachers/jim_crow_laws.htm

From 1882, when Tennessee passed a law mandating segregation on railroad trains, until 1964, when the Civil Rights Act of that year outlawed such laws, a majority of states in the United States required segregation in a variety of places where members of the public were most likely to meet, from parks to restaurants to prison cells. Up to 1954, when the Supreme Court declared the practice unconstitutional in the famous Brown v. Board of Education *decision, 17 different states demanded segregated schools, including all 11 states of the Old Confederacy. It was in those 11 states that Jim Crow laws were most rigorously enforced. The laws listed below segregate everything from circuses to hospitals to schools, and even to telephone booths. At the end of each example, the name of the state in which the law was imposed is listed. It should be remembered that Jim Crow laws extended far beyond separating U.S. citizens in public places, because they included laws that prevented African Americans from voting and laws that kept black Americans from marrying white Americans. Jim Crow laws established an entire legal system dedicated to making African Americans second-class citizens, without any of the constitutional rights, freedoms, and protections offered to the white majority. Until 1954, of course, the U.S. Supreme Court held that almost all of such laws were protected by the Constitution. Individual Americans had the right to discriminate on the basis of skin color, as the court had ruled in 1883 when it declared the Civil Rights Act of 1875 unconstitutional.*

Nurses: No person or corporation shall require any white female nurse to nurse in wards or rooms in hospitals, either public or private, in which negro men are placed. *Alabama*

Buses: All passenger stations in this state operated by any motor transportation company shall have separate waiting rooms or space and separate ticket windows for the white and colored races. *Alabama*

Railroads: The conductor of each passenger train is authorized and required to assign each passenger to the car or the division of the car, when it is divided by a partition, designated for the race to which such passenger belongs. *Alabama*

Restaurants: It shall be unlawful to conduct a restaurant or other place for the serving of food in the city, at which white and colored people are served in the same room, unless such white and colored persons are effectually separated by a solid partition extending from the floor upward to a distance of seven feet or higher, and unless a separate entrance from the street is provided for each compartment. *Alabama*

Pool and Billiard Rooms: It shall be unlawful for a negro and white person to play together or in company with each other at any game of pool or billiards. *Alabama*

Toilet Facilities, Male: Every employer of white or negro males shall provide for such white or negro males reasonably accessible and separate toilet facilities. *Alabama*

Intermarriage: All marriages between a white person and a negro, or between a white person and a person of negro descent to the fourth generation inclusive, are hereby forever prohibited. *Florida*

Cohabitation: Any negro man and white woman, or any white man and negro woman, who are not married to each other, who shall habitually live in and occupy in the nighttime the same room shall each be punished by imprisonment not exceeding twelve (12) months, or by fine not exceeding five hundred ($500.00) dollars. *Florida*

Education: The schools for white children and the schools for negro children shall be conducted separately. *Florida*

Juvenile Delinquents: There shall be separate buildings, not nearer than one fourth mile to each other, one for white boys and one for negro boys. White boys and negro boys shall not, in any manner, be associated together or worked together. *Florida*

Mental Hospitals: The Board of Control shall see that proper and distinct apartments are arranged for said patients, so that in no case shall Negroes and white persons be together. *Georgia*

Intermarriage: It shall be unlawful for a white person to marry anyone except a white person. Any marriage in violation of this section shall be void. *Georgia*

Barbers: No colored barber shall serve as a barber [to] white women or girls. *Georgia*

Burial: The officer in charge shall not bury, or allow to be buried, any colored persons upon ground set apart or used for the burial of white persons. *Georgia*

Restaurants: All persons licensed to conduct a restaurant, shall serve either white people exclusively or colored people exclusively and shall not sell to the two races within the same room or serve the two races anywhere under the same license. *Georgia*

Amateur Baseball: It shall be unlawful for any amateur white baseball team to play baseball on any vacant lot or baseball diamond within two blocks of a playground devoted to the Negro race, and it shall be unlawful for any amateur colored baseball team to play baseball in any vacant lot or baseball diamond within two blocks of any playground devoted to the white race. *Georgia*

Parks: It shall be unlawful for colored people to frequent any park owned or maintained by the city for the benefit, use and enjoyment of white persons . . . and unlawful for any white person to frequent any park owned or maintained by the city for the use and benefit of colored persons. *Georgia*

Wine and Beer: All persons licensed to conduct the business of selling beer or wine . . . shall serve either white people exclusively or colored people exclusively and shall not sell to the two races within the same room at any time. *Georgia*

Reform Schools: The children of white and colored races committed to the houses of reform shall be kept entirely separate from each other. *Kentucky*

Circus Tickets: All circuses, shows, and tent exhibitions, to which the attendance of . . . more than one race is invited or expected to attend shall provide for the convenience of its patrons not less than two ticket offices with individual ticket sellers, and not less than two entrances to the said performance, with individual ticket takers and receivers, and in the case of outside or tent performances, the said ticket offices shall not be less than twenty-five (25) feet apart. *Louisiana*

Housing: Any person . . . who shall rent any part of any such building to a negro person or a negro family when such building is already in whole or in part in occupancy by a white person or white family, or vice versa when the building is in occupancy by a negro person or negro family, shall be guilty of a misdemeanor and on conviction thereof shall be punished by a fine of not less than twenty-five ($25.00) nor more than one hundred ($100.00) dollars or be imprisoned not less than 10, or more than 60 days, or both such fine and imprisonment in the discretion of the court. *Louisiana*

The Blind: The board of trustees shall ... maintain a separate building ... on separate ground for the admission, care, instruction, and support of all blind persons of the colored or black race. *Louisiana*

Intermarriage: All marriages between a white person and a negro, or between a white person and a person of negro descent, to the third generation, inclusive, or between a white person and a member of the Malay race; or between the negro and a member of the Malay race; or between a person of Negro descent, to the third generation, inclusive, and a member of the Malay race, are forever prohibited, and shall be void. *Maryland*

Railroads: All railroad companies and corporations, and all persons running or operating cars or coaches by steam on any railroad line or track in the State of Maryland, for the transportation of passengers, are hereby required to provide separate cars or coaches for the travel and transportation of the white and colored passengers. *Maryland*

Education: Separate schools shall be maintained for the children of the white and colored races. *Mississippi*

Promotion of Equality: Any person ... who shall be guilty of printing, publishing or circulating printed, typewritten or written matter urging or presenting for public acceptance or general information, arguments or suggestions in favor of social equality or of intermarriage between whites and negroes, shall be guilty of a misdemeanor and subject to fine not exceeding five hundred (500.00) dollars or imprisonment not exceeding six (6) months or both. *Mississippi*

Intermarriage: The marriage of a white person with a negro or mulatto or person who shall have one-eighth or more of negro blood, shall be unlawful and void. *Mississippi*

Hospital Entrances: There shall be maintained by the governing authorities of every hospital maintained by the state for treatment of white and colored patients separate entrances for white and colored patients and visitors, and such entrances shall be used by the race only for which they are prepared. *Mississippi*

Prisons: The warden shall see that the white convicts shall have separate apartments for both eating and sleeping from the negro convicts. *Mississippi*

Textbooks: Books shall not be interchangeable between the white and colored schools, but shall continue to be used by the race first using them. *North Carolina*

Libraries: The state librarian is directed to fit up and maintain a separate place for the use of the colored people who may come to the library for the purpose of reading books or periodicals. *North Carolina*

Militia: The white and colored militia shall be separately enrolled, and shall never be compelled to serve in the same organization. No organization of colored troops shall be permitted where white troops are available, and while permitted to be organized, colored troops shall be under the command of white officers. *North Carolina*

Transportation: The . . . Utilities Commission . . . is empowered and directed to require the establishment of separate waiting rooms at all stations for the white and colored races. *North Carolina*

Teaching: Any instructor who shall teach in any school, college or institution where members of the white and colored race are received and enrolled as pupils for instruction shall be deemed guilty of a misdemeanor, and upon conviction thereof, shall be fined in any sum not less than ten dollars ($10.00) nor more than fifty dollars ($50.00) for each offense. *Oklahoma*

Fishing, Boating, and Bathing: The [Conservation] Commission shall have the right to make segregation of the white and colored races as to the exercise of rights of fishing, boating and bathing. *Oklahoma*

Mining: The baths and lockers for the negroes shall be separate from the white race, but may be in the same building. *Oklahoma*

Telephone Booths: The Corporation Commission is hereby vested with power and authority to require telephone companies . . . to maintain separate booths for white and colored patrons when there is a demand for such separate booths. That the Corporation Commission shall determine the necessity for said separate booths only upon complaint of the people in the town and vicinity to be served after due hearing as now provided by law in other complaints filed with the Corporation Commission. *Oklahoma*

Lunch Counters: No persons, firms, or corporations, who or which furnish meals to passengers at station restaurants or station eating houses, in times limited by common carriers of said passengers, shall furnish said meals to white and colored passengers in the same room, or at the same table, or at the same counter. *South Carolina*

Child Custody: It shall be unlawful for any parent, relative, or other white person in this State, having the control or custody of any white child, by right of guardianship, natural or acquired, or otherwise, to dispose of, give or surrender such white child permanently into the custody, control, maintenance, or support, of a negro. *South Carolina*

Libraries: Any white person of such county may use the county free library under the rules and regulations prescribed by the commissioner's court and may be entitled to all the privileges thereof. Said court shall make proper provision for the negroes of said county to be served through a separate branch or branches of the county free library, which shall be administered by [a] custodian of the negro race under the supervision of the county librarian. *Texas*

Education: [The County Board of Education] shall provide schools of two kinds: those for white children and those for colored children. *Texas*

Theaters: Every person . . . operating . . . any public hall, theatre, opera house, motion picture show or any place of public entertainment or public assemblage which is attended by both white and colored persons, shall separate the white race and the colored race and shall set apart and designate . . . certain seats therein to be occupied by white persons and a portion thereof, or certain seats therein, to be occupied by colored persons. *Virginia*

Railroads: The conductors or managers on all such railroads shall have power, and are hereby required, to assign to each white or colored passenger his or her respective car, coach or compartment. If the passenger fails to disclose his race, the conductor and managers, acting in good faith, shall be the sole judges of his race. *Virginia*

Furnifold M. Simmons

Source: "Chairman F. M. Simmons Issues a Patriotic and Able Address, Summing Up the Issues, and Appealing Eloquently to the White Voters To Redeem the State," *News and Observer* (Raleigh, NC), November 3, 1898. Available online at the North Carolina Collection, University of North Carolina Libraries, Chapel Hill. http:// www.lib.unc.edu/ncc/1898/sources/tothevoters.html

The election of 1898 in North Carolina was an extraordinary campaign in which the Democratic Party regained control of the governor's office and the state legislature after disastrous losses in 1894 and 1896. In those two campaigns the Republican Party and the radical Farmer's Alliance had formed a "Fusionist" coalition, which won control of all state offices, including the state supreme court and superior courts, seven out of nine seats in the U.S. House of Representatives, and both seats in the U.S. Senate. In response in 1898, state Democratic Party chairman Furnifold Simmons, son of a wealthy plantation owner, led a campaign based on race appealing to voters of "Anglo-Saxon blood" to come together to defeat the threat of "Negro domination" posed by another Fusionist victory. In the following speech given shortly after Election Day, Simmons traced the history of the campaign. Two issues enabled the Democratic victory: scandals during the Fusionist years in power and white fear that another Fusionist victory would allow "ignorant, non-taxpaying negroes" to take control of the state. He pointed to the riot in Wilmington, North Carolina, the day after the election, in which white mobs killed eight blacks to overturn a black victory in the city election as an example of what might happen in the future in North Carolina had the Fusionists remained in power. The Democrats did not lose this election. The appeal to racism had worked. This speech contains the general fears and warnings expressed by white politicians throughout their successful campaigns to disfranchise black voters. Furnifold later served five terms in the U.S. Senate (1901–1931).

... In the midst of all this din and conflict, there came a voice from the East, like the wail of Egypt's midnight cry. It was not the voice of despair, but of rage. A proud race, which had never known a master, which had never bent the neck to the yoke of any other race, by the irresistible power of fusion laws and fusion legislation had been placed under the control and domination of that race which ranks lowest, save one, in the human family.

The business of two of the largest and most prosperous cities in the State had been paralyzed by the blight of negro domination.

In another city a white majority had been discriminated against in favor of a black minority, and the white man, who bore all the burdens and expense of government, had been given only one-half the representation of the ignorant and non-taxpaying negro.

WHITE WOMEN, of pure Anglo-Saxon blood, had been arrested upon groundless charges, by negro constables, and arraigned and tried and sentenced by negro magistrates.

Finally, as a result of the insolence and aggressiveness which his sudden elevation to power had engendered in the negro, a leader and representative of that race, dared openly and publicly to assail the virtue of our pure WHITE WOMAN-HOOD. Suddenly the venality, the corruption in office, the extravagance, the peculation of funds, and the miserable scandals that had disgraced the State, passed out of the public mind, and in a whirl of indignation, which burst forth like the lava from the pent-up volcano, there was thrust to the front the all-absorbing and paramount question of WHITE SUPREMACY.

Frantically, the Fusion leaders thought to stay the storm of indignation, which swept like a tornado over the State.

In their desperation, the Fusionists had recourse to their old device of denial, of evasion, of subterfuge. They said it was the "old negro racket;" they said there was no truth in it; they said there might be a negro officer here and there, but they held only minor offices and insignificant places; that the East had no cause of grievance; that it was all a baseless clamor for political effect.

Then came the evidence, disclosing the actual condition of affairs, in that section of the State, which astonished and shocked the consciences and moral sensibilities of the people.

NEGRO CONGRESSMEN, NEGRO SOLICITORS, NEGRO REVENUE OFFICERS, NEGRO COLLECTORS OF CUSTOMS, NEGROES in charge of white institutions, NEGROES in charge of white schools, NEGROES holding inquests over the white dead, NEGROES controlling the finances of great cities, NEGROES in control of the sanitation and police of cities, NEGRO CONSTABLES arresting white women and white men, NEGRO MAGISTRATES trying white women and white men, white convicts chained to NEGRO CONVICTS and forced to social equality with them, until the proofs rose up, and stood forth "like Pelion on Ossa piled."

Before this overwhelming array of evidence, the weak and puny wall of defense set up by the apologists of negro rule, crumbled away, and then there came the collapse. They had seen the handwriting on the wall. Everywhere they read in the face of the brave and chivalrous white men of the State, a cool, calm, fixed resolution and determination that these things must stop; that hereafter white men should make and administer the laws; that negro supremacy would forever end in North Carolina.

Men of less determination and less desperation than the leaders of Fusion in North Carolina, would have quietly submitted to this inexorable decree of the WHITE RACE; but they did not. One recourse was left to them. With a strange fatality they seized upon it. If WHITE MEN would not quietly submit to negro domination, then they determined to force them to submit. The arm of the Federal Government was invoked for this purpose. Armed troops were asked to be sent here to force the WHITE PEOPLE of the State, at the point of the bayonet, to submit to the continuance of conditions which to the Anglo-Saxon are worse than death. But where his honor and his conscience are concerned, the Anglo-Saxon fears not the power of mortal man. Louder and still louder, they proclaimed their defiance. Closer, and still closer, from Currituck to Cherokee, from Wilmington to Asheville, from Newbern to grand old Mecklenburg, the sympathy of blood brought WHITE PEOPLE together, until party lines and past party affiliations were wiped out, and men grown old in the service of the Republican party, men who had been strongly rooted in the faith of the Populist party, from one end of the State to the other, gave their adherence to the cause of WHITE SUPREMACY and pledged their faith to their brethren in the East, despite Federal bayonet and executive proclamation, to redeem that fair section of the State from the reign and domination of the negro. And now, right on the eve of the election, after three months of frantic denial that there was negro domination in the East, these desperate men, at last aroused to a realization that they can no longer deceive and humbug the people, and that their fate is settled, begin a process of taking down the wretched creatures, whom they had sought in some counties, to elect to office over the white people of the East, and with humble apologies (thereby admitting all the charges of negro domination that the Democrats have made), ask the white people whom they had sought to put in subjection to the black man to forget the wrongs they had done them, and compromise the issue with them by agreeing to support a mongrel ticket. But there are some things which white men who are white men do not compromise, as this whole array of office-traders are at last beginning to discover.

Driven from every position of defense, disappointed in their hope of intimidating and coercing the people into submitting to their scheme of negro domination, the desperate men, who are now at the head of affairs in North Carolina, and who are running the Fusion campaign, have still one reliance left. Their last hope is a large corruption fund, which they have extorted from Mark Hanna, the financial agent of the monopolists of the United States, under assurances which they have given him, that if they could carry the State this year it will be easier to carry the State for McKinley in 1900. With this corruption fund they still hope to save something from the wreck. They hope to import negroes from the North and South of us, to buy up votes, to procure fraudulent and illegal voting, and otherwise to obtain by various means enough votes to control one branch of the Legislature, and thus block the efforts of the people to reverse the horrible conditions of the past two years. This hope will also prove delusive. If their corruption fund were TEN FOLD as large as it is, they could not bribe the sturdy manhood of North Carolina to longer submit to negro domination.

The battle has been fought, the victory is within our reach. North Carolina is a WHITE MAN'S State, and WHITE MEN will rule it, and they will crush the party of negro domination beneath a majority so overwhelming that no other party will ever again dare to attempt to establish negro rule here.

They CANNOT intimidate us; they CANNOT buy us, and they SHALL NOT cheat us out of the fruits of our victory.

The Democratic party has appealed in this campaign to the highest aspirations of the people. It has appealed to their patriotism, to their manhood, to their pride of race, to their immemorial custom and habit of ruling every other race with which they come into contact, to their self-interest, to the peace and happiness of the family, of the home, of the fireside, in the name of good government, in the name of peace and amity between the races, in the name of religion and, finally, in the name of civilization itself. It has promised fair and just laws, it has promised to all peace and security; it has promised good government, it has promised protection to property, protection to life, protection to virtue; and it has promised to undo the wrongs which have been done to our brethren in the East. It will faithfully keep and perform every promise it has made.

What good thing does the enemy promise in this contest? What measure of relief does he advocate? What principle does he stand for? Nay, verily, NOTHING, except the perpetuation of his own power and the retention of the offices which the people were deceived into bestowing upon him. In these circumstances am I not warranted in appealing to the good people of North Carolina, without regard to past party affiliations, to go to the polls next TUESDAY, and cast their votes for the success of the Democratic ticket, State, county and National?

It has been a great fight. The issues involved are pregnant with the momentous consequences to the people and State. In view of the present terrible crisis; in view of the incalculable consequences to follow to us and to our children from failure to redeem the State from the rule of the men who have debauched and despoiled it, I feel justified in appealing to all good men to close their places of business on the day of election and give that day, exclusively, earnestly, solemnly, to the State and the great cause for which we struggle.

"Of Mr. Booker T. Washington and Others" by W. E. B. DuBois

Source: "Of Mr. Booker T. Washington and Others," in *The Souls of Black Folk*, by W. E. B. DuBois (1903), revised from "The Evolution of Negro Leadership," *The Dial* (July 16, 1901).

In his famous book of essays published in 1903, The Souls of Black Folk, *W. E. B. DuBois included, "Of Mr. Booker T. Washington and Others," an angry analysis of Washington's accommodationist approach to racial prejudice and inequality in the United States. In it he objected to Washington's belief that "economic development" should be the goal for blacks in the Jim Crow South rather than the pursuit of "the higher aims of life," such as art, philosophy, music, or full political equality. He accused Washington of accepting the racial "inferiority" of the people he represented, his own people. In DuBois's view, blacks would never achieve economic equality until they had gained their full constitutional and political rights.*

DuBois singled out Washington's assertion that "the masses of us are to live by the production of our hands." No thought could have pleased white supremacists more than the Wizard of Tuskegee's contention that blacks were fit only for lives of farming and common labor. Rather than poets and philosophers, African Americans put their "brains and skill" into mastering "the common occupations of life," such as farming, shoemaking, and shoe-shining, thereby showing the white race that they could work hard and achieve as much as they had achieved. For DuBois, that idea was insulting and degrading. Blacks could better demonstrate their abilities, dedication, and hard work by committing themselves to the pursuit of scientific discoveries, intellectual greatness, and literary and cultural achievement. Washington's way, according to DuBois and other critics, led only to lives of second-class citizenship in a country dedicated to the principles of inequality and inferiority. DuBois could not accept accommodation to such a life for himself or members of his race. Accommodationism led only to more lynching and more intimidation. Human beings could not live facing common threats like that with dignity and glory.

Mr. Washington represents in Negro thought the old attitude of adjustment and submission; but adjustment at such a peculiar time as to make his program unique. This is an age of unusual economic development, and Mr. Washington's program naturally takes an economic cast, becoming a gospel of Work and Money to such an extent as apparently almost completely to overshadow the higher aims of life. Moreover, this is an age when the more advanced races are coming in closer contact with the less developed races, and the race-feeling is therefore intensified; and Mr. Washington's program practically accepts the alleged inferiority of the Negro races. Again, in our own land, the reaction from the sentiment of war time has given impetus to race-prejudice against Negroes, and Mr. Washington withdraws many of the high demands of Negroes as men and American citizens. In other periods of intensified prejudice all the Negro's tendency to self-assertion has been called forth; at this period a policy of submission is advocated. In the history of nearly all other races and peoples the doctrine preached at such crises has been that manly self-respect is worth more than lands and houses, and that a people who voluntarily surrender such respect, or cease striving for it, are not worth civilizing.

In answer to this, it has been claimed that the Negro can survive only through submission. Mr. Washington distinctly asks that black people give up, at least for the present, three things,—

First, political power,
Second, insistence on civil rights,
Third, higher education of Negro youth,—

and concentrate all their energies on industrial education, the accumulation of wealth, and the conciliation of the South. This policy has been courageously and insistently advocated for over fifteen years, and has been triumphant for perhaps ten years. As a result of this tender of the palm-branch, what has been the return? In these years there have occurred:

The disfranchisement of the Negro.
The legal creation of a distinct status of civil inferiority for the Negro.
The steady withdrawal of aid from institutions for the higher training of the Negro.

These movements are not, to be sure, direct results of Mr. Washington's teachings; but his propaganda has, without a shadow of doubt, helped their speedier accomplishment. The question then comes: Is it possible, and probable, that nine millions of men can make effective progress in economic lines if they are deprived of political rights, made a servile caste, and allowed only the most meager chance for developing their exceptional men? If history and reason give any distinct answer to these questions, it is an emphatic *No.* And Mr. Washington thus faces the triple paradox of his career:

He is striving nobly to make Negro artisans business men and property-owners; but it is utterly impossible, under modern competitive methods, for working-men and property-owners to defend their rights and exist without the right of suffrage.
He insists on thrift and self-respect, but at the same time counsels a silent submission to civic inferiority such as is bound to sap the manhood of any race in the long run.
He advocates common-school and industrial training, and depreciates institutions of higher learning; but neither the Negro common-schools, nor Tuskegee itself, could remain open a day were it not for teachers trained in Negro colleges, or trained by their graduates.

This triple paradox in Mr. Washington's position is the object of criticism by two classes of colored Americans. One class is spiritually descended from Toussaint the Savior, through Gabriel, Vesey, and Turner, and they represent the attitude of revolt and revenge; they hate the white South blindly and distrust the white race generally, and so far as they agree on definite action, think that the Negro's only hope lies in emigration beyond the borders of the United States. And yet, by the irony of fate, nothing has more effectually made this program seem hopeless than the recent course of the United States toward weaker and darker peoples in the West Indies, Hawaii, and the Philippines,—for where in the world may we go and be safe from lying and brute force?

The other class of Negroes who cannot agree with Mr. Washington has hitherto said little aloud. They deprecate the sight of scattered counsels, of internal disagreement; and especially they dislike making their just criticism of a useful and earnest man an excuse for a general discharge of venom from small-minded opponents. Nevertheless, the questions involved are so fundamental and serious that it is difficult to see how men like the Grimkes, Kelly Miller, J. W. E. Bowen, and other representatives of this group, can much longer be silent. Such men feel in conscience bound to ask of this nation three things:

The right to vote.
Civic equality.
The education of youth according to ability.

They acknowledge Mr. Washington's invaluable service in counseling patience and courtesy in such demands; they do not ask that ignorant black men vote when ignorant whites are debarred, or that any reasonable restrictions in the suffrage should not be applied; they know that the low social level of the mass of the race is responsible for much discrimination against it, but they also know, and the nation knows, that relentless color-prejudice is more often a cause than a result of the Negro's degradation; they seek the abatement of this relic of barbarism, and not its systematic encouragement and pampering by all agencies of social power from the Associated Press to the Church of Christ. They advocate, with Mr. Washington, a broad system of Negro common schools supplemented by thorough industrial training; but they are surprised that a man of Mr. Washington's insight cannot see that no such educational system ever has rested or can rest on any other basis than that of the well-equipped college and university, and they insist that there is a demand for a few such institutions throughout the South to train the best of the Negro youth as teachers, professional men, and leaders.

This group of men honor Mr. Washington for his attitude of conciliation toward the white South; they accept the "Atlanta Compromise" in its broadest interpretation; they recognize, with him, many signs of promise, many men of high purpose and fair judgment, in this section; they know that no easy task has been laid upon a region already tottering under heavy burdens. But, nevertheless, they insist that the way to truth and right lies in straightforward honesty, not in indiscriminate flattery; in praising those of the South who do well and criticizing uncompromisingly those who do ill; in taking advantage of the opportunities at hand and urging their fellows to do the same, but at the same time in remembering that only a firm adherence to their higher ideals and aspirations will ever keep those ideals within the realm of possibility. They do not expect that the free right to vote, to enjoy civic rights, and to be educated, will come in a moment; they do not expect to see the bias and prejudices of years disappear at the blast of a trumpet; but they are absolutely certain that the way for a people to gain their reasonable rights is not by voluntarily throwing them away and insisting that they do not want them; that the way for a people to gain respect is not by continually belittling and ridiculing themselves; that, on the contrary, Negroes must insist continually, in season and out of season, that voting is necessary to modern manhood, that color discrimination is barbarism, and that black boys need education as well as white boys.

In failing thus to state plainly and unequivocally the legitimate demands of their people, even at the cost of opposing an honored leader, the thinking classes of American Negroes would shirk a heavy responsibility,—a responsibility to themselves, a responsibility to the struggling masses, a responsibility to the darker races of men whose future depends so largely on this American experiment, but especially a responsibility to this nation,—this common Fatherland. It is wrong to encourage a man or a people in evil-doing; it is wrong to aid and abet a national crime simply because it is unpopular not to do so. The growing spirit of kindliness and reconciliation between the North and South after the frightful differences of a generation ago ought to be a source of deep congratulation to all, and especially to those whose mistreatment caused the war; but if that reconciliation is to be marked by the industrial slavery and civic death of those same black men, with permanent legislation into a position of inferiority, then those black men, if they are really men, are called upon by every consideration of patriotism and loyalty to oppose such a course by all civilized methods, even though such opposition involves disagreement with Mr. Booker T. Washington. We have no right to sit silently by while the inevitable seeds are sown for a harvest of disaster to our children, black and white.

Brown v. Board of Education of Topeka

Source: *Brown v. Board of Education*, 347 U.S. 483 (1954).

The Supreme Court heard the first arguments over the cases combined in Brown *in December 1952, but the court never took a formal vote on the issue. When the new chief justice, Earl Warren, took over the court, he presided over a reargument of the case in 1953. At the justices' first meeting concerning the case, he explained that he wanted the court's opinion to be unanimous and written so that it could be understood by the public. He would write the opinion by himself, and it met both of his desires. The justices voted 9–0 to overturn* Plessy v. Ferguson, *accepting the chief justice's plea that the court could not turn back to 1896 and allow segregation. Public schooling in the modern world played a much greater role in the lives of Americans than it had in the late nineteenth century. In his opinion Warren argued that equality required more than simply making sure that the school buildings and the schoolbooks were relatively the same. The court also had to consider "intangible factors" when defining equality, such the psychological impact of sending students to different schools simply because of their skin color. In a footnote, he cited several studies by psychologists indicating that the impact was negative, especially on the minds of the minority. He convinced the two justices who seemed reluctant to join in his opinion that a divided court would only encourage resistance to the court's ruling. The decision not to order immediate desegregation came from the fear expressed by most justices that such a demand would only inspire violence and opposition. They also believed that liberal white Southerners would be able to somehow convince the white people in their states to accept integration if they were given enough time to prepare them for it. In this assumption the justices proved to be overly optimistic. A majority of Southern whites refused to accept the* Brown *decision for a very long time, and when they did they began to build all-white "Christian" schools for their children.*

APPEAL FROM THE UNITED STATES DISTRICT COURT FOR THE DISTRICT OF KANSAS*
Decided May 17, 1954
MR. CHIEF JUSTICE WARREN delivered the opinion of the Court.

These cases come to us from the States of Kansas, South Carolina, Virginia, and Delaware. They are premised on different facts and different local conditions, but a common legal question justifies their consideration together in this consolidated opinion.[1]

In each of the cases, minors of the Negro race, through their legal representatives, seek the aid of the courts in obtaining admission to the public schools of their community on a nonsegregated basis. In each instance, [p488] they had been denied admission to schools attended by white children under laws requiring or permitting segregation according to race. This segregation was alleged to deprive the plaintiffs of the equal protection of the laws under the Fourteenth Amendment. In each of the cases other than the Delaware case, a three-judge federal district court denied relief to the plaintiffs on the so-called "separate but equal" doctrine announced by this Court in *Plessy v. Ferguson*, 163 U.S. 537. Under that doctrine, equality of treatment is accorded when the races are provided substantially equal facilities, even though these facilities are separate. In the Delaware case, the Supreme Court of Delaware adhered to that doctrine, but ordered that the plaintiffs be admitted to the white schools because of their superiority to the Negro schools.

The plaintiffs contend that segregated public schools are not "equal" and cannot be made "equal," and that hence they are deprived of the equal protection of the laws. Because of the obvious importance of the question presented, the Court took jurisdiction.[2] Argument was heard in the 1952 Term, and reargument was heard this Term on certain questions propounded by the Court.[3]

Reargument was largely devoted to the circumstances surrounding the adoption of the Fourteenth Amendment in 1868. It covered exhaustively consideration of the Amendment in Congress, ratification by the states, then-existing practices in racial segregation, and the views of proponents and opponents of the Amendment. This discussion and our own investigation convince us that, although these sources cast some light, it is not enough to resolve the problem with which we are faced. At best, they are inconclusive. The most avid proponents of the post-War Amendments undoubtedly intended them to remove all legal distinctions among "all persons born or naturalized in the United States." Their opponents, just as certainly, were antagonistic to both the letter and the spirit of the Amendments and wished them to have the most limited effect. What others in Congress and the state legislatures had in mind cannot be determined with any degree of certainty.

An additional reason for the inconclusive nature of the Amendment's history with respect to segregated schools is the status of public education at that time.[4] In the South, the movement toward free common schools, supported [p490] by general taxation, had not yet taken hold. Education of white children was largely in the hands of private groups. Education of Negroes was almost nonexistent, and practically all of the race was illiterate. In fact, any education of Negroes was forbidden by law in some states. Today, in contrast, many Negroes have achieved outstanding success in the arts and sciences, as well as in the business and professional world. It is true that public school education at the time of the Amendment had advanced further in the North, but the effect of the Amendment on Northern States was generally ignored in the congressional debates. Even in the North, the conditions of public education did not approximate those existing today. The curriculum was usually rudimentary; ungraded schools were common in rural areas; the school term was but three months a year in many states, and compulsory school attendance was virtually unknown. As a consequence, it is not surprising that there should be so little in the history of the Fourteenth Amendment relating to its intended effect on public education.

In the first cases in this Court construing the Fourteenth Amendment, decided shortly after its adoption, the Court interpreted it as proscribing all state-imposed discriminations against the Negro race.[5] The doctrine of "separate but equal" did not make its appearance in this Court until 1896 in the case of *Plessy v. Ferguson, supra*, involving not education but transportation.[6] American courts have since labored with the doctrine for over half a century. In this Court, there have been six cases involving the "separate but equal" doctrine in the field of public education.[7] In *Cumming v. County Board of Education*, 175 U.S. 528, and *Gong Lum v. Rice*, 275 U.S. 78, the validity of the doctrine itself was not challenged.[8] In more recent cases, all on the graduate school level, inequality was found in that specific benefits enjoyed by white students were denied to Negro students of the same educational qualifications. *Missouri ex rel. Gaines v. Canada*, 305 U.S. 337; *Sipuel v. Oklahoma*, 332 U.S. 631; *Sweatt v. Painter*, 339 U.S. 629; *McLaurin v. Oklahoma State Regents*, 339 U.S. 637. In none of these cases was it necessary to reexamine the doctrine to grant relief to the Negro plaintiff. And in *Sweatt v. Painter, supra*, the Court expressly reserved decision on the question whether *Plessy v. Ferguson* should be held inapplicable to public education.

In the instant cases, that question is directly presented. Here, unlike *Sweatt v. Painter*, there are findings below that the Negro and white schools involved have been equalized, or are being equalized, with respect to buildings, curricula, qualifications and salaries of teachers, and other "tangible" factors.[9] Our decision, therefore, cannot turn on merely a comparison of these tangible factors in the Negro and white schools involved in each of the cases. We must look instead to the effect of segregation itself on public education.

In approaching this problem, we cannot turn the clock back to 1868, when the Amendment was adopted, or even to 1896, when *Plessy v. Ferguson* was written. We must consider public education in the light of its full development and its present place in American life throughout the Nation. Only in this way can it be determined if segregation in public schools deprives these plaintiffs of the equal protection of the laws.

Today, education is perhaps the most important function of state and local governments. Compulsory school attendance laws and the great expenditures for education both demonstrate our recognition of the importance of education to our democratic society. It is required in the performance of our most basic public responsibilities, even service in the armed forces. It is the very foundation of good citizenship. Today it is a principal instrument in awakening the child to cultural values, in preparing him for later professional training, and in helping him to adjust normally to his environment. In these days, it is doubtful that any child may reasonably be expected to succeed in life if he is denied the opportunity of an education. Such an opportunity, where the state has undertaken to provide it, is a right which must be made available to all on equal terms.

We come then to the question presented: Does segregation of children in public schools solely on the basis of race, even though the physical facilities and other "tangible" factors may be equal, deprive the children of the minority group of equal educational opportunities? We believe that it does.

In *Sweatt v. Painter, supra,* in finding that a segregated law school for Negroes could not provide them equal educational opportunities, this Court relied in large part on "those qualities which are incapable of objective measurement but which make for greatness in a law school." In *McLaurin v. Oklahoma State Regents, supra,* the Court, in requiring that a Negro admitted to a white graduate school be treated like all other students, again resorted to intangible considerations: "... his ability to study, to engage in discussions and exchange views with other students, and, in general, to learn his profession." Such considerations apply with added force to children in grade and high schools. To separate them from others of similar age and qualifications solely because of their race generates a feeling of inferiority as to their status in the community that may affect their hearts and minds in a way unlikely ever to be undone. The effect of this separation on their educational opportunities was well stated by a finding in the Kansas case by a court which nevertheless felt compelled to rule against the Negro plaintiffs: Segregation of white and colored children in public schools has a detrimental effect upon the colored children. The impact is greater when it has the sanction of the law, for the policy of separating the races is usually interpreted as denoting the inferiority of the Negro group. A sense of inferiority affects the motivation of a child to learn. Segregation with the sanction of law, therefore, has a tendency to [retard] the educational and mental development of Negro children and to deprive them of some of the benefits they would receive in a racial[ly] integrated school system.[10] Whatever may have been the extent of psychological knowledge at the time of *Plessy v. Ferguson,* this finding is amply supported by modern authority.[11] Any language in *Plessy v. Ferguson* contrary to this finding is rejected.

We conclude that, in the field of public education, the doctrine of "separate but equal" has no place. Separate educational facilities are inherently unequal. Therefore, we hold that the plaintiffs and others similarly situated for whom the actions have been brought are, by reason of the segregation complained of, deprived of the equal protection of the laws guaranteed by the Fourteenth Amendment. This disposition makes unnecessary any discussion whether such segregation also violates the Due Process Clause of the Fourteenth Amendment.[12]

Because these are class actions, because of the wide applicability of this decision, and because of the great variety of local conditions, the formulation of decrees in these cases presents problems of considerable complexity. On reargument, the consideration of appropriate relief was necessarily subordinated to the primary question—the constitutionality of segregation in public education. We have now announced that such segregation is a denial of the equal protection of the laws. In order that we may have the full assistance of the parties in formulating decrees, the cases will be restored to the docket, and the parties are requested to present further argument on Questions 4 and 5 previously propounded by the Court for the reargument this Term[13] The Attorney General [p496] of the United States is again invited to participate. The Attorneys General of the states requiring or permitting segregation in public education will also be permitted to appear as amici curiae upon request to do so by September 15, 1954, and submission of briefs by October 1, 1954.[14]

It is so ordered.

* Together with No. 2, *Briggs et al. v. Elliott et al.*, on appeal from the United States District Court for the Eastern District of South Carolina, argued December 9–10, 1952, reargued December 7–8, 1953; No. 4, *Davis et al. v. County School Board of Prince Edward County, Virginia, et al.*, on appeal from the United States District Court for the Eastern District of Virginia, argued December 10, 1952, reargued December 7–8, 1953, and No. 10, *Gebhart et al. v. Belton et al.*, on certiorari to the Supreme Court of Delaware, argued December 11, 1952, reargued December 9, 1953.

1. In the Kansas case, *Brown v. Board of Education*, the plaintiffs are Negro children of elementary school age residing in Topeka. They brought this action in the United States District Court for the District of Kansas to enjoin enforcement of a Kansas statute which permits, but does not require, cities of more than 15,000 population to maintain separate school facilities for Negro and white students. Kan.Gen.Stat. § 72-1724 (1949). Pursuant to that authority, the Topeka Board of Education elected to establish segregated elementary schools. Other public schools in the community, however, are operated on a nonsegregated basis. The three-judge District Court, convened under 28 U.S.C. §§ 2281 and 2284, found that segregation in public education has a detrimental effect upon Negro children, but denied relief on the ground that the Negro and white schools were substantially equal with respect to buildings, transportation, curricula, and educational qualifications of teachers. 98 F.Supp. 797. The case is here on direct appeal under 28 U.S.C. § 1253.

In the South Carolina case, *Briggs v. Elliott*, the plaintiffs are Negro children of both elementary and high school age residing in Clarendon County. They brought this action in the United States District Court for the Eastern District of South Carolina to enjoin enforcement of provisions in the state constitution and statutory code which require the segregation of Negroes and whites in public schools. S.C.Const. Art. XI, § 7; S.C.Code § 5377 (1942). The three-judge District Court, convened under 28 U.S.C. §§ 2281 and 2284, denied the requested relief. The court found that the Negro schools were inferior to the white schools, and ordered the defendants to begin immediately to equalize the facilities. But the court sustained the validity of the contested provisions and denied the plaintiffs admission to the white schools during the equalization program. 98 F.Supp.

529. This Court vacated the District Court's judgment and remanded the case for the purpose of obtaining the court's views on a report filed by the defendants concerning the progress made in the equalization program. 342 U.S. 350. On remand, the District Court found that substantial equality had been achieved except for buildings and that the defendants were proceeding to rectify this inequality as well. 103 F.Supp. 920. The case is again here on direct appeal under 28 U.S.C. § 1253.

In the Virginia case, *Davis v. County School Board*, the plaintiffs are Negro children of high school age residing in Prince Edward County. They brought this action in the United States District Court for the Eastern District of Virginia to enjoin enforcement of provisions in the state constitution and statutory code which require the segregation of Negroes and whites in public schools. Va.Const., § 140; Va.Code § 22-221 (1950). The three-judge District Court, convened under 28 U.S.C. §§ 2281 and 2284, denied the requested relief. The court found the Negro school inferior in physical plant, curricula, and transportation, and ordered the defendants forthwith to provide substantially equal curricula and transportation and to "proceed with all reasonable diligence and dispatch to remove" the inequality in physical plant. But, as in the South Carolina case, the court sustained the validity of the contested provisions and denied the plaintiffs admission to the white schools during the equalization program. 103 F.Supp. 337. The case is here on direct appeal under 28 U.S.C. § 1253.

In the Delaware case, *Gebhart v. Belton*, the plaintiffs are Negro children of both elementary and high school age residing in New Castle County. They brought this action in the Delaware Court of Chancery to enjoin enforcement of provisions in the state constitution and statutory code which require the segregation of Negroes and whites in public schools. Del.Const., Art. X, § 2; Del.Rev.Code § 2631 (1935). The Chancellor gave judgment for the plaintiffs and ordered their immediate admission to schools previously attended only by white children, on the ground that the Negro schools were inferior with respect to teacher training, pupil-teacher ratio, extracurricular activities, physical plant, and time and distance involved in travel. 87 A.2d 862. The Chancellor also found that segregation itself results in an inferior education for Negro children (see note 10, *infra*), but did not rest his decision on that ground. *Id.* at 865. The Chancellor's decree was affirmed by the Supreme Court of Delaware, which intimated, however, that the defendants might be able to obtain a modification of the decree after equalization of the Negro and white schools had been accomplished. 91 A.2d 137, 152. The defendants, contending only that the Delaware courts had erred in ordering the immediate admission of the Negro plaintiffs to the white schools, applied to this Court for certiorari. The writ was granted, 344 U.S. 891. The plaintiffs, who were successful below, did not submit a cross-petition.

2. 344 U.S. 1, 141, 891.

3. 345 U.S. 972. The Attorney General of the United States participated both Terms as amicus curiae.

4. For a general study of the development of public education prior to the Amendment, see Butts and Cremin, A History of Education in American Culture (1953),

Pts. I, II; Cubberley, Public Education in the United States (1934 ed.), cc. II–XII. School practices current at the time of the adoption of the Fourteenth Amendment are described in Butts and Cremin, *supra*, at 269–275; Cubberley, *supra*, at 288–339, 408–431; Knight, Public Education in the South (1922), cc. VIII, IX. *See also* H. Ex.Doc. No. 315, 41st Cong., 2d Sess. (1871). Although the demand for free public schools followed substantially the same pattern in both the North and the South, the development in the South did not begin to gain momentum until about 1850, some twenty years after that in the North. The reasons for the somewhat slower development in the South (e.g., the rural character of the South and the different regional attitudes toward state assistance) are well explained in Cubberley, *supra*, at 408–423. In the country as a whole, but particularly in the South, the War virtually stopped all progress in public education. *Id.* at 427–428. The low status of Negro education in all sections of the country, both before and immediately after the War, is described in Beale, A History of Freedom of Teaching in American Schools (1941), 112–132, 175–195. Compulsory school attendance laws were not generally adopted until after the ratification of the Fourteenth Amendment, and it was not until 1918 that such laws were in force in all the states. Cubberley, *supra*, at 563–565.

5. *Slaughter-House Cases*, 16 Wall. 36, 67–72 (1873); *Strauder v. West Virginia*, 100 U.S. 303, 307–308 (1880): "It ordains that no State shall deprive any person of life, liberty, or property, without due process of law, or deny to any person within its jurisdiction the equal protection of the laws. What is this but declaring that the law in the States shall be the same for the black as for the white; that all persons, whether colored or white, shall stand equal before the laws of the States, and, in regard to the colored race, for whose protection the amendment was primarily designed, that no discrimination shall be made against them by law because of their color? The words of the amendment, it is true, are prohibitory, but they contain a necessary implication of a positive immunity, or right, most valuable to the colored race—the right to exemption from unfriendly legislation against them distinctively as colored—exemption from legal discriminations, implying inferiority in civil society, lessening the security of their enjoyment of the rights which others enjoy, and discriminations which are steps towards reducing them to the condition of a subject race. *See also Virginia v. Rives*, 100 U.S. 313, 318 (1880); *Ex parte Virginia*, 100 U.S. 339, 344–345 (1880).

6. The doctrine apparently originated in *Roberts v. City of Boston*, 59 Mass.198, 206 (1850), upholding school segregation against attack as being violative of a state constitutional guarantee of equality. Segregation in Boston public schools was eliminated in 1855. Mass.Acts 1855, c. 256. But elsewhere in the North, segregation in public education has persisted in some communities until recent years. It is apparent that such segregation has long been a nationwide problem, not merely one of sectional concern.

7. *See also Berea College v. Kentucky*, 211 U.S. 45 (1908).

8. In the *Cummin* case, Negro taxpayers sought an injunction requiring the defendant school board to discontinue the operation of a high school for white children

until the board resumed operation of a high school for Negro children. Similarly, in the *Gong Lum* case, the plaintiff, a child of Chinese descent, contended only that state authorities had misapplied the doctrine by classifying him with Negro children and requiring him to attend a Negro school.

9. In the Kansas case, the court below found substantial equality as to all such factors. 98 F.Supp. 797, 798. In the South Carolina case, the court below found that the defendants were proceeding "promptly and in good faith to comply with the court's decree." 103 F.Supp. 920, 921. In the Virginia case, the court below noted that the equalization program was already "afoot and progressing" (103 F.Supp. 337, 341); since then, we have been advised, in the Virginia Attorney General's brief on reargument, that the program has now been completed. In the Delaware case, the court below similarly noted that the state's equalization program was well under way. 91 A.2d 137, 149.

10. A similar finding was made in the Delaware case: I conclude from the testimony that, in our Delaware society, State-imposed segregation in education itself results in the Negro children, as a class, receiving educational opportunities which are substantially inferior to those available to white children otherwise similarly situated. 87 A.2d 862, 865.

11. K. B. Clark, Effect of Prejudice and Discrimination on Personality Development (Mid-century White House Conference on Children and Youth, 1950); Witmer and Kotinsky, Personality in the Making (1952), c. VI; Deutscher and Chein, The Psychological Effects of Enforced Segregation: A Survey of Social Science Opinion, 26 J.Psychol. 259 (1948); Chein, What are the Psychological Effects of Segregation Under Conditions of Equal Facilities? 3 Int.J.Opinion and Attitude Res. 229 (1949); Brameld, Educational Costs, in Discrimination and National Welfare (MacIver, ed., 1949), 44–48; Frazier, The Negro in the United States (1949), 674–681. *And see generally* Myrdal, An American Dilemma (1944).

12. *See Bolling v. Sharpe*, post, p. 497, concerning the Due Process Clause of the Fifth Amendment.

13. 4. Assuming it is decided that segregation in public schools violates the Fourteenth Amendment (a) would a decree necessarily follow providing that, within the limits set by normal geographic school districting, Negro children should forthwith be admitted to schools of their choice, or (b) may this Court, in the exercise of its equity powers, permit an effective gradual adjustment to be brought about from existing segregated systems to a system not based on color distinctions? 5. On the assumption on which questions 4(a) and (b) are based, and assuming further that this Court will exercise its equity powers to the end described in question 4(b), (a) should this Court formulate detailed decrees in these cases; (b) if so, what specific issues should the decrees reach; (c) should this Court appoint a special master to hear evidence with a view to recommending specific terms for such decrees; (d) should this Court remand to the courts of first instance with directions to frame decrees in these cases and, if so, what general directions should the decrees of this Court include and what

procedures should the courts of first instance follow in arriving at the specific terms of more detailed decrees?

14. See Rule 42, Revised Rules of this Court (effective July 1, 1954).

"Declaration of Constitutional Principles"
Issued by 101 Southern Members of Congress

Source: Congressional Record, 84th Congress, Second Session. Vol. 102, part 4. Washington, D.C.: Governmental Printing Office, 1956, 4459–4460.

On March 12, 1956, one hundred and one Jim Crow congressmen and senators issued a document referred to by newspapers at the time as the Southern Manifesto. Nineteen senators and eighty-one members of the House of Representatives signed the Manifesto, including the entire congressional delegations from the states of Alabama, Arkansas, Georgia, Louisiana, Mississippi, and South Carolina. Only three senators from the South, Albert Gore and Estes Kefauver of Tennessee and Lyndon Johnson of Texas, refused to give their support to this "Declaration of Constitutional Principles," as its supporters called it. The document denounced the Supreme Court's 1954 decision in Brown v. Board of Education *that called for the desegregation of public schools in the United States on constitutional principles. The court violated basic constitutional principles and illustrated instead the justices' disregard for the traditions and values of white Southerners. The document repeated the long-held white Southern view that relations between "the white and Negro races" in the Southern states had been improved by Jim Crow segregation. They urged states to disobey the court's call for desegregation and to use only "lawful means" to fight the decision until it was reversed. The call for disobedience met wide acceptance among governors, legislators, and the white public; however the advocacy of using only legal means to overturn the decision was largely ignored by the same people. The manifesto did not use the term "white supremacy" in its defense of segregation, but that is exactly what its argument implied—that whites should be allowed to treat African Americans as inferior, second-class citizens and that such treatment was perfectly constitutional, no matter what the unanimous Supreme Court had decided in 1954.*

The "Southern Manifesto"

We regard the decision of the Supreme Court in the school cases as a clear abuse of judicial power. It climaxes a trend in the Federal judiciary undertaking to legislate, in derogation of the authority of Congress, and to encroach upon the reserved rights of the States and the people.

The original Constitution does not mention education. Neither does the 14th amendment or any other amendment. The debates preceding the submission of the 14th amendment clearly show that there was no intent that it should affect the systems of education maintained by the States.

The very Congress which proposed the amendment subsequently provided for segregated schools in the District of Columbia.

When the amendment was adopted, in 1868, there were 37 States of the Union. Every one of the 26 States that had any substantial racial differences among its people either approved the operation of segregated schools already in existence or subsequently established such schools by action of the same lawmaking body which considered the 14th amendment.

Though there has been no constitutional amendment or act of Congress changing this established legal principle almost a century old, the Supreme Court of the United States, with no legal basis for such action, undertook to exercise their naked judicial power and substituted their personal political and social ideas for the established law of the land.

This unwarranted exercise of power by the Court, contrary to the Constitution, is creating chaos and confusion in the States principally affected. It is destroying the amicable relations between the white and Negro races that have been created through 90 years of patient effort by the good people of both races. It has planted hatred and suspicion where there has been heretofore friendship and understanding.

With the gravest concern for the explosive and dangerous condition created by this decision and inflamed by outside meddlers:

We reaffirm our reliance on the Constitution as the fundamental law of the land.

We decry the Supreme Court's encroachments on rights reserved to the States and to the people, contrary to established law and to the Constitution.

We commend the motives of those States, which have declared the intention to resist forced integration by any lawful means. . . .

We pledge ourselves to use all lawful means to bring about a reversal of this decision that is contrary to the Constitution and to prevent the use of force in its implementation.

Glossary

Accommodationism: Booker T. Washington's program calling upon blacks to accept Jim Crow discrimination while they are educating themselves and working hard to show whites that they are able to be good citizens. When the white population recognizes their worthiness, black Americans will be granted full citizenship rights.

Badge of slavery: In 1866 the Supreme Court ruled, in *Jones v. Alfred H. Meyer Co.*, that the Thirteenth Amendment not only abolished slavery in the United States, but that it also gave Congress the power to "pass all laws necessary and proper for abolishing all badges or incidents of slavery in the United States." It did not define, however, what it meant by a "badge" of slavery, and the court has never gotten around to defining that term. Lower courts have ruled that the term is limited only to cases of actual enslavement, which the Supreme Court has defined as unpaid, forced labor. But that lower court limit is not necessarily true. The Supreme Court could rule differently in a future decision.

Black Codes: Laws passed by Southern white legislatures after the Civil War in order to control the newly freed black labor force. One example: a Mississippi law requiring all black men to sign employment contracts each January or face a prison sentence for being unemployed. The Fourteenth Amendment, ratified in 1868, outlawed the Black Codes.

Civil Rights Act of 1875: The law prohibited racial discrimination in inns, public transportation systems, and places of amusement. It was declared unconstitutional in 1883.

Civil Rights Act of 1957: This bill was the first civil rights legislation passed by Congress since 1875. Its most important provision created the Commission on Civil Rights.

Civil Rights Act of 1964:   The two most important provisions in this law prohibited discrimination in public accommodations (hotels, motels, restaurants, transportation facilities, and places of amusement) and in employment.

Civil Rights Cases (1883):   The Supreme Court ruled 8 to 1 that the Civil Rights Act of 1875 was unconstitutional because it violated the right of businesses and citizens to determine who they wanted to serve or who they could refuse to serve.

Color blind constitution: A legal principal first asserted by Justice John Marshall Harlan in his dissent in *Plessy v. Ferguson* (1896) that the U.S. Constitution of 1787 does not "know nor tolerate" any racial distinctions among citizens. In other words, race or skin color cannot be used to classify Americans for any purpose, even if race was the only factor involved in their mistreatment (or even enslavement) in the past.

Discrimination: The act of treating people differently because of their race, religion, sex, or social class.

Filibuster: A technique used in the U.S. Senate to delay or block the passage of legislation. One or more senators may try to defeat a bill by talking it to death. There is no time limit on how long any senator might speak on an issue. The idea of a filibuster is to talk long enough so that the supporters of a bill will become tired and weary or the Senate leadership will become anxious to move on to other matters and request that the bill being filibustered be withdrawn from consideration. Filibusters can be broken only by passing a "cloture petition," which requires the votes of three-fifths of the senators present on the floor.

Free blacks: In 1860, the year before the Civil War began, some 400,000 free people of African descent—most of them former slaves—lived in the United States; roughly 9 percent of all blacks in the United States. They were subjected to prejudice, segregation laws, and employment discrimination in all parts of the United States, whether residing in free states or slave states. Many of the laws that victimized them—whether prohibiting them from serving on juries, testifying against whites in courts, or voting—came back after the Civil War in the form of Black Codes or Jim Crow segregation laws. They were more black than free before the Civil War.

Minstrel shows: A popular form of entertainment in the United States from the 1830s to the 1890s. White actors who darkened their faces with burnt cork portrayed stereotypical "happy slaves" and good old "darkies," who played their banjoes and talked about the good times under the good Ol' Marster in the good old slavery days. Occasionally, black actors appeared on stage during the performances, but they appeared with their faces darkened with burnt cork so that the white audiences would not be offended by having to applaud African American performers.

Miscegenation: A word coined, probably because it sounded "scientific," in the United States before the Civil War by a journalist. He made up the word by joining the Latin *miscere*, to mix, with *genus*, species. It was used to define mixed race (usually African/European) marriages. Children from interracial marriages, which were illegal in 26 states until 1968, were *mulattos* (from the Latin word for mules). Laws prohibiting interracial marriages were declared unconstitutional by the Supreme Court in *Loving v. Virginia* (1968).

Police powers: The power of a government (local, state, or federal) to pass laws promoting its citizens' safety, comfort, health, and morals, as long as that is done in a "reasonable" fashion. The courts generally decide what is reasonable and what is not.

Privileges and immunities: One section of Article IV of the Constitution protects "the privileges and immunities" of U.S. citizens from being denied by any state. Unfortunately, the Constitution does not specify nor has the Supreme Court ever determined what those "privileges and immunities" are. The Fourteenth Amendment prohibits any state from abridging "the privileges or immunities of citizens of the United States." Again, however, the meaning of that term was not defined and remains undefined, other than including the right of citizens to travel freely across state lines and the right for all citizens to use the navigable waterways of the United States.

Reconstruction: The period after the Civil War—1865–77—when attempts were made to bring the states that had seceded in 1860–61 back into the Union.

Restrictive covenants: Contracts signed by homeowners prohibiting the sale of real estate to African Americans, Jews, and nonwhite ethnic groups. Popular in late nineteenth-century cities and considered legal until 1948, when the Supreme Court declared them unconstitutional in *Shelley v. Kraemer.*

Segregation: The physical separation of one group of people from another, usually because of race. It can be mandated by law (*de jure* segregation) or can be the result of custom and tradition (*de facto*—"a matter of fact"). Segregating people by law in public schools, for example, became unconstitutional after the *Brown* decision. For schools segregated by housing patterns in cities or neighborhoods, as was and continues to be true in almost all major U.S. urban areas, the Supreme Court has determined that such segregation does not violate the *Brown* decision unless it can be shown that school boundary lines were drawn intentionally to separate students by race.

States' rights: A political doctrine upholding the powers of the states within the United States as opposed to those of the national government. State laws are superior to federal laws in most areas of U.S. life, the exception being in the area of national defense and foreign policy. The doctrine is traditionally invoked by those opposed to a strong federal government, especially in areas such as education, police powers, and social welfare policy.

Voting Rights Act of 1965:   This law suspended the use of literacy tests for purposes of determining whether a citizen is qualified to vote. Instead, states can require only proof of a sixth-grade education as evidence of literacy.

Annotated Bibliography

Books

Alexander, Michelle. *The New Jim Crow: Mass Incarceration in the Age of Colorblindness*. New York: The New Press, 2010.

The author argues that the current mass imprisonment of young African American males in major U.S. cities and states has replaced Jim Crow laws as the modern method of trapping blacks into the status of permanent second-class citizenship. Millions of black males are either serving long prison terms or are labeled felons for life. Many states punish felons even after they have served their sentences by denying them the right to vote for the rest of their lives. She argues that black men and women now are discriminated against because they are "criminals," rather than because of their race. The modern criminal justice system is used for purposes of racial control, the same function used by Jim Crow laws for most of the previous century.

Anderson, James D. *The Education of Blacks in the South, 1860–1935*. Chapel Hill: University of North Carolina Press, 1988.

The book contains a brilliant survey and analysis of African Americans in the Jim Crow states and their long campaign for equality of education. The author describes the fight of black parents against the system of vocational and industrial education developed in Southern states by white supremacist education leaders and Booker T. Washington supporters that seemed aimed only at keeping their children poor and out of political influence and power. White Northern philanthropists provided needed money for the vastly underfunded black school systems in Jim Crow America but rarely challenged the inferior content of courses and curriculum offered at black public schools. Despite these terrible obstacles, black families persisted in challenging the structure and content of the educational opportunities offered by their separate and unequal public schools.

Bartley, Numan V. *The Rise of Massive Resistance: Race and Politics in the South During the 1950s.* **Baton Rouge: Louisiana State University Press, 1969.**

A well-written, detailed history of the popular campaign encouraging open resistance to the Supreme Court's 1954 decision in *Brown* calling for an end to racial segregation in public schools. White Citizens' Councils rose up across the South to delay implementation of the decision, to demand the impeachment of Chief Justice Earl Warren, and to prevent federal government interference in local matters, such as providing second-class education for U.S. citizens of a different skin color. The book clearly demonstrates that you did not have to wear a white mask and sheet to be a racist.

Carter, Dan T. *Scottsboro: A Tragedy of the American South.* **Baton Rouge: Louisiana State University Press, 1969.**

A history of one of the worst failures of Jim Crow-style justice, a trial (actually a series of trials over four years) during which nine young, unemployed black defendants (the "Scottsboro Boys"), were convicted and sentenced to death at least three times, for a crime they never committed. The case led to two major Supreme Court decisions protecting the rights of defendants in criminal cases, in *Powell v. Alabama* (1932) requiring adequate legal representations for defendants in death penalty cases, and in *Norris v. Alabama* (1935) calling for nonsegregated jury selection. These cases represented a major step forward in the war against Jim Crow "justice."

Cortner, Richard C. *A "Scottsboro" Case in Mississippi: The Supreme Court and* **Brown v. Mississippi. Jackson: University Press of Mississippi, 1986.**

The author presents a well-researched study based on a 1934 case that still shocks opponents of segregation and Jim Crow ideas concerning "law and order." This history of a case involving outright police brutality (even though the police involved never suffered an ounce of punishment) is based on court documents, police reports, and personal interviews that explain why the Supreme Court ordered new trials for the three African Americans who confessed to murder and were originally sentenced to death. The court ruled that evidence and confessions obtained by the police after torturing prisoners for endless hours with whips, clubs, and the "water cure," which involves "simulated drowning" of victims (now referred to as "waterboarding"), cannot be admitted into court. The book makes fascinating reading and gives a horrifying account of the meaning of Jim Crow justice as really practiced in Southern jails.

Daniel, Pete. *The Shadow of Slavery: Peonage in the South, 1901–1969.* **Urbana: University of Illinois Press, 1972.**

A carefully researched look at various forms of peonage and "debt servitude" in the South that evolved during the Jim Crow era. Based on the Peonage Collection in the U.S. Department of Justice archives, personal interviews with victims, and eyewitness accounts. The book describes the horrible conditions and treatment suffered by the mainly African American victims of this inhuman system of punishment. Daniel also discusses the long struggle in federal court led by a few Justice Department attorneys to get this racist system of "justice" outlawed by the U.S. Supreme Court.

Doyle, Bertram. *The Etiquette of Race Relations: A Study in Social Control.* **New York: Schocken Books, 1971.**

A book by an African American sociologist at Fisk University in Nashville, Tennessee, originally published in 1937, which describes the patterns and forms of daily contacts between Southern blacks and whites in the Jim Crow South. The purpose of the "etiquette" Doyle describes was to keep African Americans constantly aware of their own "inferiority" and the overwhelming superiority of the white race. Black acceptance of their racial inferiority was the key to maintaining racial peace in Jim Crow America. The book is a very interesting eyewitness account of the effects of racial subordination and intimidation.

Dray, Philip. *At the Hands of Persons Unknown: The Lynching of Black America.* **New York: Modern Library, 2002.**

The essential history of lynching in the United States based on the lynching records at Tuskegee Institute. The author discusses its causes, perpetrators, defenders, and victims. He also describes the story of the struggle against lynching led by the NAACP and antilynching crusaders including Ida B. Wells, W. E. B. DuBois, and Walter White. He describes the horror and brutality of lynch mobs and the long fight against making lynching a federal crime led by its Southern defenders in Congress. The book makes the essential link between lynch mobs, the passage of Jim Crow legislation, and the victory and long duration of Southern white supremacist culture. The author makes it very clear that lynchers were not only Ku Klux Klansmen but had the support of the vast majority of white Southerners.

Egerton, John. *Speak Now Against the Day: The Generation Before the Civil Rights Movement in the South*. Chapel Hill: University of North Carolina Press, 1995.

A massive and eloquently written account of those African American and white Southerners who dared to challenge the attitudes and customs associated with Jim Crow thinking and Jim Crow "justice." Written by a white Southerner, it tells the story of the "prophets of Tomorrow in the South," whose "better vision" of equal justice and equal rights for all people regardless of race eventually brought about a revolution in the crusade for freedom and equality.

Finley, Keith. *Delaying the Dream: Southern Senators and the Fight Against Civil Rights, 1938–1965*. Baton Rouge: Louisiana State University Press, 2008.

A very readable, well-researched history of the fight by Southern senators in Washington, D.C., against any and every civil rights bill, voting rights bill, or any other attempt to promote equal political and constitutional rights for African Americans. It does an excellent job of describing the use of the filibuster, or just the threat of a filibuster, to block any attempt to weaken Jim Crow segregation in the states of the Old Confederacy. This book presents an excellent portrayal of how the legislative rules of the U.S. Senate can be used to prevent passage of legislation that promotes equal rights and equal justice for all Americans, and a useful lesson in how a small group of determined legislators can prevent U.S. citizens from enjoying their full constitutional rights.

Gilmore, Glenda Elizabeth. *Defying Dixie: The Radical Roots of Civil Rights, 1919–1950*. New York: W. W. Norton, 2009.

The story of how white and African American communists, socialists, liberals, union leaders, radical lawyers, and a small group of historians, psychologists, and sociologists at the University of North Carolina and a few other institutions of higher learning in the Jim Crow states helped lay the groundwork for later achievements of the civil rights movement. The book is especially interesting in describing the lives and struggles of the U.S. Communist Party and its leadership and influence in the long fight against Jim Crow laws and attitudes, which are closely associated with the anti-union, anti–social justice, anti–women's rights, and anti-equality ideology expressed and supported by advocates of white supremacy.

Griffin, John Howard. ***Black Like Me***. **New York: Signet Books, 1962.**

John Howard Griffin, a white, Texas-born journalist, used chemicals and medication to darken his skin in 1959. He then set out on a journey through the South to report on what it "is like to be a Negro in a land where we keep the Negro down." He spent about six weeks hitchhiking and taking the bus across Louisiana, Mississippi, Alabama, and Georgia, trying to discover what life was like on the other side of the "color line." His eyewitness account of his experiences provides example after example of the fear and threat of humiliation faced by African Americans every time they encountered a white person. The author's compassion for the oppressed Americans he briefly lived with in his travels led to daily threats to his life and his being called a "traitor to the white race" by residents of his hometown when he published his book. Life for his family became so difficult and unpleasant that they eventually moved to Mexico.

Harlan, Louis R. ***Separate and Unequal: Public School Campaigns and Racism in the Southern Seaboard States, 1901–1915***. **Chapel Hill: University of North Carolina Press, 1958**

The author has produced a detailed, scholarly comparison of African American and white public school education in the Jim Crow South. Based on reports from state school inspectors, education departments, and manuscripts in the Southern Education Collection at the University of North Carolina Library, the author concludes that the "gentle approach" practiced by white and African American reformers lacked the ability to produce significant change. The book is a well-argued refutation of Booker T. Washington's call for compromise and cooperation with the better class of whites he felt would eventually accept equal rights for their black employees and neighbors. The "dual systems" approach benefited only white Southerners—they saved money because taxes paid by African Americans supported white schools far more generously than the meager amounts states gave to the "colored schools."

Johnson, Kimberley. ***Reforming Jim Crow: Southern Politics and the State in the Age before*** **Brown. New York: Oxford University Press, 2010.**

A study of white and African American progressive education reformers and their efforts to improve "separate but equal" schools in the Jim Crow South. Though they never challenged the system of segregated education, they tried to create a progressive program of vocational education within Jim Crow schools. The reformers struggled to build a curriculum that stressed racial progress by training black students to careers in various trades (plumbing, construction industries, accounting, and office work), while accepting their position as citizens without equal rights. Apparently, this acceptance of second-class citizenship helped some students achieve modest levels of economic self-sufficiency, but it also generated more demand—at least among their children—for true equality in U.S. society.

Kennedy, Stetson. *Jim Crow Guide: The Way It Was*. **Boca Raton: Florida Atlantic University Press, 1990.**

First published in Paris in 1956 by Jean Paul Sartre because the author could not find an U.S. publisher, the book is written in the form of a travel guide. It covers every style of Jim Crow law and order, custom, and bias found in the American South. It covers where and with whom a person could live, work, study, travel, eat, sleep, play, marry, or be buried. It also includes rules for how to behave (as late as the 1970s) for people of color while in or travelling through Jim Crow states, such as: "Never assert or even intimate that a white person may be lying," or "the farther you stay away from white people," the happier you will be. The author also invented a term for the system of relations found in the post–civil rights American South, "desegregated racism."

Klarman, Michael J. *From Jim Crow to Civil Rights: The Supreme Court and the Struggle for Racial Equality*. **New York: Oxford University Press, 2004.**

A complete history of the U.S. Supreme Court's decisions on race, from *Plessy v. Ferguson* (1896) to the *Brown* ruling of 1954. Klarman concludes that the court's decision in *Brown* was more important in energizing white opposition to school desegregation than in encouraging the growth of the modern civil rights movement. But the book provides more than a commentary on the difficulties of desegregating public schools; it also provides a detailed study of cases involving discrimination in voting rights, criminal trials, police procedures, transportation, and other areas of life that were effected by Jim Crow attitudes.

Kluger, Richard. *Simple Justice: The History of* **Brown v. Board of Education** *and Black America's Struggle for Equality*. **New York: Vintage Books, 2004.**

The highly regarded history of *Brown v. Board of Education*, originally published in 1975. The 2004 edition includes an essay marking the 50th anniversary of the ruling that covers the subsequent impact of the ruling on schools and race relations in the United States. The book is especially detailed in its description and analysis of the team of African American lawyers that success-fully challenged the system of "separate but equal" facilities supposedly estab-lished by *Plessy v. Ferguson*. There is excellent coverage of all of the cases included in the *Brown* decision, a lengthy analysis of the controversial remedy offered in *Brown II*, and a dramatic account of how Chief Justice Earl Warren achieved the unanimous decision he so desired in *Brown I*.

Litwack, Leon F. *Trouble in Mind: Black Southerners in the Age of Jim Crow*. **New York: Alfred A. Knopf, 1998.**

Without a doubt, the best history of Jim Crow America yet published. A com-plete account of what the victims of Jim Crow racism had to endure and suffer. Based on personal accounts from both African Americans and white segrega-tionists, the book portrays life in the bloodiest, most repressive period in race relations in U.S. history. It also describes, through the music and literature of the victims of white supremacy, the spirit of resistance that emerged among people severely injured by discrimination, constant fear, and daily reminders of their alleged "inferiority."

Litwack, Leon F. *How Free Is Free? The Long Death of Jim Crow*. **Cambridge, MA: Harvard University Press, 2009.**

The author's Nathan A. Huggins Lectures delivered at Harvard University show the changes produced by World War II on U.S. race relations. The war against Nazi Germany did little to disturb Jim Crow attitudes—as a matter of fact, Afri-can American soldiers faced the same humiliations, hostilities, and denial of equal rights that their fathers had faced during World War I. Many black sol-diers saw little difference between the white soldiers they fought with and the Nazi soldiers they fought against. The civil rights movement produced modest advances toward equal rights, but white attitudes concerning race had barely changed even 50 years after *Brown*. Neither the 1964 Civil Rights Act nor the Voting Rights Act of 1965, in the author's view, had much impact on the prob-lem of African American poverty.

MacGregor, Morris J. *Integration of the Armed Forces: 1940–1965*. **Washington, D.C.: Department of the Army, 1985.**

A history of the desegregation of the U.S. Army, Navy, Marines, Air Force, and Coast Guard. The book actually goes back to World War I in its description of the various attempts to overcome a Jim Crow military and break down the tra-ditional views of African American "incompetence" in battle that dominated the thinking of the white officers who dominated military culture from the American Revolution almost to the very end of the Second World War. Because of manpower needs during that war, however, some of the traditional racist assumptions of military planners that kept African Americans out of anything but construction battalions and burial squads began to weaken. Harry Truman's desegregation order violated those assumptions, but successful integration of military units still took a long, long time.

McMillen, Neil R. *Dark Journey: Black Mississippians in the Age of Jim Crow*. **Urbana: University of Illinois Press, 1990.**

A book that covers all of the horrors faced in the day-to-day lives of African Americans living in Jim Crow Mississippi. Interesting and detailed descriptions of Jim Crow courts, Jim Crow "justice," and Jim Crow versions of "law and order." Mississippi sheriffs liked to administer what they called the "water cure" to black prisoners if they refused to confess to whatever crime they were charged with. Water would be poured into a prisoner's nose, causing "intense pain," as deputies held him to the ground, giving the victim the feeling of drowning. It only stopped when he confessed ("waterboarding" as the practice is called today). Eventually the Mississippi Supreme Court found the "water cure" unacceptable, ordering lower courts to reject any confessions gained through this method of torture.

Newby, I. A. *Jim Crow's Defense: Anti-Negro Thought in America, 1900–1930*. **Baton Rouge: Louisiana State University Press, 1965.**

An excellent, detailed, study of anti–African American thought based on the author's reading of newspapers, speeches, pamphlets, and books from the Jim Crow era that demonstrates the hostility and racism that dominated the thinking of an overwhelming majority of Americans, in the North, the South, the East, and the West. A vast majority of Americans, not just Ku Klux Klansmen and other crackpots, in the early twentieth century believed that African Americans were inferior beings just a few generations away from their savage, cannibalistic ancestors. The book provides detailed evidence that the race problem in the United States was not "the Negro" but white Americans' attitude toward their fellow African American citizens. The book is a frightening but scholarly analysis of racial thinking in the United States.

Oshinsky, David M. *"Worse Than Slavery": Parchman Farm and the Ordeal of Jim Crow Justice*. **New York: Free Press, 1996.**

The story of Parchman State Penitentiary in Mississippi, considered the most brutal and cruel prison in the United States, especially because of its treatment of African American inmates. Based on prison records, police reports, interviews with former prisoners, and blues songs, the author describes the life of prisoners from the days of cotton-field chain gangs to the experience of hundreds of Freedom Riders held in the prison during the 1960s. Imprisonment was meant to break the will of the civil rights workers; that it did not testifies to the strength of character and the deep commitment to justice that motivated the group.

Perman, Michael. ***Struggle for Mastery: Disfranchisement in the South, 1888–1908***. **Chapel Hill: University of North Carolina Press, 2001.**

A detailed, well-researched history of the successful campaigns in Alabama, Arkansas, Florida, Georgia, Louisiana, Mississippi, North Carolina, South Carolina, Tennessee, Texas, and Virginia to deprive almost all African Americans of their voting rights. The new laws and constitutions adopted by those states during that time had one purpose and only one: to protect white supremacy. The study also explores the role of the federal government and federal courts in aiding and abetting the move toward disfranchisement and legal segregation. Jim Crow dominated life in Southern states for much of the twentieth century, but that could not have happened without the aid of the Supreme Court and the cowardice on the racial question shown by U.S. presidents and members of Congress.

Schneider, Mark Robert. ***"We Return Fighting"***: ***The Civil Rights Movement in the Jazz Age***. **Boston: Northeastern University Press, 2002.**

The book begins with a brief survey of African American soldiers and their experience during World War I in a racially segregated army and navy. The fact that many black soldiers felt that their white fighting mates showed more respect to their German enemies than they showed toward their African American countrymen turned many black veterans into militant defenders of full equality and an immediate end to Jim Crow laws and attitudes when they returned home. The author describes the emergence of a new movement for civil rights in the United States that is greatly influenced by and inspired by the racist treatment experienced by black veterans of the war "to make the world safe for democracy."

Sullivan, Patricia. ***Lift Every Voice: The NAACP and the Making of the Civil Rights Movement***. **New York: The New Press, 2009.**

The history of the National Association for the Advancement of Colored People, the organization most responsible for the final victory over Jim Crow segregation. The book describes the NAACP's successes and failures from its beginning in 1909 through the assault on Jim Crow beginning with the *Brown* decision in 1954. The author explains the various NAACP strategies used to fight the seemingly impossible battle against legal segregation. It provides brief biographies of the men and women engaged in the campaign for full equality and describes the brutality and terror used by the various white supremacist groups organized to defend the white "southern way of life."

Weiner, Mark S. *Black Trials: Citizenship from the Beginnings of Slavery to the End of Caste*. New York: Random House, 2004.

The book covers 14 legal cases involving the question of race in America, from the 1741 grand jury investigation of people involved in a slave plot to burn down New York City to the 1991 Senate confirmation hearing for Supreme Court Justice Clarence Thomas, in which he was confronted with sexual harassment charges by Anita Hill. It includes the cases of *Plessy v. Ferguson* (1896) and *Brown v. Board of Education* (1954). The author presents the legal doctrines associated with each trial as well as detailed biographical information concerning the participants, lawyers, judges, and defendants involved in each case.

Woodward, C. Vann. *The Strange Career of Jim Crow*. Commemorative Edition. New York: Oxford University Press, 2001.

A classic history of Jim Crow in America first published in 1955. Considered a "landmark in the history of American race relations," the book aims to show that segregation was not a longstanding Southern tradition and "way of life," but a post–Civil War response to changing political conditions in the former Confederacy. Jim Crow emerged as a method of preventing cooperation between poor whites and African Americans by the white economic elite made up of planters and business leaders. Had such a coalition emerged, the new majority of poor blacks and whites could have demanded major changes in the Southern economy, including things such as higher wages, unions, and more money for public education. Appeals to white supremacy prevented any of those costly reforms from being considered or implemented.

Electronic Resources

American Experience: Freedom Riders. CD, DVD, and accompanying Web site.

A documentary focusing on the extraordinary journey of civil rights activists who called themselves the "Freedom Riders," who set off on a remarkable bus journey across the Jim Crow South in 1962. Their goal was to get to New Orleans by bus in order to test the response to a recent federal court decision outlawing segregated seating on buses crossing state lines. This remarkable documentary of the dangers they faced—several Riders were almost killed, and one of them was permanently disabled by a savage beating—testifies to the Riders' courage and determination. The fact that they did not complete their journey because of fires set to buses, beatings at the hands of local and state police, and imprisonment in some of the South's most notorious jails, bears witness to the great hostility and hatred aroused among white Southerners by any challenge to the Jim Crow system.

Library of Congress. Jim Crow in America. http://www.loc.gov/exhibits/ african/intro.html.

The best of several sites maintained by the Library of Congress that includes primary sources such as images, photographs, song sheets, articles, legal documents, newspaper files, political cartoons, and sound files devoted to the history of segregation. The site also provides a gateway to dozens of other sites and materials available online from the Civil War to the civil rights movement.

The Jim Crow Museum. Ferris State University. http://www.ferris.edu/ jimcrow/index.htm.

A site organized and maintained by Dr. David Pilgrim, professor of sociology at the university. It contains exhibits, videos, racist caricatures, racist cartoons, and brief scholarly essays discussing racist attitudes and the history of racism in the United States. This very well-maintained, well-organized site is affiliated with the Jim Crow Museum at Ferris State, which also sponsors travelling exhibits devoted to "images that force a person to take a stand for or against the equality of all human beings."

The History of Jim Crow. http://www.jimcrowhistory.org/home.htm.

A site that provides source material on the long history of segregation in every area of American life, from politics to education to sports. It includes material covering the geography, literature, and popular culture associated with Jim Crow America. It begins with a historical overview contained in a series of scholarly, in-depth essays titled "From Terror to Triumph," focusing on creating, surviving, resisting, escaping, and defeating Jim Crow. Also included are images and narratives of many events, from an essay illustrating the racist views of black Americans presented at the World's Colombian Exposition of

1893 in Chicago to a discussion of images in popular art, "Embedding Racial Stereotypes in the American Mindset—Jim Crow and Popular Culture." This is a marvelous site for students, researchers, and teachers.

The Rise and Fall of Jim Crow. CD, DVD, and companion Web site. http://www.pbs.org/wnet/jimcrow/.

A four-hour television history of the African American struggle for civil and constitutional rights, first presented on PBS in 2003, is available for purchase. The companion Web site contains a wealth of information on segregation in the United States, including photographs, images, first-person narratives, historical essays, timelines, court cases, Supreme Court decisions, maps, biographies, newsreels, public opinion polling data, and government reports and documents covering the Jim Crow era from the end of the Civil War to the dawn of the civil rights movement.

Index

Abernathy, Ralph, 141
Accommodationism, 28, 41, 155, 156, 175, 189
Agricultural Adjustment Act (1933), 83
Agriculture Department, U.S., 83, 84, 94
Alabama, 48, 125, 138, 141–44; Birmingham campaign in, xxii, 141–43, 159; bus segregation in, 130; convict-leasing system in, 23–24; "false pretenses law" in, 54–55; labor law in, 55–56; police brutality in, 149–50; Scottsboro Boys, xx, 78–80, 163; Wallace as governor of, xxiii, 80, 143–44, 149
Alexander, Will, 92–94
Amendments, Constitutional. *See* Constitutional Amendments
American Dilemma, An (Myrdal), 4–5
American Federation of Labor (AF of L), 77
Arkansas: Little Rock Nine in, xxii, 133–34; race riot in, 65–67
Armed forces. *See* Military, black soldiers in
Arthur, Chester, 25
Association of Southern Women for the Prevention of Lynching, 88
Atlanta, race riot in (1905), 52–53, 96

"Atlanta Compromise" speech (Washington), xviii, 28, 154–55, 165–67, 178

Bailey, Thomas Pearce, 37, 38
Bailey v. Alabama (1911), xix, 55–56
Baker, Ella, 136
Barnett, Ross, 141
Barry, Marion, 136
Berea College v. Kentucky (1908), xix, 45–46
Bethune, Mary McLeod, 95
Birmingham (Alabama), 70; antisegregation campaign in, xxii, 141–43, 159
Black Codes, 3–4, 5, 7–8, 189
Blackface minstrels, 1–2, 191
Black men, white women and. *See* Interracial marriage; White women, black men and
Blacks, education of. *See* Education, of blacks; School segregation
Black soldiers. *See* Military, black soldiers in
Bolling v. Sharpe (1954), 119–20
Boll weevil *(Anthonomus grandis)*, 59–60
Boyton v. Virginia (1960), 137
Bradley, Joseph P., 19, 31
Brewer, Earl, 92
Briggs v. Elliott (1951), 118–19, 183–84

Browder, Earl, 93
Brown, Henry Billings, 30, 31
Brownsville (Texas) race riot (1906), xix, 51–52
Brown v. Board of Education of Topeka (1954), xxi, 98, 122–27, 129, 167; precedents for, 119; remedies offered, 123–24; Southern Manifesto and, 126, 187–88; text of, 179–87; white resistance to, 124, 126–27
Brown v. Mississippi (1936), xxi, 90–92
Buchanan v. Warley (1917), xx, 72
Buckley, John J., 72
Bulah v. Gebhart (1952), 119
Bunche, Ralph, 86
Bus segregation, xxi, 69, 129, 168; Freedom Riders and, 109–10, 137–40; Montgomery Bus Boycott, xxii, 129–30, 158–59, 163–64
Byrnes, James F., 68

Carnegie, Andrew, 154
Carter, Robert, 118, 120
Chambliss, Robert "Bomber Bob," 144
Charles, Robert, 50–51
Chicago, 160; race riot in (1919), 64–65
Church bombings, 144
Citizens' Committee, 29
Citizenship, xvii, 5, 19, 20
Civil Rights Act of 1866, 8
Civil Rights Act of 1875, xviii, 12–13, 18–19, 189
Civil Rights Act of 1957, 132–33, 146, 189
Civil Rights Act of 1960, 146
Civil Rights Act of 1964, xiii, 17, 146–48, 159, 190

Civil Rights Cases (1883), 17–19, 31, 73, 190
Civil rights legislation, 111, 116
Civil rights movement, 54, 136, 142, 159. *See also* King, Martin Luther, Jr.; NAACP
Clark, Jim, 149
Clark, John, 90–92
Clark, Kenneth B., 118, 123, 186
Cleveland, Grover, 25, 27
Clyatt v. United States (1905), 55
Coal mines, convict-leasing in, 23–24
Colfax (Louisiana) Massacre, 11–12
Colleges, integration of. *See* University entries
Color blind constitution, 32, 190
Colored Advisory Commission, 75
Color line, 7–8, 69, 140
Columbia (Tennessee) race riot, 111–12
Commission on Civil Rights, 146
Commission on Interracial Cooperation (CIC), 92–93
Commission on Job Opportunity Under Government Contracts, 135
Committee on Civil Rights, 113, 146
Communist Party of the United States (CPUSA), 76–79, 93, 95, 124, 158; Scottsboro Boys and, 78–80; textile worker strikes and, 76–78
Confederate states, 5–7, 49
Congress, U.S., xiii, 81, 86, 135; African Americans in, 21, 49; Agricultural Adjustment Act and, 83; antilynching laws and, 87; Civil Rights Act of 1875 and, 12–13; civil rights bills and, 144–48; electoral commission, 15; minimum wage and, 85; Southern Manifesto, 126, 187–88; voting rights and, 8, 25,

About the Author

LESLIE V. TISCHAUSER is Professor of History at Prairie State College in Chicago Heights, Illinois. Dr. Tischauser has written *Race Relations in the United States, 1920–1940* and *The Changing Nature of Racial and Ethnic Conflict in United States History*.